W9-ATZ-334

Where the Words Come From

Where the Words Come From

CANADIAN POETS IN CONVERSATION

Edited by Tim Bowling

NIGHTWOOD EDITIONS

Roberts Creek

2002

Copyright © 2002 by the authors

All rights reserved. No part of this publication may be reproduced, stored in a retrieval system or transmitted, in any form or by any means, without prior permission of the publisher or, in case of photocopying or other reprographic copying, a licence from CANCOPY (Canadian Reprography Collective), 214 King Street West, Toronto, Ontario M5H 3S6.

Nightwood Editions
R.R. #22, 3692 Beach Avenue
Roberts Creek, BC
Canada V0N 2W2

Edited for the house by Silas White
Printed and bound in Canada

Nightwood Editions acknowledges the financial support of the Government of Canada through the Canada Council for the Arts, and the Province of British Columbia through the British Columbia Arts Council, for its publishing activities.

THE CANADA COUNCIL | LE CONSEIL DES ARTS
FOR THE ARTS | DU CANADA
SINCE 1957 | DEPUIS 1957

National Library of Canada Cataloguing in Publication Data

Main entry under title:

Where the words come from

ISBN 0-88971-184-4

1. Poets, Canadian–20th century–Interviews. I. Bowling, Tim, 1964–
PS8155.W43 2002   C811'.5409   C2002-910266-9
PR9190.5.W43 2002

Sleep softly spirit of the earth
as the days and nights join hands
when everything becomes one thing
wait softly brother
but do not expect it to happen
that great whoop announcing resurrection
expect only a small whisper
of birds nesting and green things growing
and a brief saying of them
and know where the words came from

– Al Purdy, from "The Dead Poet"

Photo Credits

Margaret Atwood: DeNeen Brown
Margaret Avison: Joan Eichner
Roo Borson: Silas White
Don Coles: Cheryl Bellows
Lorna Crozier: Barry Peterson & Blaise Enright-Peterson
Don Domanski: Jeannette Gaudet
Patrick Lane: Barry Peterson & Blaise Enright-Peterson
Dennis Lee: Susan Perly
Tim Lilburn: Degan Davis
Don McKay: Don McKay
Michael Ondaatje: Linda Spalding
Eric Ormsby: Terence Byrnes
P.K. Page: Barry Peterson & Blaise Enright-Peterson
Sharon Thesen: Barry Peterson & Blaise Enright-Peterson
Phyllis Webb: Barry Peterson & Blaise Enright-Peterson
Jan Zwicky: Don McKay

The lines from Al Purdy's "The Dead Poet" in the book's epigraph were taken from *Beyond Remembering: The Collected Poems of Al Purdy* (Harbour Publishing, 2000).

In his introduction Tim Bowling quotes lines from Czeslaw Milosz's "Ars Poetica," taken from *New & Selected Poems 1931–2001* (Ecco Press, 2001).

Contents

Introduction

Interviews with poets can enhance our appreciation of their art. That is the main reason this book exists. It's not intended to defend Canadian poetry or to raise its profile (after all, a raised profile only makes a poet a better target). As Robert Frost wrote, "We love the things we love for what they are," and I love Canadian poetry for what it is – a refuge from the trivial and an affirmation that life is worthy of reverence. For good poets, no matter their style, tone or literary alliances, share one important characteristic: they take life seriously to the extent that they think and feel deeply about it.

Where the Words Come From began as a response to Al Purdy's death in April 2000. On hearing the news, I decided that I wanted to find some way to honour Purdy's work and the work of the many fine poets, living and dead, who have written and published in Canada. A collection of interviews pairing younger and/or less well-known poets with some of our country's most celebrated practitioners of the art seemed a fitting homage. And so, starting several months later, I made a few phone calls, wrote some letters and e-mails and, due to the generosity, enthusiasm and hard work of thirty-four poets, these interviews began to accumulate.

My role has been a minor one, mostly concerned with bringing the poets together. However, I did require each interviewer to ask the following three questions, which were designed to generate a range of responses to some general issues surrounding the poet's life and work:

In his poem "The Dead Poet," Al Purdy, speculating on the origins of his poetry, asks "how else explain myself to myself/ where does the song come from?" Do you have any explanation of where your voice came from, of why you became a poet?

How important have reviews, awards and other honours been to your feelings about your work? Is competition healthy or unhealthy for a poet?

How have your feelings about poetry, the reading and writing of it, changed since you were in your twenties?

For the most part, the interviewers asked these questions as I wrote them, so I have edited out any references within the interviews themselves to the questions being mandatory, except where an interviewer expressed some dissatisfaction with this requirement.

The format of the interviews varied according to geography, personal preference and convenience. It was financially prohibitive to fly poets around the country for in-person conversations, but as it turned out, several poets *preferred* to answer questions by post or e-mail. For the record, eight of the interviews were done in person (Atwood, Crozier, McKay, Ondaatje, Ormsby, Page, Waddington and Webb), three by mail (Avison, Lilburn and Zwicky), and six by e-mail (Borson, Coles, Domanski, Lane, Lee and Thesen). Obviously, these differences in format resulted in a greater or lesser degree of formality.

As for the content of the interviews, I'd prefer not to generalize, since that would be a disservice to the poets and the distinct differences between them. But I will just point out how often the idea of silence comes up. Phyllis Webb, for example, describes silence as her natural mode; Don McKay refers to the perfect gesture of speechlessness; and Don Domanski believes that at the core of poetry there is the silence of a world turning. It perhaps comes as no surprise to poets, but might to others, that the act of writing poetry is so often informed by the idea of not writing poetry. After all, as most poets readily concede, silence is perfect in a way that language never can be. Yet it is the poet's joy and curse to be forever seeking a companion perfection in words for the purity of silence.

All of which means I'm even more grateful that the poets agreed to speak out of their preferred form, especially since the results are so informative and entertaining. Indeed, putting this book together often felt less like editing and more like hosting a party (to use Tim Lilburn's apt description). It's only fitting, then, that not long before I sat down to write these words, I came across the following stanza from "Ars Poetica?" by the Polish poet, Czeslaw Milosz:

> The purpose of poetry is to remind us
> how difficult it is to remain just one person,
> for our house is open, there are no keys in the doors,
> and invisible guests come in and out at will.

So, welcome. I hope you'll find much pleasure in the conversation as you come and go through these seventeen rooms. And once you're done, I encourage you to head to the library to find the poets' books, for, after all, that is where the conversation of any poet really matters.

TIM BOWLING

Looking at the World Through Topaz

P.K. PAGE

Interviewed by Christine Wiesenthal

P.K. Page's most recent books are *The Hidden Room: Collected Poems* (Porcupine's Quill, 1997), *A Kind of Fiction* (Porcupine's Quill, 2001) and, with Phillip Stratford, *And Once More Saw the Stars: Four Poems for Two Voices* (BuschekBooks, 2001). *Planet Earth: Poems Selected and New* is forthcoming from Porcupine's Quill. She lives in Victoria.

Christine Wiesenthal has recently published her first collection of poems, *Instruments of Surrender* (BuschekBooks, 2001). She lives in Edmonton.

CW: Well, your career is now into its seventh amazing decade.

PKP: I can't count in decades. But it is a long time. I do know that.

CW: And so many people have remarked upon the fact that it has been an exceptionally multi-faceted creative career.

PKP: I suppose it has. I've had to turn my hand to things in order not to be bored – not that my *life* has been boring – but painting or drawing or getting involved in puppet shows – anything creative, in fact, has been both natural and essential.

CW: Or children's books, or fiction . . . .

PKP: And children's theatre when I was younger. A whole lot of things. "Jack of all trades" is the saying. "Master of none" is how the saying ends!

CW: In your poetry there is a recurrent concern, I think, with both the idea of multiple selves, a proliferation of selves, and also a resistance to any form of entrapment or stasis. It seems to me that one might draw a parallel there between the working through of those themes with your broader career as an artist. That is to say, your artistic life – always innovative, trying a variety of art forms – stands as a kind of testament in practice to these themes in your poetry. Is that a correlation you would also draw?

PKP: A very interesting observation. I really don't know a lot about my own work. But I am aware of the fact that we are multiple – all of us. I remember in my twenties, thinking I had some kind of an identity, an indelibility, something that was monolithic in some way. As if I had been born as a wound-up toy – born programmed. And then I began seeing things differently. I now think there are many I's in us – not E-Y-E-S – but the vertical pronoun, as my husband would have said. For instance, let us say I decide to go on a diet. The I that gets up in the morning full of resolve is not the I that goes out to dinner and has a drink and finds the food awfully good, and goes to bed full of remorse. Somehow we are deluded into thinking that all these I's are one, but I don't think they are. Perhaps if we could see them all and let them act out their little lives they might ultimately fuse. But in the unregenerate state – I was going to say *we* are in, but let me just say I am in – we can't bring them all together.

CW: You can use the plural pronoun, as far as I'm concerned.

PKP: *[laughs]* That's kind of you.

CW: Now, you said in your twenties you had thought there was a kind of solidity to identity. Was there something that precipitated your change in thinking about identity?

PKP: Reading, I expect. It has been a great teacher. New ideas have led to wider experience.

CW: One of the questions that you anticipate with that response – and this is a big question, given the extent of your career – is how your ideas about the reading and writing of poetry have changed since you were in your twenties.

PKP: That's a full-bodied question! In a funny kind of way, I don't think I've changed that much. Sandra Djwa is working on a biography of me, and we've been going through some of the books I read when I was young. Heaven knows I've lost half of them in my wanderings around, but I still have anthologies of poetry with notes in the margins. I find it quite interesting, actually, to discover that my preoccupation with craft was evident very early. What age was I in 1934? Seventeen perhaps, something like that. And in the books dating back to 1934, my comments in the margins are almost all about craft: the use of alliteration, of assonance, of consonance. Clearly I saw it, heard it in the work. I cannot believe anybody taught me, for the teaching in school was abysmal, abysmal, *[laughs]* and very minimal, too. Already the analytical school of teaching had come into being – "What does the poem mean?" – a method I'm unsympathetic to. Of course the meaning is significant, but it is only one of many significant elements. What does a surrealist poem mean?

 At any rate, I don't think I got my *love* of craft from what I was taught in school or from my parents. I got my love of poetry from my parents, both of them, actually, but my mother especially, who had an actor's repertoire. She must have had a photographic memory, judging by the amount she could quote – from Shakespeare to nonsense rhymes. So I heard poetry all the time. I was aware of rhythms, and wordplay and alliteration – in nonsense rhymes you get an enormous amount of alliteration. ("Betsy Better bought some butter, but she said 'This butter's bitter'" . . . "'Round the rugged rock the ragged rascals ran . . .") I must have been taking it in through my ears without knowing it. So I think my attitude to the way I read now is not so very different from my attitude to the way I read then. I am still very, very aware of craft as I read and I'm more attracted to crafted poetry than to some of the looser work that is written today.

 As to the writing of poetry . . . my early work was flooded with images, an embarrassment of them. In the poem "After Rain," written in the early fifties, I wished to write a poem "clear of the myriad images that still –/ do what I will – encumber its pure line." Certainly I got my wish, to the extent that now I might wish for a greater flooding with images. I think my work has become more cerebral.

CW: This leads to another question, which relates to your poetic voice: Al Purdy, in a poem called "The Dead Poet" asks the question, "how else explain myself to myself/ where does the song come from?" Do you locate the origins of your voice as coming from your mother's words, her recitation of poetry in the house, or is it the case, as you have said, I think, in the past, that you first came to writing by "being an adolescent, which is enough to make anybody write."

PKP: All those hormones raging around. Oh, Lord, what else can you do with them except go out and get pregnant? *[laughs]* I don't know. You can do both, of course; it isn't necessarily an option. I don't think my voice came from one particular place. I think hearing all that verse was certainly a factor. But I also think we bring a lot of stuff with us – that our origins are not here, on this planet. When I say that, people immediately say, "Oh, do you believe in reincarnation?" I don't know that I believe in reincarnation. I think the word is probably too gross a word to encapsulate the infinite subtleties that exist in the idea of our coming from somewhere else or returning to where we came from. I have no understanding of it. All I have are intimations caused perhaps by a remembrance of some other state.

CW: I guess it gets back to the idea of identity, as being perhaps trans-individual?

PKP: Racial memory?

CW: Maybe familial, the idea that there is a kind of ancestral part of us.

PKP: Possibly. I don't know. But I certainly don't think we began when we emerged from our mothers' wombs. We come trailing clouds of glory, or clouds, at any rate. The onset of puberty creates a great longing in one. I suppose to a large extent it's a sexual longing, but it's very difficult to know the difference between a yearning for the erotic and the yearning for 'God.' This is not an original thought. Northrop Frye and others have had quite a bit to say about it. But anybody who has experienced either knows that there's some very curious connection between the two.

CW: Christina Rossetti comes to my mind right away. Lots of devotional poems where you really can't discern whether it is a secular love or sacred love that she's talking about.

PKP: Indeed, Emily Dickinson's another example, and many of the great mystic poets – the Middle Eastern poets of the Middle Ages and *Song of Solomon*, for Pete's sake, just to coin a poem.

CW: I like the tag, *Song of Solomon, for Pete's Sake*. Good title. Now, when you were in your late twenties, you were in Montreal and you were associated with the *Preview* group of poets. That's going back to the beginnings of your career. I wonder if you could say something about your experience as an aspiring young writer in that time and place, in a time that people talk about as the phase of literary modernism in Canada, at a time when you are surrounded by a group of older male mentors like A.J.M. Smith, F.R. Scott, Patrick Anderson, A.M. Klein. Were adequate models of a poet's life ever an issue for you?

PKP: Adequate models of the poet's life. What do you exactly mean by that?

CW: I mean that you were one of the relatively few women aspiring to a serious writing career at that time, and so many other women artists of the period speak of struggling to reconcile what they see as a poetic vocation or a writer's life that is implicitly gendered male, and then – on the other hand – the realities of life as a woman. Was that ever an issue for you?

PKP: No, no. It didn't occur to me that gender had anything to do with being a poet. I was brought up in a family that didn't denigrate women. I was always encouraged to believe I could do it, whatever "it" was. My father taught me as many male skills as my mother taught me female – in fact, perhaps more. He taught me how to change fuses and light gas furnaces, all those sorts of things.

CW: Survival skills.

PKP: Yes, indeed. There wasn't a strong demarcation between men's work and women's work in our household – gender wasn't an issue – but I was slow to mature, slow to get a sense of myself. So I was surprised when, as a little girl from the sticks, I went to Montreal and found myself accepted by this group, not because they were men. I don't think I thought of them principally as men. I thought of them as poets, more accomplished than I, more educated than I, and I was surprised they accepted me because I was less educated, not because I was less male! They clearly didn't see poetry as the preserve of men either for they nourished a talent that I didn't know I had. Also they took me seriously. My editorial opinion was respected, and I learned at the speed of light. I read until I went practically blind. Being forced to see larger issues than the self was perhaps one of the biggest things that happened. I became tremendously aware of the labour situation in Canada and the situation in the world. We were at war, for God's sake.

CW: You have described yourself in the past "as a feminist but not a feminist writer." Can you elaborate more fully on how you understand that distinction?

PKP: That's a good question. Some of the things I've said in the past absolutely baffle me when I hear them today. *[laughs]* I can't imagine what I was thinking. But there is a distinction for me between a feminist and a feminist writer. I'm rarely polemical; I don't write to support causes. But I'm very much a feminist in my conviction that we have the same rights men have, rights my mother's generation were denied. I think I've lived my life as a feminist, although certainly not as an activist.

CW: Yes. It's an interesting question. At one level as a woman writing about experience, you're writing as a woman writer; it's hard to maintain any distinction. I was reading a book by the Irish poet Eavan Boland, and she talks about the fact that being a woman and a poet obliges you to ask certain questions about the nature of voice, authority and self, and the relationship of poetry to acts of power. She says, though gender obliges you to ask those kinds of questions, it doesn't liberate you to "subcontract a poem to an ideology."

PKP: *[laughs]* Very articulate, very articulate.

CW: Yes, really. I thought that was a helpful way of putting it. The politics can't predominate.

PKP: The poem is usually ruined if they do. It becomes something else; it becomes a tract.

CW: But it is a carousel of a question. Because even though, as Boland argues, no one is "free to demand that a bad poem be reconsidered as a good ethic," the question comes round again when you consider that the judgments we make about "this is a good poem," or "that's a bad poem" are so thoroughly conditioned by our culture and by cultural biases.

PKP: Right. We're so conditioned we can't see ourselves. Who was it first discovered water? It certainly wasn't a fish. We're immersed in whatever our mindset is, and it's very difficult to break out of it, to even glimpse we're in it.

CW: And the problem of perspective has always been one that your poetry takes up and engages: vision, optical illusions, the nature of seeing, kinds of seeing, ways of seeing, the impossibility of seeing, limitations of vision. This I find very interesting. It's an abiding theme in your work. Do you see your working through of the problem of vision as having helped you at all with the issue of self-perspective on your own work?

PKP: The working through has more to do with my psyche than with my work. I'm very unconscious in my work. I never think that I'm working through a theme or even that I have a theme. I can't plan a series of poems. I could never have got a Canada Council grant – had I applied – because you have to present a ground plan. I can write only what I write when I'm writing it. I haven't a great sense of a body of work, or of themes. After the fact, reading, I can say, "Yes, all right, that relates to something earlier."

CW: Your body of work is like a kaleidoscope to you in the sense that you do habitually go back and regroup poems all the time. In *The Hidden Room*, for example, the poems are not chronologically arranged. So there's always a new syntax to your body of work.

PKP: I like it that way. Incidentally, I didn't choose the arrangement of poems in *The Hidden Room*. Stan Dragland chose it. With my approval. That was the way he saw it, and I liked what he saw. I could have vetoed it. Some academics were irritated by its lack of chronology. But there is another order that has nothing to do with time and Stan showed it. The need to know what came before what is a very linear approach. I think a poem can be judged simply as a poem, a body of work as a body of work. I also sometimes think the whole body of one's work exists at the outset. Dorothy Livesay and I used to argue about chronology. We used to argue about almost *everything*, I might add, but this was one of the major things. I said that if I came back to a poem after some years and thought changing the word from "green" to "blue" would make it better, I would change it. She would say it was dishonest, that my poems in chronological order and unaltered were my autobiography. And I would say, "You may think your work is *your* autobiography; *I* don't think of mine as my autobiography. What I'm trying to do is make a thing as good as I am capable of making it, and if ten years later I can make it better than it was then, it's *my* poem."

"But it's dishonest," she would say. "You couldn't have done it ten years before or you would have done it." It's a totally different approach.

CW: Yes, absolutely. Your argument with Livesay involves a very different conception of one's craft. Do you approach it as an ongoing work-in-progress that is always open to revision and change? Or should a body of work remain fixed? I can understand Livesay's point . . . .

PKP: I can understand it.

CW: – to the degree that some people are embarrassed by their early writing or ashamed of it. The temptation is sometimes there, I think, if not to disown it, then to feel – "Oh God!" – somewhat embarrassed by it, and I think that you need to be thoughtful about that. It's an early, honest effort; you were doing what you could, right? So to some degree I am sympathetic with those who say, "Don't tinker with it." I guess it's more a question of motive.

PKP: I have sympathy with it. I think it's a perfectly legitimate point of view, but it isn't my point of view, that's all. If I can make it better, I will. It's mine.

CW: At any rate, it's interesting you raise Livesay, because one thing that I wanted to ask you involves a comment that she once made to a younger poet. She once said that "sometimes a poem has to be accepted, even if it fails. Its very failure may be its meaning, or its meaning may not be for today, but for tomorrow." Is that a comment that you would also disagree with?

PKP: I don't fully understand what she's saying. I think it's quite possible that one is writing for a time that hasn't yet come, and by that I don't mean writing for posterity; I mean that you have had a glimpse of the future, or known something you don't yet understand. I think of the last lines of my poem "Stories of Snow": "through to the area behind the eyes/ where silent, unrefractive whiteness lies." I had no idea what the lines meant when I wrote them but I instinctively felt they were right and that I shouldn't change them. It wasn't until probably forty years later that I read in Rumi, "A blue glass shows the sun as blue, a red glass as red/ when the glass escapes from colour it becomes white. It is more truthful than all other glasses." So a poem that may not make sense when it is written may, in the future, make perfect sense. I can believe that.

CW: How about the idea of a poem that has to be accepted even if it fails, or that its failure may be its meaning?

PKP: I don't know what she means by "fails." Fails as a poem?

CW: Yes. Let's say a poem doesn't come together . . . that's how I'm construing her remark.

PKP: But surely if it fails as a poem, it doesn't have a place in the future. It has to be viable as a poem in order to have any significance at all. There seem to be two things here – writing as therapy and trying to create a work of art. The subjective and the objective.

CW: Maybe she means in the sense that you might learn from it in the future, looking back on it, maybe learning why it did fail, or something else from it. I guess I'm trying to ask you about the value of failure. We've all had poems that just refuse to be written, right?

PKP: Oh! Dozens of them, mm-hmm. My body of unfinished work is infinitely greater than the body of my finished work. All those false starts where you didn't have the lift to get over the jump.

CW: Yes. Or they stay in some kind of inchoate form, and no matter how many times you rejig them, they just will not come into being.

PKP: But that's all part of the process of learning how to write, I guess, which one goes on doing forever, as far as I can make out. Somebody said to me, a very good poet too, I might say, said to me, "Now that I know how to write a poem, it's so easy." I was astonished, actually, because I have no idea how to write a poem. Sitting here like this, now, there's no way I know how to write a poem. It seems to me each poem has its own rules, its own structure, its own essence, its own being.

CW: The subject of a poem's rules and structure makes me think of some of my more illuminating writing failures, many of which have involved experiments with traditional forms. With my first attempts at sonnets, I couldn't believe the kind of language that was coming out of me. It wasn't completely archaic, but it made very manifest to me the power of form to . . . .

PKP: Yes, mold language.

CW: – mold language, exactly. Now, in your foreword to *Hologram*, you talked about some of the technical challenges in writing the glosa, and you got around that eventually.

PKP: Certainly I know what you mean about trying to write a sonnet, that one slips into a kind of language one doesn't normally write in. The glosa was so unfamiliar to me that it didn't impose a vocabulary upon me at all. But to break out of a certain vocabulary that is associated with a particular form is difficult. I have great difficulty with sonnets, myself. I find myself slipping into love sonnets, to begin with. They seem to ask me to write about love. But in these last sonnets that I wrote with Phil [Stratford], *And Once More Saw the Stars*, the fact that we didn't rhyme gave us a greater freedom. I found the unrhymed sonnet form a great deal less draconian than rhyming sonnets.

CW: But you have said you enjoy the constrictions that form imposes on you.

PKP: I do; I contradict myself. But both are true. I love restrictions because they force me into new thoughts: if I can't go through I have to go around or up or over. Like travelling over rough country. Masochistic all the way.

CW: Masochistic, but also . . . .

PKP: It isn't masochism really.

CW: It's a fascinating process of discovery. Lately I've been experimenting with the villanelle.

PKP: Hardest of all. No, perhaps the pantoum is hardest, but a villanelle is *very* tricky.

CW: How would you describe your sense of the value of experimenting with traditional forms such as the glosa or the sonnet?

PKP: There is an intellectual pleasure in discovering what subjects fit what forms. You can't force the right hand into the left-hand glove. A villanelle is a compulsive form. It doesn't lend itself to pastoral subjects, for instance. I also found interesting the response to the glosas. People from all over the country sent me glosas. Some of them excruciatingly awful, *[laughs]* some of them remarkably good, while some people couldn't do them at all. Perfectly good poets couldn't write them. So I guess you find what you need. It's highly individual, the whole process. I don't know if I've gained anything beyond great pleasure in experimenting with traditional forms, which after all is no small thing. The real, real pleasures we have in our lives aren't – I was going to say aren't that many, but that's absurd. They are multiple; they're all around us all the time – what our eyes can bring us and our ears and our hearts if we can stay awake. But beyond the pleasure – there's something in me that likes to be challenged. I've always said that if I'm frightened of a thing, I have to do it. There's some of that in confronting a form that's too difficult for you, that's unknown territory. It brings out things in you that you didn't know you had. And so when a person says to me, "Now I know how to write a poem," I think already they're cutting themselves off from that enormous world that is filled with sharks and mermaids and constellations you never imagined . . . .

CW: Has recuperating traditional forms also given you a more historical perspective on the craft, so that you see yourself in the context of a much longer poetic tradition?

PKP: No. I don't see myself. I am not self-conscious in that respect, so it's always surprising when other people say they see me.

CW: You're a hologram.

PKP: *[laughs]* That's me.

CW: How important have reviews of your work have been to you, generally, over the course of your career?

PKP: I don't think they've been all that important. By that I don't mean that I am impervious to praise. I'm not; I don't think any of us are. It's a pleasure if I feel I've communicated with somebody, because that's really what it's all about. Or is it? One of the things, at any rate. "Only connect," as Forster said. It's wonderful when you receive the ball back over the net. You know you've made a connection. I always read my reviews and try to hear what the reviewer is saying.

But I'm never wildly depressed by a bad review or wildly elated by a good one. I know it's only one person's opinion; and I also know that if I am at the mercy of what other people think about me, I am nothing more than a shuttlecock being batted about. I think there's a centre-place between elation and despair that it is important to maintain. At the same time I'm not made of iron or stone. I suppose I got some very bad reviews when I was young. But on the whole, with a few exceptions, my reviews have been favourable. What I like best is a thoughtful review, and you don't get that too often.

CW: Yes, right, one that reads closely and attentively.

PKP: That points out your strengths and weaknesses. I'm really not, I think I can honestly say, looking for praise. That's not why I'm doing it.

CW: But the problem of – and this is why I asked about perspective earlier – the problem of keeping faith in one's work can be a real challenge at times, the sense of belief that one needs in order to keep on writing at some point.

PKP: In terms of creativity my life has been bizarre. I've never had a game plan, as I said earlier. In Brazil, for the first time in my life I couldn't write. I went through a bad period. If I hadn't been in love with the country, I might have been in trouble. My ego must have been fairly exaggerated at the time that it seemed so important that I write. What was the world going to lose, after all? Or perhaps it wasn't ego so much as a need for the balance writing gave me.

CW: Well, you had just won a Governor General's Award; you had been producing poetry that was being acclaimed. So I think even now, from what I've read, there is a fascinated incomprehension that borders on horror on the part of critics who are flummoxed by your silence, this ten-year silence. It seriously unnerves people. Ten years and not a poem published! And on the heels of a Governor General's Award yet! What's going on?

PKP: I have various theories about it, probably none of which is true, or all of them are. I was immersed in a different language. I wasn't hearing my own speech rhythms. I was trying frantically hard to learn Portuguese. I was overwhelmed by the world I was in, a totally baroque world in terms of the vegetation, architecture, people.

CW: Sensual, yes.

PKP: I drowned in it almost. And although I thought I wasn't writing I was writing copiously. It just didn't happen to be poetry. I was writing a journal, and also

I was drawing. That was what saved my life, the drawing. I got every bit as much satisfaction out of drawing as I did out of writing, and I didn't question it. I was perfectly happy learning how to put paint on paper, learning the different widths of nibs, the intricate, extraordinarily wonderful implements of the craft of art.

CW: Even though you were writing in your journal at that time, that somehow didn't count to you?

PKP: Oh, that didn't count, because writing to me was poetry.

CW: The responses that I have come across to that period of silence made me go back to this book, *Silences*, by Tillie Olsen. She talks about the distinction between silences of renewal, as with natural cycles, where something goes fallow for a while, and silences that are a kind of "unnatural thwarting of what struggles to come into being." In her own case, she talks about having to let writing "die in [her] over and over again" for all the wrong reasons; that is to say, she had a young family to support and so had to go out and get a series of dumb jobs to feed them. So that made me think: your silence, even though you were panicked by it at the beginning, it seems to me, it was ultimately one of these silences of renewal.

PKP: I think maybe you're right, because I was taking in an awful lot at that point, yes. With incredible pleasure, all my senses involved, looking at the world through a topaz. So after the first shock, because by that time I'd just assumed I was a writer, and that what a writer does is write, it was very weird not to.

CW: Do you think that silence is an underrated or misunderstood phenomenon in today's literary culture?

PKP: I think it's undervalued in our culture. Talk, talk, talk, talk, talk, talk, talk; turn on the radio for a music program and what do you get, blah, blah, blah, blah, blah; and his nickname was, and he had – who cares about his nickname? This is a great composer, and we want to know his nickname? Blah, blah, blah. But it gives the disc jockey an opportunity to sound off. Silence has been a matter of considerable interest to me one way and another. I married a very silent man, and he probably was more profound than most of the people I've known in my life.

CW: He was the one that brought you the drawing paper.

PKP: He was. Socially you're also expected to fill conversational gaps. Why? There are sounds out there. If you stop for a minute, you can hear all kinds of things that you don't even know are going on. We ask a good price for talking parrots, but what about those thinking parrots, as Nasrudin said. *[laughs]*

CW: The emphasis, increasingly, in both literary and intellectual circles, seems to be on early and constant production, and our culture is all about quick consumption. So as soon as you've got one thing, you've got to get another thing out.

PKP: That's true. It must be terrible for novelists. It seems to me that that sort of pressure cannot be borne. It could drive people to either writing very badly or saying to hell with it.

CW: Yes, and similarly, I think that many of the speculations about your period of silence say more about the critics' own preoccupations with the importance of publishing than anything essential about the experience as it was for you.

PKP: I read something the other day about my silence. Somebody was taking a psychoanalytical look at it, and it seemed to me they were talking rubbish. But even *there* somebody is trying to fill a void. It's the same thing.

CW: Psychoanalysis, literary criticism and the discipline of art history, too, as people point out, also involve such filling – art historians and critics filling up the painting with words, telling the narrative behind the painting. That too is forcing a kind of silence.

PKP: Mm-hmm, as if the painting can't speak for itself.

CW: And this gets back to your resistance to the analytic approach to poetry – always making the poem speak, or speaking for it.

PKP: Mm-hmm. Misinterpretation a lot of the time, too. Removing the legs from the fly, again. It seems to me too close a reading can lead you to emphasizing one thing over another and not getting the balance right because the glasses you are reading through are your own biases.

CW: You just intimated earlier that while you were learning Portuguese, it seemed to be displacing English in your mind. In retrospect, though, do you think that learning another language and the patterns and the rhythms of another language has actually enhanced your dexterity writing in English?

PKP: I doubt it very much, because I'm poor at languages. I've never mastered any language I've attempted to learn . . . I don't think that the bones of the language got into me enough to do that. I remember reading [Robert] Graves at one point in which he said that a good writer knows all the meanings of every word he uses, and it's a sort of micro attention to . . . .

CW: God, that would bog me down completely.

PKP: I think it would clip my wings. I wouldn't know how to move those feathers. *[laughs]*

CW: You'd be just a thinking parrot, then.

PKP: Just a thinking parrot, exactly. *[laughs]*

CW: You've written interestingly in ways that resonate for me with the way that learning a new language does change your personality, and your analogy was, one is a toy at first – a doll –

PKP: Mm-hmm. Say "Mama."

CW: – then a child. It's actually a very good, I think, experience to go through for that reason.

PKP: It strips you down to your naked self, whoever that is.

CW: In 1964 you came back from Mexico to Canada, to Victoria, with your husband. For a lot of poets who were writing in the sixties, the west coast would have been a very exciting place to come back to.

PKP: I suppose. The *Tish* movement was over by then, wasn't it?

CW: 1963 was, I think, the big summer school where the Black Mountain poets came up, so it was still very much in the air, I believe.

PKP: It wasn't exciting for me. I wasn't excited by the Black Mountain poets; they didn't talk to me particularly. And I had to find my way in a country that had forgotten me. It was a difficult time for me, one of the more difficult times in my life, coming home, which I thought was going to be lovely. I think I've said this before: your country has changed in the time you are away; and you, unbeknownst to yourself, have changed, too. Nothing really fits when you come back. You can't find a match. Nobody seemed much interested in me or my work. Another thing – the confessional poets were dominant, the influence of Plath and Sexton. By nature I'm not a confessional poet – which doesn't mean that I haven't written some poems out of my own experience.

CW: It's true, you began with a fairly impersonal voice.

PKP: "Man with One Small Hand," "Stenographers," "Typists." I was a camera. I was more a painter in a kind of way, a portrait painter – but not self-portraits, although every portrait is a self-portrait, I guess. I didn't really feel the self was the stuff of poetry. I always believed that poetry was something much bigger than me.

CW: So there were trends that –

PKP: That I felt I was at odds with, out of step. It took me a long time to find my voice again. To begin with I was not sympathetic to the Black Mountain people. I might be more sympathetic now than I was then. I wasn't sympathetic to the confessional poetry, although I admired Plath immeasurably. For her genius, not for her subject matter. Then I had a roadblock in Victoria. Robin Skelton was the major literary figure in Victoria at that time and he excluded me from anything literary that was going. I had come home and I didn't fit in. It was a bad time. But my husband was useful as always. He'd say, "Go and work. Work is your best friend. Go and work." *[laughs]* But that changed. Things do change in life, and all that changed.

CW: I was very intrigued that in John Orange's book, *P.K. Page and Her Works*, you mentioned some of the contemporary writers who were an influence around this time period. No, not an "influence" – you don't like that word! Affinity. You mentioned, among others, Patrick Lane, Gwendolyn MacEwen, Margaret Atwood and Jay MacPherson. Can you elaborate on what you felt poets like that offered you, why they intrigued you, why you felt an affinity with them?

PKP: I felt a great affinity with Patrick through his language – wonderful language. Gwendolyn's whole vision was – ennobling to me in some way. I didn't know her. I sat on a Governor General's jury with her once. I knew her to say hello to, but we were never friends. Because I was here and she was there we never got to know each other. But I loved what Gwendolyn was doing. Her T.E. Lawrence poems, I think, are among the best poems the country's ever produced. I think she's one of our very big poets, and she's hardly remembered at the moment. She will be again. Jay McPherson has an extraordinarily antic mind. I've known her since she was a child. I read her earliest poems and then saw her blossom into a poetry I hardly yet understand. I've forgotten what her metre is called. It's a Greek metre, I think. Sapphics? In *The Boatman* she seemed to be lifting poetry to a higher level. What intrigued me with Atwood was the fact that we used very similar images in a totally different way, to different ends. I don't think there was an affinity with Atwood. But I admired her immensely, *immensely*.

CW: How did the formation of the League of Canadian Poets in 1968 affect your career?

PKP: It was invaluable to all of us, perhaps especially to me, because I was an outsider coming in. At the AGM's we met each other, exchanged ideas, addresses.

The League also organized readings. When I left Canada in the fifties, poets didn't read. None of us in *Preview* gave readings. But when I came back, everyone was reading, and I thought, " There's no *way* I could get up and read." When Al Purdy was writer-in-residence at Simon Fraser, he suggested to Sandra Djwa that they ask me to come and do a reading. I was appalled when I got the invitation. To do a reading was bad enough, but to read to a university class . . . ! I have no university education, and at that point I imagined that people who had were learned. *[laughs]* Some *are* learned, of course, but in my imagination I didn't discriminate. They were all on a pinnacle for me. Then one morning I was wakened by a voice that said to me, "The only reason you don't want to read is because you're frightened of making a fool of yourself. Okay, so make a fool of yourself." And I went, and to my surprise I discovered I didn't read too badly and that I actually enjoyed it. There's enough of the ham in me to get a charge out performing. From that beginning I got onto the League's reading circuit, which gave me a chance to travel and meet poets in Nova Scotia and Edmonton and all over the place. So, at that time, for me, the League was invaluable.

I don't have a great deal to do with it now. I'm a member, but I'm not wildly sympathetic to the way the League has gone. Perhaps it is fine for the times – times I don't belong to. It has become large and expensive. I remember being at an annual general meeting – in Fredericton and our membership fee was – I think – five dollars a year. We were in grave financial difficulties and I had the temerity to suggest that we put the membership up to seven dollars. I was almost hooted out of the meeting. "Impossible! You may be able to afford seven dollars; but we can't." What is it today? $160 or $200? Of course, the value of money has gone up, but not that much. Arlene Lampert was the executive director in those days, there was little overhead and the poets were scrutinized by a membership committee of their peers.

One year I proposed that we make tapes of the poets reading – a good proposal, I think – a pity they dropped it. It was based on a program financed by the Library of Congress. Our National Library didn't – and I think doesn't – finance such a project. I thought it should, but if it didn't, then the League should do it. So we made up a hit list. *[laughs]* Of course a hit list doesn't work perfectly because you don't know who's going to die; you can only surmise on the basis of age. Pat Lowther I don't think was ever on tape. And Alden Nowlan died before we got to him. The idea was to give a set of tapes to the National Library and market them to universities and schools. I think that is the kind of thing the League should do. But for you, the League as it is today, may be equally valuable. I don't know, Chris. I'm not a young writer, so I don't know.

CW: I asked you earlier about reviews. But what about prizes and awards and honours? How important have they been to you?

PKP: I've had some prizes – not many. But I have had an extraordinary number of honours, which is interesting. I never know how to read that. I haven't been even shortlisted for any of the prizes in the last – I don't know – twenty years. And yet the honours come in. It gives me a sort of double vision of myself – on the one hand; on the other hand. How important are they? It's awfully difficult to know.

CW: Is competition a good thing for a poet?

PKP: Which poet? I'm not competitive. I've never entered a contest. I'm not sure of my motive – do I not want to compete or am I frightened of losing? For some writers it's marvelous; some love the competition. I know two writers who enter every competition going, and win prizes and so add to their incomes.

CW: The importance of awards is a question that I think is worth asking at this point, because there are now increasingly well-endowed and well-publicized awards, right? Like the Giller or –

PKP: The Griffin.

CW: – the Griffin, yes. Very sexy prizes. And yet poetry, on the whole, as an artistic practice, it seems to me, is ever more obscure in the wider culture.

PKP: It is funny, isn't it? On the one hand; and on the other hand, as I was saying a minute ago, but in a different context. People turn out in *droves* to hear poetry readings. I don't think half the audience is remotely interested in poetry; I think it's a sense of getting something for nothing, or a manifestation of the aimlessness that seems to have overtaken our culture, or the hope of titillation. You only have to say the word "fuck" and you bring the house down! *[laughs]* It's bewildering to me. And then there are open mics where people get up and read stuff that should never have been written in the first place. Or if written, written as therapy. Rather than developing an ear for poetry, this practice diminishes, reduces it. It may well contribute to the place of poetry in our society. It doesn't treat it as a holy thing, which at best, I think it is.

CW: Yes, it's a disturbing trend. Poetry is often quite unselfconsciously spoken of as one stop on the way to the Holy Grail of fiction. I've heard people say things like, "Oh, well, I'm sure she would have *made the leap* to writing fiction if she hadn't died first, writing her skinny little poems" or something to that effect. So there's this assumption that fiction signals some sort of inherent progression.

PKP: The "progression" from poetry to fiction is possibly a takeover by the linear left hemisphere of the brain. I suspect it's the more linear part of the brain that writes fiction and we are living in a left hemisphere culture. I throw that out as a possible explanation.

CW: I hadn't made that connection. It's certainly true that poetry is difficult, and ours is not a culture that embraces difficulty, not intellectual difficulty.

PKP: But some poetry isn't even intellectually difficult.

CW: You're right. The neglect of poetry is so manifest though, isn't it? When they announced the Governor General's Awards this past spring on CBC-TV, Peter Mansbridge announced the fiction winner and the nonfiction winner –

PKP: I know.

CW: – and could not take a nanosecond to say, "And for poetry, Don McKay."

PKP: I know. Want to kill them! But perhaps I should modify that! It might be taken as a threat.

CW: So how do you think about the role of poetry in contemporary culture? Is it a shift that's concerning you, or how do you think we need to think about writing poetry today?

PKP: I think it could save the world, actually. Delusions of grandeur? But to return to the two hemispheres – I don't know how much you know about the brain; I don't know much myself. But to oversimplify what little I do know, we're a left-hemisphere culture, and the left hemisphere you could say is the masculine hemisphere – rational, linear. The right is the female hemisphere – intuitive, musical, lateral. Perhaps the dreaming hemisphere. And when I say "female" and "male" I don't mean sexual; I mean the female and the male principle. The more the left dominates, the more we are out of balance, and the worse the world will become. So, without the poet – and when I say "poet" read "female principle" – we're in deep trouble. There was a very curious paper in *Poetry Chicago* some years ago that analyzed the effect of poetic metre on the brain. Apparently there are certain rhythms in the English language, and in other languages too, that are healing rhythms. And when we eliminate them from our lives, we are more subject to lunacy and breakdown. And sickness. *And indoctrination.* Now, they may be wrong, I don't know. I'm not in a position to argue with them but my instinct persuades me they are right. I think it's deep in us – like our blood.

CW: One of the glosas from *Hologram*, "Planet Earth," was recently read on international ground locations around the world, including a radio station in Antarctica and the International Space Station.

PKP: I don't think it was read in the Space Station. They had to negotiate it and I don't think the negotiation came off. But I believe it was read on Mount Everest. If you're reading to emptiness, does emptiness hear? It's the old question, if a tree falls in the forest when no one is there . . . ? Takes you right back to that early teenage query.

CW: Yes. At some level, I guess, the question of "Who is listening?" or "Who's out there who might be hearing?" has to preoccupy the mind at some point.

PKP: We don't know, that's the whole truth, do we? We don't know if ghosts are walking among us here today, this afternoon, if this room is peopled. We have no idea. We know you and I are in it, or we think we are, but whether there are more of us here than that, we don't know. And in terms of space, Lord help us – when you look at it, it's enough to dazzle you. We can't be the only humans. Can't be the only entities. There must be others out there, and who knows who's communicating, what's going back and forth.

CW: You alluded earlier to Philip Stratford, and I do have a question about this latest book, *And Once More Saw the Stars*, jointly authored with Stratford. I see this book as a logical or natural progression from *Hologram* . . . in the sense that *Hologram* involves a kind of collaborative process . . . .

PKP: Yes, it is; that's very true.

CW: – with the poets whose lines you've chosen to "launch" your glosas.

PKP: Yes, you're quite right. Two voices. In each case two voices.

CW: "A marriage of sensibilities" you called it in the foreword to *Hologram*. But in the correspondence that you exchanged with Philip, which is reprinted in *And Once More Saw the Stars*, he says at one point, "I don't even feel the impulsion to discuss the experience of co-authoring, although some day I'd love to sit down with you and discuss the adventure." Now, that day didn't arrive, right?

PKP: No.

CW: Because he died. But if one of the presences in this room now was Philip – what would you have to say to him about the process of poetic collaboration as you experienced it?

PKP: It was very stimulating . . . the connection between our two minds. A friend of mine who is a poet, when I told her I was writing this renga with Philip, began one with a friend of hers. "But," she said, "it didn't go anywhere. I'm trying to figure out why yours worked. I think, to begin with, you chose big themes. We didn't. We chose quite a small theme that didn't give us much space. Another reason was that we didn't choose a form to work in." I would say also that the voices have to match, but not perfectly, and the minds have to surprise each other. Philip's being different from mine pushed me just as a form does – forcing me into areas I would probably never have thought of going. He'd leave a line dangling, and I'd have to pick it up and run with it. I loved it. It was very stimulating. A game.

CW: It's funny: you call it the "ding dong, ping pong" method of composition.

PKP: Playing this game with Philip was almost like a fast little game of tennis.

CW: Has the computer affected your process of composition at all?

PKP: It must have, and yet it would be very difficult for me to analyze it. When I first started using the computer I had to print everything as I went along. And as I really do care about the planet, it bothered me that I was using so much paper. But little by little, as the computer and I got to know each other, I didn't mind losing the early versions. Today, I would find my earlier method cumbersome. There was a point when I felt I could physically feel something changing in my brain. And now I can hardly write any other way, in spite of the fact I've been fiddling with a pen all the time we've been talking.

CW: Yes, but maybe the nib is reassuring for somebody who's also –

PKP: A visual artist? Perhaps, but I *love* the computer now; I just *love* it.

CW: I used to write everything longhand first as well, and now I compose on the computer, too. It does give you that sense, though, that you can tinker endlessly, right?

PKP: And you do!

The Company of Great Thieves

MICHAEL ONDAATJE

Interviewed by David O'Meara

Michael Ondaatje is a poet, novelist and editor of *Brick* magazine in Toronto. His most recent novel is *Anil's Ghost* (McClelland & Stewart, 2000), and his poetry collections include *The Cinnamon Peeler: Selected Poems* (M&S, 1992) and *Handwriting* (M&S, 1998).

David O'Meara is the author of *Storm still* (Carleton, 1999). A new collection of poetry is forthcoming in 2003. He lives in Ottawa.

DO: What do you look for in a poem? What tells you that it's not merely competent, but good?

MO: Oh, I expect to have my life changed by it. That's what I'm looking for, always. I guess in some ways I react *against* a simply competent poem. Essentially I want to be changed, steered to a new place, have something fulfilled. Is that asking too much? Now and then that happens. I might read a four-line poem by Patrick Kavanagh and be altered . . . .

DO: Is it just the message, or is it the way it's written, or both, how this comes about – this sort of confluence of the poet's technique with the actual content of the poem?

MO: Well, it is a confluence. The message also comes through in the style, and the craft, the pitch and tone of it.

DO: And maybe it must also be clear that the writing is coming from an inner compulsion, that the writer feels it's absolutely necessary to say it. And when it's put down on the page, it's done in such a way that you connect with that compulsion to some degree?

MO: It's to do with my recognition of it. There are lots of good reasons why we are moved by poetry. But one also might recognize, with a writer like Robert Lowell for instance, that the poetry seems too "cooked." At least to me. Even in *Life Studies*, I think. Whereas John Berryman's *Love and Fame*, for example, represents something much deeper and certainly more raw, for me. . . . It is that mixture of being focused but also half-made, as if the whole thing is only just being held together. That sweet disorder in the dress.

DO: It's almost as if you lose something if it's too polished. That it needs a bit of that rough edge to it to suggest that it has come from somewhere more honest. There's also the question with Lowell, not that he was creating drama in his life to write the poems, but using it for a dramatic advantage. There was the backlash with *For Lizzie and Harriet* – that he was taking very personal things from letters and correspondence and incorporating them into his fourteen-line poems. It's something that I often question a bit, that when a poem is being written, particularly if it's something personal, there's always the danger in sort of looking at our personal lives as *material* – only – rather than honestly wanting to articulate something that you feel strongly about. There are times that you'll hear someone say about a planned trip or some upcoming event "That will be good material," and I'm a little wary of that, because I never plan something thinking, "This might lead to a poem." The experience is simply the experience. A poem might come afterward but you can't be cooking it up like that. Sometimes I can see that falseness, the agenda behind it, when I'm reading that stuff.

MO: That brings up a whole other can of worms – Leonard Cohen speaks about poets as "the company of great thieves" . . . I tend not to think of poetry as something preconceived. I don't sit down because I have an idea I want to get across, or even an emotion that I am clear about. I'm not quite sure what is going to happen. I might start a poem thinking about traffic but it could end up being about a sparrow, and then I'll rework it and rework it and it will turn into being about something else. For me the poem is discovered during the process of making it.

DO: I think Stephen Dobyns also says something to that effect. That the worst a poet can do is sit down and know exactly what they're going to say when they start it. And he cites the weakness of late Wordsworth, where it's clear that he is imparting his wisdom, rather than enacting a search. That he's passing out "improvement pills" in the late poems, just working towards a very pat conclusion, whereas maybe his earlier stuff was just coming out of a feeling, and he was moving towards re-enacting that. At the beginning of the Age of Modernism, perhaps free verse derived its power not only from a new-found freedom with subject matter, but also with breaking with our expectations of form, breaking from our anticipation of certain patterns of established verse, and something like surprise became an integral element to poetry's effectiveness. Do you think, now that we have almost a century of free verse behind us, that it still has the power to surprise? And how does it do it?

MO: Well, I never thought free verse was "free." And in that way Pound and the Imagists were the most important pointers for me when I began to write.

DO: What did they suggest to you?

MO: That the precision and sharpness of every word counted. I think that became the first essential thing, more important to me than the eventual structure of the villanelle or the sonnet. And also what Pound said: if the hawk is going to become a symbol of something in a poem, the hawk first of all has to be a real hawk. It's got to have feathers; it's got to be active as a creature. So I mean nearly all the principles of the Imagists appealed to me, and that was where I began in a way. I think all good poems are "formal" or "structured," but not necessarily so in the sense of them all having or living in a pre-existing pattern.

DO: Maybe the question leading from that is: do you think that contemporary poets are taking free verse for granted? Do they even think that there is such a thing as technique in free verse? That there are still choices?

MO: A lot of poetry doesn't have a focus or precision. But that is not limited to free
       verse. A good deal of poetry, free and formal, is just too verbose – it hasn't
       been distilled. What I look for in a poem is a balance of the seemingly casual
       voice, with a carefulness. That it's said as simply as possible, but also as *sug-
       gestively* as possible. That four-line poem by Patrick Kavanagh suggests more
       than an entire book.

DO: When you talk about how something is too cooked, it can also be too raw, and
       it's hard to say where the balance is. You want to write powerfully, but being
       quiet or subtle in a poem is just as difficult.

MO: I know in my earlier poems I was almost too casual, too lackadaisical. Wild
       and woolly, someone said. With *Handwriting* I really wanted to write the
       poems as if there was a limit to the number of words that could be used. You
       do have to work at being simple. I really wanted to take off, remove, all those
       extra clothes that were there in the earlier poems.

DO: There certainly seems to be a decided spareness to the language in
       Handwriting, as opposed to the earlier poems. Bare narrative and the use of
       lists – a kind of catalogue verse. I got the sense that it was an excavation – you
       were bringing these images up and just sort of placing them there unadorned
       for the reader to make their own decisions about these things, rather than try-
       ing to influence the reader with charged metaphors and language. It is far more
       spare writing than anything you had done before. Do you think that the mate-
       rial itself brought that out, that the content suggested the form and language
       of what you were writing?

MO: The content always does influence the form, and vice versa. I might begin
       the poem as a whisper, and that will govern what I say about the world
       around me. But I was definitely piecing together fragments of history, so that
       kind of rune-like voice was necessary. And, also, as I said, there was less
       assurance of what exactly one can say about this situation. I remember the
       other book where the poetry was manically tight was *The Collected Works of
       Billy the Kid*, but there you had the prose as well, so in a way, you didn't
       have to do the work of the prose in the poetry. In the poems the words were
       sharpened and gnarled. But I was able to do that because one third of the
       book was prose, where I could go all over the place. Whereas I think in the
       early books of poetry, I was carrying both the prose and the poetic side, car-
       rying armfuls of clothing from one room to another one. With *Handwriting*
       I also knew I was going to try to write, or was already writing, a book of fic-
       tion as well. And though the subject seems to be very similar, in the poems
       I wanted a lighter kind of pointing. The content of *Anil's Ghost* and
       Handwriting are very different for me. When you are writing prose you are
       in the mud, you know, you are constantly in the mud. With poetry you can

look down, you can fly over something, and connect two very different things up almost simultaneously.

DO: Do you mean you have more perspective of what you're examining, or . . . ?

MO: There is a kind of stylistic leaping that is possible in poetry that cannot really happen in prose. Prose, if you compared it to a painting, needs to be realistically grounded, (this is a simplification, I know), whereas poetry can be more impressionistic.

DO: Do you feel like you've found a new way of writing poetry? That there's been a leap, or at least a sea change of some kind? What have you got from the experience of writing *Handwriting*, deliberately writing in that more spare style?

MO: Well, I don't think I can go back to an earlier style, but at the same time, *Handwriting* did feel like a kind of ending to me. It's like the thin end of the wedge that I'd got to. But *Handwriting* is the kind of poetry that, I suppose, I am closest to.

DO: I seem to recall – somewhere in the back of my mind where one stores these things – you once saying about your fiction that whenever you write a new novel, you have to wrestle with a new technical challenge. Do you feel the same way about verse?

MO: Yes I do. I think that's exactly the state I'm in right now. I don't want to go and start to write another book of poetry that's going to sound and look like *Handwriting*. It would look closer to *Handwriting* than *The Dainty Monsters*, for sure, but . . . I think it's a matter of changing your verbal patterns and habits. You don't want to go back and retread those techniques.

DO: I think with a first book you spend a lot of time just learning, trying different things, and once you put it out, then you spend some time trying to "not write like yourself." Whether it's after the first book, or maybe it's after the third, and maybe it continues, and you repeat that cycle. And so there's sort of an aggression, I guess, to go somewhere else and find a new way to enter the original experience, and consequently, the material. With this different style in *Handwriting*, where do you want to go now? Do you have anything in mind, or are you waiting for it to happen, that you'll hit upon something?

MO: No, I haven't got anything in mind, but I think that what you say is true: it is this odd thing of sitting down to write and surprising yourself about the way you're writing. And also what you are writing about. I guess repeating oneself is like hell to me. Not that I dislike what I've done, but I want to be able to discover something new about myself and the way I think and articulate those things.

DO: At the end of your poem "Tin Roof," you evoke Rilke, expressing the desire to find the same creative space that he entered when composing much of *The Duino Elegies* – how the lines sort of announced themselves and came out of him, as pure inspiration, as if he were simply acting as a conduit for already-composed lines. Is that something that haunts you? What are your thoughts on inspiration? What is inspiration, do you think?

MO: I'm not sure. Practically everything I write is a surprise to me, so in that sense, it's inspiration. I don't sit down with an idea or a plan. I sit down to write and see what happens. There will be a subliminal craft at work with the first thing you write, and that path will somehow affect what you do. There will be a kind of pattern and discipline. But it's when you've written fifteen lines and you go back and look at it and realize that in the shaping of those fifteen lines you can find another different seven-line poem that you hadn't even thought about when you were writing the fifteen lines. And that process of editing, shaping, rewriting the poem, is where a lot of inspiration also happens.

DO: Do you think the process can also happen in reverse? Obviously a poet has to be prepared, and know their technique, know what's a good line, what's important to keep or throw away, and consider thoughtfully the experience they are writing about, or the historical event, or whatever. If they're prepared technically for it, the inspiration comes more easily. They can simply recognize that this is going to be something worth using. I guess I have a sort of "blue-collar" attitude to writing poetry. That it's real work, a lot of slogging to get to that magic moment. Certainly there's room to just be hit by something that suddenly comes out and it's "there." Yes, I agree that you must be surprised by what you're writing. But also, to know your tools. To know alliteration, and know how to use line breaks, to understand the tension between stressed and unstressed syllables, and how metaphors work, and that an image, no matter how fanciful, must be accurate to be powerful. Those kinds of things. To have learned how those tools work allows you to understand how you can use inspiration when it happens, I guess. There's a certain preparation involved in claiming that inspiration.

MO: What I am saying is the inspiration doesn't only happen in the first draft of writing; it happens when you're rewriting. Where you see that in fact the alliteration is over the top in this poem, or that you need to slow down the pace in some way, or add a couple of beats of air in there when you feel the line going too fast. All these things. All the technical things that you've learned, or you are learning in fact *as* you are writing – which is always more interesting. I know when I was editing *The English Patient*, I started shifting the pronouns or the time frames, and that kind of doubled all kinds of meanings. And I think that came out of reading Rilke, probably, more than anyone else. His floating pronouns. Sometimes it's that kind of influence that a poet can have on a novel. But I think the act of editing for me is where you bring all your skills as a reader and a writer to bear on the page, and to recognize that yes, this is good, but maybe it's a bit too well-made here. Let's pull back a bit, or . . . The stresses or the line breaks – all these things are kind of at war and you need to balance them.

DO: Often the most enjoyable part of writing the poem is those revisions, where even tweaking a word and suddenly the line lives, where maybe before it wasn't working. Just the change of an adjective or dropping part of a phrase, and suddenly "*Bang*, there's the tone I want to suggest . . ."

MO: But to go back, I'm not necessarily waiting for inspiration. I decided I was going to write a book about Billy the Kid, I had no idea how long it would take. For three years I was doing that – sometimes something happened, sometimes nothing happened. If you're focusing on a certain subject, the way you do with explorers in your book, you're in a mindset of receiving anything to do with that. You might be living on Galley Street, but you're really thinking with half your head about this explorer or the astrolabe or whatever. What I loved about your book, actually, was the fact that it was still so contemporary. You had a historical line and a contemporary line, where an explorer's astrolabe can continue to exist alongside that lovely poem about someone who has lost himself.

DO: The "Turtle Soup" poem on Darwin is maybe a good example of what we've been talking about. I had been trying to write that poem for quite some time, and I'd just stopped working on it, because it wasn't happening. I had done tons of reading on Darwin – biographies and essays. And one day, thinking about it again, the three-line stanzas suggested themselves and I started again. It just kind of came out, it kind of flowed. It was a very easy poem to write once I'd hit that point, although I'd done forty drafts before it, in different styles and different kinds of tones. I had all the information, but it took those forty drafts to find that entry point. So maybe that's an example of preparation leading to inspiration.

MO: I know in the novels, what I sort of wait for is when I can get a voice from the characters. I can do all the research ad nauseam, plot or story or whatever – but about two-thirds of the way through *The English Patient*, Almasy started talking, and he was saying things I never would have thought of saying. It was like – not quite speaking in tongues – but he was making grand statements about nationalism and post-nationalism, and things I was not even interested in. But it was like I'd set him up, as if I'd stoked a fire. So you wait for that aspect to come out. It's not *just* out there, it's a combination of something out there and something within you. And I think that happens in poetry, too, when you are on a roll. You are waiting for that thing that will happen, which is a result of much preparation.

DO: The two most difficult things to write about might be love and politics, and humour might be the most challenging tone. Do you find one subject or tone more difficult than another?

MO: Well, the thing about the love poem is that there is such a great tradition, and so everyone can accept it. So it's easier to write definitely than the political or humorous. Not that it's easy to write a *good* one. But it's acceptable for us to sit down and want to write something that is a term of endearment. The political poem is a killer. The political *anything* is a killer because we don't trust anybody who speaks that way out there. I don't, anyway. The minute I start reading a tract I get suspicious. So really, you have to do it perhaps from the point of view of an individual as opposed to an ideology. Some of Brecht's political poems are pretty great, but you can't do a lot of that, sustain that . . .

DO: You look at an example like Neruda, who was supportive of Stalin. He couldn't have known the reality behind the ideal. Yet he wrote these very human poems . . . .

MO: But you see, I think an ode of Neruda's on salt is more politically successful than his "bigger" poems about the history of South America.

DO: It's quite easy to slip into propaganda, isn't it? And it's such a surprise and delight to come across a poem that manages to be political and yet very human. Michael Redhill's poem "Via, Outside Quebec City," from *Asphodel*, is a good example. He's talking to these two vaguely foreign children on the train, joking with them, asking them what they like, when the elder brother says "He no like tear gas." There's a stanza break, and then the line, "Now we sit quietly and dusk is coming," and so much happens in that break! The suggestion of strife, pain, history. The jolting of consciousness in the narrator. The poem doesn't end with descriptions of bloodshed or riots, just the onomatopoeic train-sound "Bogota Bogota Bogota . . ." Nothing and everything is said. He's not telling us what we should think, just presenting a picture of individuals . . . Now *humour*, how can you know if your intention is coming across on the page. You've written some very humourous stuff – I'm thinking of, say, "Claude Glass," with the self-deprecating narration . . . .

MO: You can't sit down and *try* to be funny because it's just so leaden. One thing I found interesting when I did "Elimination Dance" was that the humour doesn't come in the actual line of content, but in the synapse *between* two lines. So there's a line about the Rosicrucians – "Anyone who's written to the age-old brotherhood of Rosicrucians . . ." – and the next line is "Anyone who's lost a urine sample in the mail." And it's just that strange jump from that pompous little example to the other thing that makes it funny. Neither line is actually funny by itself. And *Elimination Dance*, which was more like a joke than anything else – actually taught me a lot about humour and pacing and timing. And it was fun to write and rewrite and I still change it every now and then.

DO: There's a British anthology published by Faber and Faber, called *News That Stays News*, with a hundred poems – one poem for each year of the twentieth century. A small percentage of the poems are about everyday life, but a lot of them are dealing directly with events that are happening in that specific year, written by a poet contemporary to the time. It got me thinking about writing about contemporary events. Is there a responsibility to comment on events as they happen? How can you do that successfully?

MO: There's no solution to this one. Often the way you respond to something as a human is different (in terms of time) to the way you respond as a writer. I'm one who takes a long time to respond, in terms of art anyway. I *will* respond in fury or pleasure to something political, but to then write something that is not just for the moment, but for longer than that, takes longer. I wanted to write about Sri Lanka for a long, long time before I actually wrote about it. I didn't know how to write about it without demeaning or just "using" the subject, you know? I think, again, it has to come from a human perspective – from some personal angle.

DO: In his poem, "The Dead Poet," Al Purdy, speculating on the origins of his poetry, asks "how else explain myself to myself/ where does the song come from?" Do you have any explanation of where your voice came from, of why you became a poet?

MO: I was pretty much alone as a kid. I didn't really feel *lonely*, but I felt very much alone. And I think I became an avid *reader* when I was about nine or ten. And that was the great pleasure for me growing up, and is so even now. But I didn't think about becoming a writer until I was at university in Canada, and it was a complete surprise to me. It was almost like all that stuff I had access to before then had made me ready to start writing. Again, it wasn't prepared or thought of beforehand. I also grew up with English and some Sinhala – which I lost when I left Sri Lanka. So somehow in the middle of my teens I lost a language. And I always imagined it got submerged into English somehow, and that helped it. But I feel there was a lot of luck, you know. When I began to write it was a time when I wanted to express myself or discover myself, and I was in a new country, and I also had Arthur Motyer, a great teacher for the first time in my life, and all those things happened simultaneously and kind of merged and allowed me to write, to even *think* of writing.

DO: Were there particular poets who touched that off?

MO: I remember picking up an anthology by Brinnin and Read called *The Modern Poets*, which had pictures of poets. It was my first book with pictures of poets in it. *[laughter]* And I read all these poets I'd never heard of. I read Ted Hughes for the first time and Philip Larkin, I guess. It was mostly some English and some American. I went out and bought their books. Thom Gunn's *My Sad Captains*; Ted Hughes's *The Hawk in the Rain*. About the same time I was discovering W.B. Yeats and Robert Browning at university. And about that time I started reading the poets who were writing in Canada. And then later on it was William Carlos Williams and Robert Creeley. It took me a while to get to them, but they were also crucial to me. Williams's "No ideas but in things" was an opening door.

DO: I don't remember getting into poetry right away. One thing I remember – probably thirteen or fourteen years old – is taking out a book of quotations, "great" quotations from essays and speeches, and I was fascinated by the *choice* of words. I certainly didn't know what most of those quotes *meant*. But in a literary essay or in speechmaking, it's always about choosing words carefully for the best effect, which is what poetry is. And maybe that love of the well-worded phrase influenced the way I look at poetry.

MO: The other thing that we never think about is how many song lyrics we have within us. We grew up on years and years of song. How many are in my head right now? Whenever I go to England, they always seem to be playing the same songs they were playing thirty years ago. Like "Toreador" or some damn song like that. The minute I get there, I hear these songs I heard in the fifties or sixties, and I can immediately join in on the song. And I know every word. And so the fact is, that whatever generation we are part of we are carrying about four hundred songs in our heads, at least. And that must influence how we talk and how we speak and how we write.

DO: A friend of mine once commented that after Shakespeare, he thinks the most quoted person is Elvis Costello. *[laughter]* How have your feelings about poetry, the reading and writing of it, changed since you were in your twenties?

MO: One of the things that has happened is that all the arts have become much more prominent in terms of the media. Which is a good and bad thing. I think poetry might be more popular but we are less educated about it. Much of the criticism is appallingly facile, even in our serious journals – more involved with quick judgments, a rave or a dismissal, placing a person on a ladder of talent as if that was a final slot for the rest of their life. So there's a sense that a writer has to hit it out of a ballpark right away. Or your first novel has definitely got to be a hit; otherwise you won't be picked up by the publisher again. In comparison, when I began writing in the sixties, I think there really was a sense that you could fall down and it wouldn't make much difference. I mean Patrick Lane wrote a few quite bad books of poetry, and then a really wonderful book of poetry, and then became a very good poet. So there was that kind of nurturing that existed at that time in the late sixties and early seventies. Because poetry was not important in a public way. So you learned in a way in private, while being published by small presses or publishing in magazines. And there was an awareness of the writers around you in Canada at the time. I mean, my specific interest in Larkin, Hughes, Gunn was over very quickly, and I was conscious of Al Purdy and Phyllis Webb and David McFadden and John Glassco and Victor Coleman. So there was a real sense of a company of people around you that you could learn from, and even meet. I guess you have that now, but there's more of a professional thing going on.

DO: It's unfortunate, because the sense of individual exploration has been replaced by workshops and writing programs. I *do* think that one needs to enter into some critical dialogue, maybe with just another person or a small group of individuals, but there's also a danger in becoming a workshop junkie, a person who will not write without being directly involved with a workshop, who needs that fix or gratification of others commenting on the work all the time. There's a fear of solitude, of educating yourself, of learning that poetry is, *really*, reading, and writing and writing and writing and working out the bumps . . .

MO: One of the things that was good for me when I was at university was that about three or four of us would get together once every two weeks and we'd read each other's poetry and rip each other to shreds. But it was not personal in some odd way. There was Tom Marshall, and David Helwig, and Douglas Barbour, and Tom Eadie in Kingston. And that was so important to me, because it's difficult to find people who will call you on something that has become too much of a habit. But also you need time alone. You need time to spend – half a year kind of burrowing into some little corner, and finding something that's specifically your voice. But you know, now, everything is so speeded up, it's very difficult. You write three poems and then there's a workshop, and then somebody approaches you to do to a book, or something or other, and it's on a T-shirt before you know it . . . *[laughter]*

DO: And if you write something that might be surprising to you, in a style that you weren't expecting, and you bring it to a workshop and three of the people in your class say, "Well that's cute, or derivative, or doesn't hold with such-and-such a theory," then you'll just abandon it. Whereas you might write ten, fifteen more shitty poems like that, and then eventually you'll see how that works, or doesn't, but it will be your own process.

MO: And sometimes having a flawed poem is a good thing, because that can lead to the next breakthrough.

DO: How important have reviews, awards, other honours been to your feelings about your work? Is competition healthy or unhealthy for a poet?

MO: I think what's good about awards is that they're a kind of alternative to what the media present as going on in writing. So if there's a really good book that comes out and gets overlooked, maybe because it's not published by a big press, that book will disappear quite possibly unless it's recognized by an awards jury. That for me is the main value of awards and short lists.

DO: But what happens to that book that was very well-crafted and didn't get short-listed?

MO: That's the problem. One of the problems with awards and short lists is that the general public thinks that those are the only five books of poetry that came out that year.

DO: I guess if I hear from someone who I trust that such-and-such a book is very good, then that means more to me than hearing that someone won this prize. It's wonderful when a book that really deserves it wins, but I rarely pick up a book because I hear it's won this or that award. I'll leaf through it, and if after three or four pages I see it's strong writing, then I'll buy it.

MO: Yes, for me, if someone I admire writes to me and says they like this book of poems, or that novel, that will mean more than an award.

DO: Auden once said that "Every poet has his dream reader: mine keeps a lookout for curious prosodic fauna like bacchics and choriambs." *[laughter]* Do you have a dream reader? Maybe this brings us around from the opposite direction of my first question. What do you want people to appreciate in what you've written?

MO: I'm not sure who that reader is. It's not one individual; it's a kind of mixture of people. Someone pretty smart, who keeps you from being too much of a smartass. But I don't really think of the reader actually reading the poem – I sort of imagine the reader pushing me towards a thought. And again it's not a specific person. I suppose this is useful for me because he or she replaces the idea of an audience while I am writing. Because if I think of an audience when writing, I become self-conscious. That's my first principle of writing: in order to write I have to kind of not think that this will be read by anybody. That it's something that's utterly private, this is just for myself. That's crucial for me.

DO: Also, I think it's important, at certain stages, not to send poems out to maga-
zines until I've finished the manuscript. It's really what you've been saying. If
I'm thinking about "Oh, I'm going to send this poem to the Such-and-such
Review when I finish it. Or I'm going to send it off here," then other aesthetic
choices may enter into it. And whether a poem is rejected or accepted, that
affects the poet's relationship with the poem. I may eventually say, "Oh I don't
think it's very good," or "Yes, I'm happy with it," but there's an outside influ-
ence there – the publishing fever – I don't want entering the work until I've
finished the whole manuscript.

MO: Yeah. Poems exist in a context. The third poem might have more power
because it comes after the first two poems, or after the eighteenth poem. So to
read a poem by itself is to see one side of it. When I wrote *Billy the Kid*, I really
wanted to keep that book unread until it was, you know, all of a piece. And a
lot of the time when I'm writing, even for a novel, I don't show the work to
anyone until it's all done. As far as I can take it, anyway.

DO: Has there been a heyday of Canadian poetry?

MO: I really don't know when the heyday was. I mean . . . Lampman? *[laughter]*.
Poetry doesn't really fit into a calendar for me. It's difficult to think of poetry
belonging to one age or another. I mean they all seem to exist in a room *up
there* . . . .

DO: And really, what's a heyday, anyway?

MO: It makes you think about the poets you like, and you realize they're all in dif-
ferent periods of time. Is Anne Carson a classical poet, as opposed to a
contemporary poet? The main problem is there's so little knowledge or aware-
ness of where the great poems are. It's difficult to find them. We tend to rely
on the familiar and well-worn, or the English-American axis. So it is really
exciting when you find a *really good* poem, that was written not necessarily
this year, but forty or four thousand years ago . . . That's one purpose of life, I
suppose. To look for and find those great ones.

The Appropriate Gesture, or Regular Dumb-Ass Guy Looks at Bird

DON MCKAY

Interviewed by Ken Babstock

Don McKay's most recent collection of poetry is *Another Gravity* (McClelland & Stewart, 2000). A book of (mostly) essays entitled *Vis à Vis: Field Notes on Poetry and Wilderness* was published by Gaspereau Press in 2001.

Ken Babstock was born in Newfoundland, grew up in the Ottawa Valley and currently lives in Toronto. His two poetry collections are *Mean* (Anansi, 1999) and *Days into Flatspin* (Anansi, 2001).

KB: When you left Cornwall were you one of those small-town people dying to get out of their small town?

DM: Was I even thinking? Wide world beckoned. I still have these paper-mill-town sinus passages, though.

KB: You went to university.

DM: I went to university. And then my parents moved while I was at university so I didn't get the chance to go back and hang out with the people I knew there, and there was a break and I'm bad at keeping in touch, so . . . .

KB: – so Cornwall drifted into the distance for a while.

DM: It did, but my parents had a property there that they were going to retire on. An old, abandoned farm.

KB: This is the one you still go back to.

DM: The farm's actually just inside Glengarry County. It's become a kind of retreat, really. It's a place to go away to and write.

KB: You went to university where?

DM: Bishop's

KB: You did post-grad there?

DM: No, I went to Bishop's for two years then I went to Western. Did an M.A. there, then went to Saskatchewan. In those days places like the universities of Saskatchewan and Alberta would let you teach with an M.A. for two years – with the understanding that that was it. Going to Saskatchewan made sense . . . that and getting out of southwestern Ontario for a while.

KB: I didn't know you'd ever lived on the Prairies.

DM: From '65 to '68, something like that. I did the two years, then went to Wales.

KB: That was the Dylan Thomas Ph.D.

DM: Yeah. It held a tissue of sense – go to Swansea to study Dylan Thomas – but it was only superficial. There are few of his manuscripts there.

KB: Really. Just the cottage where he lived.

DM: Well, yeah, all the Dylan Thomas tourist stuff, you know, though it wasn't so touristy in those days. You could always go down to the pub and claim it was research. They'd all tell you he drank in that particular pub every night of his life. Every pub in Swansea, especially those in Mumbles. Have you ever been?

KB: No. I wanted to go after the year in Dublin. We'd planned to see Wales and then go over the southern border into Dorset to see where my family came from. There's a tiny village in Dorset, England called Baverstock, or something very similar.

   How important, Don, have reviews, awards, honours been to your feelings about your work? Is competition healthy or unhealthy for a poet?

DM: Whoa . . . *[silence]* It would be nice to say, "Competition is unhealthy and awards mean nothing." That would be the high mind, but in some ways people need . . . I mean, poetry is such a lonely business. So an audience is important, and probably an audience apart from just your pals, those people you can go and show your work to.

KB: Some glimmering of a readership somewhere.

DM: The glimmering of a readership. Well put. *[speaking into the mic]* Get that recorded for posterity. I don't know about competition. I think in the arts, it's imported. But it's so ingrained now that we talk inside that framework all the time.

KB: Everything being a meritocracy.

DM: Yes, it's looked at that way – and it's not that there isn't merit but it's more that: is competition in your mind so much when you're writing? You may have a different view on this, I don't know, but people I might really admire, like Ted Hughes, was I really competing with him? I don't think I was. It's not competing in the same key anyway. There's probably an element in all male relationships that involves competition – an element – but with poetry it's more like, "Gee, that bugger really did it. I wish I could do it like him." I don't know if that's competition so much as . . . .

KB: Yeah, I don't know how I would translate that word into the world of poetry. I think I can recognize – especially once you've tagged someone as being great, or whatever – that there's a standard there that you want very badly to be in conversation with, so it becomes an effort at getting up there . . . .

DM: There's no doubt that reading other poetry can be totally inspiring, finding someone who's found some kind of fresh knowledge or has broken into some fresh territory in that problematic interface between language and the world.

Or some fresh music. But how much of that is competitive? You know it's not even imitation, or influence, all those words go bad too, but there's something in the energy of reading others . . . I might say, "I want some of Louise Glück's hardness in this." But if I try it I'm not going to get any of Glück's particular tone. It'll emerge as something with its own spin – if it works.

KB: It's very elastic, reading others, I might find the work really powerful but essentially it will send me bouncing off in the opposite direction than the one that poet happens to be moving in.

DM: Yes, with your stuff, for example, the Brits are important, right? People like Armitage, maybe Motion . . . .

KB: Heaney, Hughes, Patterson, Muldoon . . . .

DM: . . . etc., but even though a person would say they can hear that stuff in the background, it's far from imitation.

KB: I hope.

DM: No, because your own energies have invaded this. The influence is so thoroughly digested.

KB: If I tried to trump up that British cheekiness and wit, it would fall really flat. But there's a topography to English, Irish, Scottish vernacular and slang that I find Canadian English poor on. It feels as though they have thirty-five different expressions for putting on your shoes, you know, so often the topography of those breeds of English feels much more colourful and jagged and active, so I envy them that. But I guess it forced me to try and make the English I use somehow more jumpy. Look for another word – some other way to say it.

DM: You know there's something about the way Purdy inhabited Canadian English . . . .

KB: Made the vernacular beautiful . . .

DM: Yes, and yet you think, "Gee, this guy really read his Auden as well." Those sentences and that weight to the declarative stance. He matched his own stride to it, somehow, took it over, assimilated it. Thinking of David Solway's dismissal of him, I mean, Solway wanted to say that poetry is essentially *written* so we can get rid of all that stuff, but – I mean, saying poetry is *written* is a truism but at the same time it's written *with the ear*. If you don't hear something, it's not working. It has to be called music – whether vernacular music or what have you . . . And Heaney said something really good about that, about his attitude to his own Irish English. I think it's the essay where he's talking about Hughes, Larkin and Hill.

KB: Yeah, he'll use Hughes to demonstrate, is it Middle English?

DM: Hughes is Old English, and Geoffrey Hill, I think, represents the Middle.

KB: Hill is Middle and . . . oh shit, I'm thinking of a Hughes essay where he's on about the importation of French into English, I'm off base –

DM: But what you're picking up is the sense those writers seem to have of existing in a laddered, very heavily textured, linguistic surround. And I'm not sure we actually inherit that, unless we go after it. I mean Hughes is so aware – he has such a sort of Poundian sense (what a strange coupling) but he has a kind of Poundian sense of this huge inheritance. English as a sort of massive carpentry shop that you go into and take what you need, but more of a jumble, a bricolage shed or something where you just pick stuff off the wall: "I need this, it suits me at this point in time."

KB: You said we don't have that inheritance, or perhaps are unaware of it. Does this mean North American English is poorer? Is it thinner or shallower?

DM: I wonder if it's a colonial sense of inferiority. There's a certainty in the UK of what the current thing is. They don't have to establish the current lingo; there's BBC English. There's this standard where we hadn't – and maybe this is retrospective by now – we hadn't established a kind of Canadian *talk*, a Canadian speech. Maybe it's got more to do with Don Cherry than we care to admit. And then there's the old reserve, being colonial, always referring to somewhere else: if it's elegance we're looking for we look to the UK, if it's hip we look to the States.

KB: I was just thinking I was possibly attracted to all that because, as far as regions in Canada go, the Maritimes and especially Newfoundland, have an incredibly thick linguistic resource.

DM: Exactly, yes, and you can feel that in your work.

KB: But I've lost it. Having moved to Ontario when I was two, I'm essentially linguistically separated from that tradition. I no longer sound like a Newfoundlander, don't use the same vernacular. So it's the regret of *I could have had it, it was so close.*

DM: I would say that's true of your work. That you're trying to bring back a certain linguistic texture.

KB: It is about the ear, for me. I have to confess to concentrating more attention on what I'm hearing in a line than to what the line might actually be saying.

DM: You know, if you're going to have an imbalance I think that's the right one to have, isn't it? I find most beginning poets want to *say* something and they're worried about getting the statement out there and not really hearing that music. Even line breaks.

KB: Speaking of Purdy, in his poem "The Dead Poet," speculating on the origins of his voice, he asks, "how else explain myself to myself/ where does the song come from?" Do you have any explanation of where your voice came from, of why you became a poet?

DM: Do I want to know? Good question. Historically, it just came from being a poetry junkie. The music. Being a Blake junkie for years and years, being a Shelley junkie, different kinds of voice break on you kind of as a revelation. There was certainly a lot of reading in the early days . . . and writing very badly.

KB: It's a cumulative process then.

DM: Yeah there was a definite breakthrough, though, with the love of landscape. In terms of recognizing myself as a linguistic creature. It being beyond words . . . out there. To me, landscape at first was very Group of Seven: blue skies and rocky shores. And then the birdwatching, that was the major heave, acknowledging that I was hooked. So, yeah, the nature-poet thing is being inarticulate in the face of these things – while also being a language-animal needing to articulate *something* – so it's really mainly gestural. With, I hope, the acknowledgement that language is not going to pretend to do justice to it, to wrap it up. And trying not to cash in on the Romantic imagination.

KB: That leads into my next question. You just identified yourself, and have elsewhere, as a nature poet. How do you relate to the Romantic poets, to their view of nature, to Coleridge's idea of pantheism? Do you have an argument with them, or did you learn from them?

DM: Definitely learned. For a while there I could recite whole swatches of the Prelude. It's got that great iambic sentence to it. It's kind of like Purdy staying in the mind; you can tell it's necessary speech. But the more I got serious about being a quasi-naturalist the less happy I became with the aeolian harp idea, you know, that nature is playing through you and translating itself into language. And the more I became a sort of crude phenomenologist, the more I had to acknowledge the separation in the act somehow, or hopefully . . . .

KB: The separation between the human and what it's confronting?

DM: And the inevitable reduction that language involves . . . while still making some pretty elaborate linguistic gesture. I think probably Gary Snyder would say something different: that making the gesture should be easy, natural. Make the natural gesture as if you're letting go of the linguistic apparatus. It's no longer there, or it's become transparent. For Snyder, words just flow, whereas I try to acknowledge the artifice.

KB: The artifice of language.

DM: Yeah.

KB: Okay, I was going to ask where in that scheme of the human and the natural would language fit? Is it a human artifice, is it separated from nature?

DM: Yes . . . even though there are linguistic animals, I know, you always have to enter that caveat, but language is our big tool. That's where the big brain went; it's what separated us from it all and is also our glory. It's our fire. Our fire is really language. That's our separation from the other. That cooked from the raw. Being a poet, loving language, I don't think there was any energy in my work until I got to that point. Energy requires tension and paradox.

KB: If language is what separates us from the rest of the natural world, and yet we evolved this way which I'm assuming happened pretty naturally, why is language not part of the natural world? I guess I'm asking if you're a Darwinist?

DM: I know that argument . . . *[long pause]* . . . I think we have to live in the paradox. That's part of it. It is quote-unquote natural for us to have evolved to acquire language, for that to have developed. We can't lobotomize ourselves and pretend that's not there. So if you're interested in that world – the world of the object – and feel that, language's marvelous capacity for simplification, its capacity for symbolic structures, separates us. Yet poetry is trying to make a back-flow inside that context and using the same instrument. There's a kind of jiu-jitsu in poetry, for me anyway – that's a paradoxical stance I'm comfortable having. Well, it's actually an uncomfortable stance but a familiar one.

KB: Something that strikes a reader almost immediately when reading your work is its sheer playfulness of imagination. The poems often revel in metaphoric inventiveness – an example that springs to mind is "We wave goodbye to Christmas in cubism" – an image like that is immediately striking but is also coloured with so much humour and playfulness. Is your voice naturally inclined this way? And are you having as much fun composing them as the poems themselves seem to be having?

DM: I'm not having as much fun initially because there's this hope . . . you're just trying to get it right. Still, I think that humour is natural to metaphor, because it's surprise. To me, even if the metaphor uses something pretty dismal like a corpse or a dead pig, to take Hughes again – "scoured it like a doorstep" and so on – you're still going, "yeaaah." You don't get there by following a chain of logical arguments, where each point says yes, yes, yes, yes . . . .

KB: And it's settling down into rightness –

DM: It's settling down into rightness, exactly, whereas there's a kind of jump contained in metaphor and you say "Whoa, I made it," and there should be some kind of fresh insight and zap that comes with it – some kind of possibly illicit knowledge, or knowledge that language doesn't usually have. You know, metaphor gives analytic philosophers a *bad* time.

KB: Because it does communicate something but the point of a metaphor is that what's communicated can't be re-said in another way.

DM: And I think that's implied in all metaphorical activity, to tell you the truth. The world is so complicated and so beyond us; this fridge is so beyond us, linguistically, that if we tried to describe it . . . .

KB: . . . as a "fat armless weeping willow" . . . what was it?

DM: Oh yeah, [laughing] the armless weeping willow of the kitchen. Who thinks this up? Sorry, fridge.

KB: Maybe the mischief and fun comes in knowing the philosophers do have such trouble with metaphor.

DM: Well, when I try to figure some of those things out for myself, looking back at my own experience, I think there probably is an element of teasing propositional language, like kidding an overly serious friend. But metaphor also springs from a need to confront or contemplate the world and say something, rub up against it with language. Maybe the pure gesture – made by a saint or a mystic – would be speechlessness. So propositional language isn't adequate on the one hand, and silence isn't an option; you get metaphor stepping up to make the linguistic gesture when the world is beyond language. Metaphor lives in the paradox, I think. I go on about this obsessively in *Vis à Vis*. I have 2.6 ideas and I say them five times each in the book. Of course there are all new costumes and different animal acts each time.

KB: [laughter stemming from the suspicion this might be true] In your 1997 collection, *Apparatus*, you seem to focus the lens more on objects, their usefulness or practicality; their lives as objects – am I way off base with regards to that book? And I was going to ask when does an object, or an experience for that matter, descend into the realm of the useless? Does that condition interest you poetically?

DM: Yeah, yeah. *Apparatus*, working on it, was important for me because I could get beyond nature in a narrow sense. We don't just have to be focusing on thrushes. Another bird poem! Not that! Being a birdwatcher, after a while you realize you can really indulge yourself; it can begin to feel like viewing soft porn. The natural world is either in decline or gone, depending on your degree of pessimism. *Apparatus* was an attempt to focus on those elements of the natural world that we've claimed, and made tools of. Taking the word "tool" very broadly, that's apparatus. I made a very conscious effort to do that, and to look at landscape that has been made into apparatus, or even worse. So apparatus – this is one of my 2.6 ideas – is wilderness that we have relieved of its anonymity, its autonomy, and made ours, owned for the life of that object. But there's still that sense that it may go back, that it may return, die out of tool-use.

KB: Like a thing being haunted by its own prior uselessness.

DM: Yes, it used to not have use and we've made it useful. I was also interested in this because of environmental devastation and my sense that it stems partly from our capacity to own tools permanently, to extinguish their wilderness. The thing will be ours forever. A manic ownership. That's what I called "Matériel" – a long poem in *Apparatus* – where I looked at this military base as land that had become *matériel*. They just bombed it and bombed it, so it'll never be unchemicalled; it'll never be *not* a pseudo-war site. We deny it the capacity to die.

KB: The last section of that long poem, "Matériel," the end of the section called "*Stretto.*" Do you feel like parsing that for me? It's a darkly hilarious prose piece, and it feels like there are eight or more streams of mangled language happening.

DM: That's the very end of "*Stretto.*" I borrowed an idea from Celan, from his poem "The Straitening," for an increasing of intensity at each successive level. So you take the last line make it the beginning of the next section with, hopefully, an increased intensity at each step, so you eventually get to the quintessential voice of *matériel* – that manic voice – which, in that context is the voice of Cain. It's supposed to mangle English and become a great ugly thing doing ugly barbaric things to the English tradition and language.

KB: You've lived in London, Ontario; Fredericton, New Brunswick; Saskatchewan;

and now Victoria, BC. That's the east, central, some time in the prairies and the west coast. What do you think might have entered into your work had you spent ten years in the Northwest Territories?

DM: Boy. Probably much the same as what's going on for me out on the west coast right now. A lot of field work – just wandering around looking at this and that, trying to take in both the physical landscape and the cultural landscape . . . and the cultural history of the natural landscape. That would involve logging etc., on the west coast, but up in the NWT, well, that would be a whole other fascinating problem. I'd welcome the opportunity, but on the other hand I think how much stress – not stress, work I suppose, it would entail.

     The west is so eloquent yet so sad at the same time. You can feel it slipping away. Amazing how the loggers and logging poets – even Robert Swanson the bunkhouse balladeer – can be elegiacally aware of the loss even while celebrating a Paul Bunyan spirit.

KB: They don't *not* know what's going on.

DM: Right.

KB: Landscape. You've been overseas but I can't think of a poem that's set outside of Canada. Can a place mean something to you if you're just passing through?

DM: It's possible. If you acknowledge your own tourism – and I'm removing the negative connotations from that word. Not that it's necessarily a pejorative term. There are really good tourism poems where the stance is being acknowledged; the speaker is either appalled or in awe of whatever they're looking at. They're honest. I have to be in a place for some time . . . get into the landscape, it has its particular ethos that will probably always want to be beyond us but . . . I mean, that would be true if I went to the Ottawa Valley.

KB: So even inside Canada's borders there are places where you'd still feel like a tourist.

DM: Oh yeah, we're so diverse. I feel Zwicky for example, or Crozier, can write straight out of the prairie experience. If I tried to do that . . . I wrote a poem called "Poplar" and it is prairie poplar I'm thinking of there but I'm not pretending to be able to speak out of the land.

KB: How have your feelings about poetry, the reading and writing of it, changed since you were in your twenties?

DM: Did my twenties exist? . . . *[long pause]* . . . Well, it isn't any easier, probably more difficult. There's also less emphasis on the personal and more respect for, more awareness of, the importance of reading a lot of other people. And that probably goes along with realizing that poetry is a big project. A huge hydra-headed beast, really, rather than "I gotta get my own voice out there." Reading other people's work reflects less on me, personally. My attitude to my own projects has changed, too. I'm more patient with what's called in basketball *working off the ball*. You're not actually writing, not sinking the shots, but you're . . . .

KB: Looking for the open lane.

DM: Yeah, the poetic surround becomes important. At some point in all that, during all that birdwatching, the idea of poetic attention came up for me. It's a very bad term for a genuine recognition. Somewhere I realized that poetic attention was more important for me than poetry was. Going for long dry spells is still frustrating though I'm not saying to myself "I'm not writing" whereas I would've been back then, in my twenties. It's proven to be a wonderful reassurance, not to mention a great excuse to get away from the desk and into the bush.

KB: The term poetic attention, the time spent away from the ball, if you had to give it a short definition –

DM: Well, I've called it a kind of longing without the desire to possess. Most longing, including sexual longing, is involved with possession and ownership. I realized that that's what I was into while birdwatching – that want is a kind of pure applause for the being of something else. At that point it was all birds . . . but it extended to fridges, hammers, etc., so there's nothing that you can't approach that way. The attention is the important thing . . . and I think I need a whole lot of that to support the poetry. It's like how some animals need a huge ecosystem. I'm a kind of grizzly bear. So I guess the west coast is going to defeat language unless I can get in and give it enough of that kind of attention.

KB: When you use the word wilderness, is that term referring to the other being's existence that you don't want to possess?

DM: Yes, exactly, it's what's outside the mind. The complete "other," which I think we lose completely when we're living mostly with tools. Because we own them or we want to own them – and we need them to work, etc., wilderness experience is cherishing the uselessness of the other, in a deep sense.

KB: Your partner, Jan Zwicky, is also a poet and a professor of philosophy, what would we overhear at the breakfast table? You losing?

DM: "How about another bagel?"

KB: That was a stupid question, sorry. You've been writing two ongoing series or modes that pop up frequently in the books: songs and meditations. When is a poem one and not the other? Do they sound differently? Think differently?

DM: Well, formally the songs tend to be lyrics; I put myself right in that lyric mode. And I started them partly because I really wanted to write about birdsong, without describing or imitating. To perform some linguistic gesture which would be in homage: "So, this is *for* you but not *about* you." It's trying to make the appropriate gesture, one I hope somebody else could also find appropriate.

In this book of essays I mention the possibility of actually reading the field guide entry *to* the thing that you're looking at. Especially if it's a flower, something stable, trying to run around after a bird while reading to it might prove more difficult . . . You know, "these are our big brains and we loved you so much, this is your picture, a description of you in our iconography" and so on and so forth, then actually giving it to the critter. As opposed to taking the critter and trying to translate *it* into language, into our taxonomies etc. So it's trying to undo the taxonomical ownership of the gesture. And I've actually done this, you don't want anyone to come up the trail while you're doing it, but I have and it puts you in an interesting place, especially if you're thinking of yourself as the creature with language approaching the non-linguistic entity. Inevitably, language is going to be trying to pull it into it – how do you get some back-flow toward the other? The songs were deliberately trying to enact that lyric gesture that would seem conspicuously inadequate to the creature but might seem, to me and hopefully to somebody else, an appropriate gesture toward the white-throated sparrow.

KB: I'd like to ask about the "somebody else," being the reader. You describe that whole exchange as happening between you the linguistic creature and the non-linguistic creature. Is the reader there as that attention is going on, or during composition, or is it only afterward, once it's a poem in a book?

DM: The reader's not there in the initial act of composition, except of course in the person of the poet's ear, but then there'll be readership at the level of editor, someone I choose to show it to. If I show it to a reader and get a "huh?" then, well, maybe it's not coming off so well.

KB: There's a third energy there at some early stage to make sure it's communicable to another linguistic creature.

DM: Yeah, and we're going to have to activate some things we already know. We know metaphor and we know song so we can see if these things are working inside the language. And some don't work, even when they seem to be working to me.

KB: And what about the meditations?

DM: I think the meditations are a different thing. Probably Dennis Lee's influence shows here: enacting a meditation is a very big thing for him, this sense of it as a process. The process of thinking inside language with a lyric sensibility. And also Al Purdy: "I can see that I have been foolish in a poem." Instead of the perfect lyric gesture, the meditation is a little more prosy, a little more moosey-faced. Often the poem will use a walk and notice this and notice that, so it's a little more time-bound – what they would call in the theoretical seminar rooms "diachronic." *[raising of eyebrows at the use of a word heretofore unknown to the Interviewer]*

KB: You've spent some time thinking about the relationship between lyric and narrative – wait . . . I didn't ask you this already, did I?

DM: Well it's been six hours, Ken!

KB: Thinking about lyric and narrative –

DM: I'm really surprised you can afford this penthouse here, and such a beautiful view of the lake.

KB: Don't mention the Porsche.

DM: Debbie, could I have another martini please?

KB: Lyric and narrative. Are they allies or do they squabble?

DM: It's really interesting, I think they're quite diverse and they have an erotic relationship with each other. So I often find that pull of the narrative when I'm in the lyric mode and vice versa. And I think the poem only works when I feel that pull. A lot of lyric or metaphor implies a whole story – or at least a context, a setting. In the flash of metaphor there's a whole whack of implied narrative outside of it, and part of the surprise is turning things forty-five degrees and seeing it from a totally different angle. All of that implies a life, a context, your relationship with your grocer, how far you are from the beer store, etc. Similarly, without the lift of lyric, narrative is just flat. Thank god for lyric novelists, I say. And prose poets.

KB: Is there such a thing as pure lyric?

DM: I don't think so, but possibly the Romantics and people like that would fight me off on this one.

KB: The Symbolistes.

DM: Or the Symbolistes. I guess I'm an impure poet, or impurity is a study of mine, to put it more positively.

KB: You do make use of humble things: Esso stations, shovels, hockey sticks, a jumble of things poetry doesn't often look at in the lyric mode. You have an affinity for –

DM: An affinity for low life . . . *[a long pause occurred here wherein the Interviewer and Interviewee can be heard lighting cigarettes and gazing at their respective boots]* . . . . Ordinary Dumb-ass Guy Looks at Bird. You know? I don't think there's the pure Keatsian moment. Even in Keats, in the nightingale ode, there's an implied narrative going on: he walks out into the garden, he's feeling suicidal and all that. Well some impure poet in me is going to think "Have you tried aspirin? One too many drinks? One too few?" I couldn't write like that, I'd have to include some of the sense of context out of which this came.

You know those structuralist diagrams where they have lyric going up one axis and narrative going along the other, that makes some kind of crude sense to me. It's a radical simplification, but narrative's going along historically – "and then, and then, and then" – the lyric can at any point leap out of it, with an implied eternity.

KB: The eternal moment.

DM: "Now it's fit to die because we'll never get beauty like this again" – lyric attempts to pause there, but I think even while doing that there's an implied gravity. The narrative goes on to the next day. The meditative approach acknowledges this: that one moment will inevitably lead to the next. We accept mortality instead of fighting it off.

KB: That's the diachronic – being locked in time.

DM: I guess. Whatever that lyric aesthetic is, it probably has something to do with the momentary retardation of time's erosions, just for that moment. The narrative acknowledges, "Yes, it is just for the moment, now we're getting back into the flow, so fasten your seat belt."

KB·   Speaking of narrative and history, I was just reading an essay on Czeslaw Milosz and he's made some disparaging remarks – or at least disappointed remarks – over his career concerning American poetry (and I assume he's including Canadian) stating, in effect, that much of it has little of any weight

to say because of a lack of historical awareness. Its practitioners – and this
seems an unfair criticism – were fortunate enough not to have lived through
this century's greater evils.

DM: Well, you can see it from Milosz's perspective, living in California, where his-
torical awareness does not seem to get much grip on the public imagination.
He may be partly right about North American writing not carrying the burden
of this – what can we call it? – the bitter wisdom and weight of much modern
European poetry, its conditioned skepticism and hardened core. I'd go to
Zbigniew Herbert, probably, before Milosz to find it in a somewhat purer, less
defended form. I do feel the pull of that kind of poetry, its critique of all forms
of idealism. Like that great Milosz elegy, "Dedication," which rejects poetry
that does not save nations or people.

KB: So, obviously neither of us have lived through the twentieth century's larger
horrors. Can one think about suffering and evil without an immediate cultural
consciousness of it? Your aesthetic seems to be a moral stance concerning the
world around you, the "other."

DM: It's a moral stance, but it's born out of a pure aesthetic enjoyment. The sort of
soft porn of watching, or hard porn depending on the species. Soft porn if it's
sparrows, hard if it's osprey or sea otters.
    But don't you think we're in the middle of increased historical awareness?
I mean, because of historical circumstance, I couldn't be a nature poet in the
old sense; you turn to nature as the kindly nurse and it soothes your cares and
reminds you of the still, sad music of humanity – well, when you're standing
in a clear cut that still, sad music starts to sound like the grinding machine of
humanity. So it is going to overtake you one way or another. I, personally,
experienced the fall inside nature poetry. And we're all going to do that in dif-
ferent ways, September 11 or no. Somebody in Hamilton, at Redeemer College,
asked me where I stood on Adorno's statement that poetry is impossible after
Auschwitz. An interesting question to which I probably didn't have a satisfy-
ing answer at the time; but think *what is Adorno talking about?* I thought it
might actually be a cutting gesture directed at Celan. But Celan proved that it
is possible, something happened to poetry in his work, something devastating.
It takes on the burden, and I think language has to do that . . . if we're going
to persist. And what does Adorno mean, anyway? If we unpack it I think it
really means that high German Romanticism is impossible after the Holocaust.
Celan takes those high German Romantic poems and turns them inside out.
Think of the anti-Rilke, anti-Heine poems.
    So, the moral or political stance I believe will just happen to you, if you're
involved with poetic attention and not reserving it only for things you think
deserve your attention. "That's beautiful and that's not. I won't look at urban
nature. I won't look at *matériel*." There was a conversion factor there for me

– having forced myself to look at *matériel* with *Apparatus*. With Celan, well it's an unaesthetic poetry. But there *is* an aesthetic to it, and a great, brave, courageous sense of gesture. Some poems like "Tenebrae" – "pray God we are near" – seem devastating, yet exactly right: calculated blasphemy. He seems to be more and more important to me. As we look back at the twentieth century, he emerges –

KB: More and more important. Yet he's so close to silence it's hard to – I mean, I imagine him as a blockage for poets the same way I think of Beckett for prose writers who are into that aesthetic. He's *this* far away from silence.

DM: Yeah, "I can't go on, I will go on." It's almost as if Celan took silence and smelted it, like his work had *gone there* before it spoke at all. So, Milosz's stance is a bit like Adorno's stance: it's true in a limited sense. It's true if you understand the perspective he's coming from. In North America the whole agon is, perhaps, still unwinding itself and I don't have any optimistic sense that we're going to avoid that. It's still to come. We inhabit a continent that has been through *relative tranquility, is comparatively stable*; it hasn't owned up to its own inherent violence with regards to its Native peoples, or the environment. But that's bound to happen. It is happening.

KB: It still has to play itself out.

DM: So it's a historically bound statement – while, at the same time it would be inappropriate not to acknowledge that there are elements of wilderness left here: if you were living in wartorn Europe maybe all you could do is mourn. You can't move without that sense of history, without that sense of damage to the radical "other," the wilderness. So, if you just add that history that Milosz is invoking to counter North American poetry in general, then I think his statement undoes itself – just wait long enough . . . *[long silence]*

KB: Right . . . now I'm depressed.

DM: Well, you can look at Europeans like Tomas Tranströmer. Even though he's a great elegiac poet, he still walks off into the woods and finds the clearing that can only be found by someone who has lost their way. But his work is still steeped in historical loss. He's a very mournful poet but he still has that lift – or that reach toward that lift. And Hughes found himself back at that point when he started publishing the European poets. Poets who lived in a context where people die in the streets daily. And Neruda, another nature poet (among other things), arrived there in the Spanish Civil War: it happens over and over again.

KB: What else do you see contemporary North American poetry doing these days?
       Any little flare-ups? Who are you reading?

DM: I recently finished Jose Saramago's *Year of the Death of Ricardo Reis* – you
       know, one of Fernando Pessoa's four personae. Great fluid treatment of the
       sentence and dialogue, blends voices like impressionist painting. I'm travelling
       right now with Susan Mitchell, Tranströmer and Ulrikka Gernes in my carry-
       on. Gernes is a very delicate, very fine-boned Danish poet recently translated
       by Patrick Friesen and Per Brask. And then of course there are those wild
       young Canadians like Babstock. *[much laughter, honestly]* . . . Because I'm
       involved with editing here and there, I get to read quite widely among the
       younger poets. They seem much more streetwise and maybe worldly wise.
       Tough skeptical wisdom strikes people earlier, I think. And I've been
       impressed by their formal daring and sense of wide linguistic possibilities.

KB: Does linguistic possibility offer any kind of solace?

DM: This may be naive, but I think it has some of the solace of the blues. We could
       go back to Celan – is there solace? Perhaps there's some in naming the pain.
       Getting an accurate take. Or your poem where you're walking in High Park,
       given the context, you're actually seeing what's there: the garbage and natu-
       ral devastation and whatnot. I'd probably have to fight my way out of the
       Romantic inheritance. My indulgence would be going around birdwatching
       rather than seeing those things first off; I had to make some kind of major
       move in my aesthetic to get myself into the *matériel* mode.

KB: Though it might be a laziness, an easy cynicism in my generation. I know my
       first inclination would be to walk out the door and see the garbage etc. *as
       opposed to* noticing that there *is* a green space there, you know, there are
       hawks in High Park!

DM: Hawks. Probably coyotes, too.

KB: Exactly, but one of the early images in "Public Space" [*Days into Flatspin*] is
       the children punching and kicking at geese, so I go there before really see-
       ing the geese. There's a risk of cynicism, of not lunging into that other
       approach –

DM: This may be a generalization, but I think there may be a besetting peril for
       each generation. Maybe we should just talk about ourselves, but what you're
       calling cynicism might be a radical skepticism.

KB: Yes, cynicism is an ugly word.

DM: That might actually be your starting point, or your natural tendency whereas I'm probably still a mildly reconstructed Romantic –

KB: If we shifted the generational thing into pop-culture terms, what music were you listening to when you were fourteen or fifteen? It was my English teacher who introduced us to punk rock when I was thirteen or fourteen.

DM: Is that right? Used to be Bob Dylan was the high school poetry star. And Cohen before that.

KB: I guess the first ethos or world view I was submersed in would've been Joe Strummer and Johnny Rotten and all that gloomy business. It's probably more of an effort for me to get to a point where I can offer praise as opposed to pointing out the kids punching the geese –

DM: But it still comes to that. Just given the metaphors, we still get that energy. The long "tassels of ick" out of the cow, for example . . . .

KB: Maybe I was thinking of Johnny Rotten when I wrote that "tassels of ick" bit. *[more laughter and general mirth]*

DM: *[suddenly stops laughing]* Wasn't that a sci-fi novel?

KB: What do you think Don, you have anything else you need to say?

DM: I don't think so. I think we've about covered it. 2.6 on the nose.

KB: Then I'll thank you for sitting in my tiny kitchen.

A Brooding Upon the Heart of Things

PATRICK LANE

Interviewed by Russell Thornton

Patrick Lane presently resides in Victoria, BC. His most recent poetry collection, *The Bare Plum of Winter Rain*, came out in 2000 with Harbour Publishing. A new collection will be published in 2003. He is presently completing a meditation on gardens entitled *What We Are Is a Garden*.

Russell Thornton is the author of *The Fifth Window* (Thistledown, 2000) and *A Tunisian Notebook* (Seraphim, 2002). He won first prize in the League of Canadian Poets National Poetry Contest in 2000. He lives in North Vancouver, BC.

RT: In 1970, you wrote a prose piece called "To the Outlaw" that seems to me to have turned out to be a seminal outcry – possibly containing the whole of your life's writing crushed into it. I wonder if you'd like to say something about what was going on in your life around the time you wrote "To the Outlaw."

PL: John Gill, whom I met at Expo '67 in Montreal, editor of the fledgling *New: Canadian and American Poetry* (a magazine that was inspired in John by a conversation with Earle Birney in 1966), asked me to write a statement of poetics when I was staying at his farm in Trumansburg, New York, in 1969. I left and travelled north and west to my old wandering home of BC. Extremely ill with some nameless disease, I was in hospital in Quesnel for a month, and when I left I stayed on a week at my brother John's home there. It was a difficult time for me. The past six years since 1964 and my brother [Dick "Red" Lane] and fellow poet's tragic, early death from a brain hemorrhage in Vancouver had been difficult. I was quite deranged back then. His death was followed by my move to Vancouver in February 1965 where my marriage began the last stages of disintegration, finally ending Christmas 1968. My mother-in-law died Christmas 1967, my father was killed by a gunshot in February, and I deserted my family in March or April going out to Toronto, Montreal and New York City, then returning at the end of August where I got a job at Small & Boyes Furniture Factory and tried to start the family going again. We separated four months later and were divorced in the fall of 1969, my wife remarrying a rich professor, leaving me without the need to pay either alimony or child support.

         A traumatic time for a young man. I was emotionally wrecked by the decade. The "Outlaw" essay was written the next summer, I think, but am not sure. I haven't read it in many years. It's hard to go back and understand what I was feeling at the time. I was quite suicidal and self-destructive, I know that. I had several near-misses at death in car accidents (Margaret Atwood forecast two of them in a tarot reading at her home in Edmonton in 1970, warning me I might die in the next two or three months. I almost did.) Suffice to say, I was not in good psychological or emotional health. I ranged around North America in a kind of frenzy, bouncing from city to city, friend to friend, lover to lover. Looking back now I think I should have been institutionalized for a while or at least in the hands of a good psychiatrist. I lived excessively in every possible way: alcohol, drugs, women, etc., etc. I was, to put it mildly, quite wild and extremely irresponsible to say the least.

RT: I've always been captivated by some of the statements you make in "To the Outlaw" regarding the nature of poetry and the poet. You refer to Irving Layton's poem "Whatever Else Poetry is Freedom," for example, and say: "but I tell you, Layton, poetry is a Grand Inquisitor waiting in the next cell for your coming – catharsis leading into bondage." And later: "whatever else, poetry is beauty in bondage . . . a poet . . . is the outlaw surging beyond the only freedom he knows, beauty in bondage." And, finally, in a footnote: "What follows is silence." I've often wondered how you might elaborate on the connections you make here between freedom, beauty, confinement, release . . . Can you talk about these statements?

PL: "Beauty in bondage?" I meant that the poem, all art if you like, my drawing, etc., was bondage to me as a man, liberation to me as a poet. I was immensely frustrated by my art, the need to cage emotion and spirit within the confines of poetry. That cage of poetry was a kind of freedom to me but the freedom was the same as Rilke's leopard, something remembered and not experienced. The past has always been a burden to me, but then I suppose it is to everyone. It all sounds very romantic, but I was a very romantic young man back then. The last time I read the essay I was struck by how angry I was and how the essay was as much a cry for help as it was a manifesto toward action. The final footnote, "What follows is silence," spoke to my own self-destructive desires as much as about the poem, though they are somewhat the same, aren't they?

    A Jungian psychiatrist I spoke to in the late seventies read my work. She had studied with Jung and was quite old. She was the first practicing Jungian in Ontario. I met her in Ottawa. She wanted to come out of retirement and treat me but I was afraid of that. She told me all my poetry was a search for God and I think she may have been right, though what that means I'm not sure. Perhaps a search for a positive spiritual path. The one I was on was Dionysian and destructive. I was influenced at the time by many poets. At the time I wrote the essay I had been deep into Neruda's work and his essays on poetry and poetics. I liked his attention to the high calling of poetry, but also to the plight of the workers of the world, the lowly and disenfranchised people of society. I had been one of them – a wage-slave in mills and camps, etc. I identified very strongly with the slant of his poetic, the "soiled with our shameful behavior, our wrinkles and vigils and dreams . . ."

    I, like the Romantics before me, especially Baudelaire and Rimbaud, but also the Beats of the fifties, wanted derangement and excess in my life and in my art. I wanted to burn, not out, but constantly. Strange how my struggle with the poem was a struggle toward order, in my life a struggle toward disorder. How I laboured over the poem. I remember, back in the early sixties ('61 or '62) spending weeks trying to get twenty-seven words to obey me. It was a little poem but it wouldn't do what I wanted it to. Long gone and lost now, that poem. But I learned from it just as I learned in the four or five hours a day I spent on my craft when I was married, the hours from eleven to three o'clock in the morning after the family slept. But that's another story. "Catharsis leading into bondage." The life lived entering the strict confines of the poem, a caged animal.

RT: In a number of my own poems, I find I'm trying to look back at the people I was closest to in my childhood and a little later in my life – those people I first, and without any choice, came into contact with. It seems that a lot of poems originate in one way or another in an individual's experience of that time of initial powerful relationships, and that those particular poems define much of whatever poethood a person might possess. Can you talk about your childhood and early manhood? What contributed to your earliest development as a writer of poems?

PL: I always wanted to be an artist from the time I was a small child – a painter, not a poet. I've always thought I missed my true calling and might have been a good visual artist had I followed my dreams. My family was a storytelling family. My mother was a storyteller. She had long, complex tales of family history, glorifying her roots back in the USA through her father and mother, plantations in Virginia, murders, Indian massacres in Tennessee, family feuds from Bloody Williamson County. My father as well, though he was silent about his past much of the time and what I now know I had to dig out of my mother and her horrifying sisters, my aunts, and the few relatives of my father I still knew. ("The Weight" came out of stories I dug up about my father's past and mother's, too.) My brothers and I told endless stories about our childhood, mythicizing it really. It was very competitive, our storytelling. It was a demand for the attention of our parents, but also and more importantly, arose from a desire to name ourselves and our experiences in a grand fiction of family. My mother's influence, I'm sure.

As a boy I read voluminously and wildly everything I could find. I had no perceptible taste and read farm almanacs and Mark Twain at the same time and with the same intense vigour. Anything with words in it was grist for the mill. I practiced my vocabulary, building it up so I could win competitions with my brothers when we did the *Reader's Digest* "Word Power" quiz each month. I read encyclopedias and dictionaries like you'd read novels. Mickey Spillane and Leo Tolstoy were equal in my young eyes. I read very little poetry until I was sixteen when I wandered about spouting Eliot's "The Hollow Men," Pound's "Mauberley," and Stevens's "The Idea of Order at Key West" to my friends. I still have an image of me in Vernon in 1955 standing on the courthouse steps reciting "The Hollow Men" to the disinterested citizens of Vernon who passed me by as if I were mad. How charming I must have been! Quite the little showman. I first read Rimbaud and the rest in an anthology of poetry out of New York by Selden Rodman. At that time it was very important. It was the first modernist poetry I'd ever read. I was quite the little pedant when I think back on it.

My brother Dick went into the air force in 1954 where he became friends with George Bowering and began writing short fiction and poems. We were intensely competitive and he was rather superior about his new role as a writer. An early short story of his was considered by *Esquire* magazine, but finally not accepted. I too began to write largely in reaction to his arrogance, but poems not stories. This would be when he came out of the air force in

1957. Within a year my two brothers, Dick and John, and I had all had shot-gun marriages. We were the "wild boys" of our little, nowhere town. We lived together in Kamloops for a year in 1959, perhaps the happiest of my life, though we were all very poor. The three brothers together for the last time. I look back on that year or so with great, sad fondness.

Both Dick and I were writing poems all the time. He was a troubled young man, hated his marriage, and spent much of his time running away from it. He reunited with George in Vancouver around 1960. And so began his connection to the early poetry scene of Vancouver: Birney, Newlove, bissett, Bowering, Acorn, Kearns, Marlatt (Buckle then), UBC and my own weekend visitations to their readings and parties from Avola on the North Thompson. *Tish* was alive and kicking. Dick was seen by George as a kind of Neal Cassady to George's Kerouac. To me he was just a brother. John, who wrote a novel and poetry in the mid-seventies, was not writing back then. He wanted a secure and stable life, due as much to his troubled youth and my mother's dis-like of him as anything else.

By '64 Dick was dead, the academics like George had left and I moved to Vancouver where I took up with Seymour Mayne, Acorn, Jim Brown, bissett, Copithorne, Jamie Reid, etc., the hippies and the Summer of Love just up the road a bit. I published my first poems in *The Canadian Forum* in 1962, I think. Very Stone House started in 1966. My first book, etc. They were the early writing years. I was deeply passionate about poetry, though I didn't finally learn to write it well until the late sixties and early seventies. The first mature work came the year after I returned from South America in 1972. The poems of *Unborn Things* were written in late '72 and early '73. *Passing Into Storm* was written in 1970 and 1971 in Toronto, Smithers, Vernon and Vancouver. Atwood approached me in 1973 to do a selected that became *Beware the Months of Fire* with Anansi in 1974. From what I've heard over the years it was a rather sem-inal book to a lot of people at the time. I'm pleased it was. God knows it took a lot to write it.

RT: In your thirties, it seems to me that you reached the culmination of an early phase in your poetic development with poems like "Stigmata" and "Albino Pheasants" (both widely anthologized now) and one of my favourites, "Wild Birds." Then, in 1979, you won the Governor General's Award for poetry for your *New and Selected Poems*. How important for you was winning this award at this particular point in your life? What effect did it have on you? You've received other awards since. How important have these awards been to you?

PL: "Stigmata," "Wild Birds" and "Albino Pheasants" were all written between 1973 and 1975 when I was living at Middlepoint up the Sunshine Coast in my second marriage. Winning the Governor General's in 1978 was anti-climactic for me. I had been irritated I hadn't won it earlier like Ondaatje and Atwood and Nichol. I was ambitious and competitive just as had been as a boy and as a young man. The awards were still very much Torontocentric back then. I thought *Beware the Months of Fire* should have won in 1974. This sounds like I spent my time worrying about awards. I didn't from one year to the next, but when I did my first selected I thought it deserved more than it got. When I did get it in 1978 I thought of refusing it but didn't. I needed the money. I'd left my second wife and gave her the $5000 to help with the kids. Mine was a prancing arrogance modified by reality. The awards over the years have been affirmations, of course, but they have made little difference to my poetry. They gave me a national name later than most of my peers but that has had its own negative side, distracting rather than focusing my writing. I liked getting awards and always thought I should have won more for years when I knew my work was better than that of other recipients, but that sounds like arrogance. But why not be honest? I've irritated and alienated a lot of people in my wild and selfish life, some of whom have sat on juries. What goes around comes around. Ah well. Enough of that. It all sounds egotistical and arrogant in the extreme. Awards are good, the money, the prestige, etc., but you're still left with the blank page at eleven o'clock on a Sunday night, aren't you?

RT: Often I find I can only write when I've put everything in the place where I live into some sort of satisfyingly non-irritating state. I have to make sure I "sweep the floor beneath my feet" (to quote from what I think is some Zen saying). I suppose I have to clear and clean away my obstructions on the literal level before I can get down to producing new things or new orders for myself on any other level. What sort of work habits do you have? Do you write daily? Do you have a favourite place to write, or can you write anywhere?

PL: When I was young back in my twenties (1960 to 1968) I wrote after the kids and my wife went to bed. I was working at a regular job back then so would go to my typewriter and work from eleven o'clock till three or four in the morning. This would go on all week until I was exhausted and then begin again the next week. Did this for ten years. I was quite driven, still am, I suppose. When my marriage ended in '68 I wrote in bursts. A binge writer. Weeks and sometimes months would go by without writing at all. I was travelling from '68 through to '74, not paying rent, living off friends, relatives, in old vans, wherever, but once I found a place where I could settle for a month I'd write non-stop. My early books are the result of such intense work. I didn't write at all when I was in South America, only when I got back. In the past twenty-five years I've written almost every day, usually from nine in the morning till twelve. The late evening is a time for meditation and reflection, reading and drifting in my mind. Poems often come from that twilight zone, a daydream state really. When I'm writing fiction or non-fiction I'm quite disciplined and try to write two or three pages a day of prose. Poetry is very different. It is much more inspired and occasional because of that. When the poem comes I write. I work in my office mostly on computer. I wrote on typewriter when I began and still feel comfortable composing on the machine. The last ten or twelve years I will handwrite first drafts, but then it's to the computer to fiddle the words. I can't write just anywhere, never write when I travel, don't write in hotel rooms or in airplanes.

RT: I have a couple of friends I might show my poems to when I know the poems probably aren't actually done. Do you read or show your work to others while it is in progress?

PL: Almost never show my work in progress to anyone. Sometimes to Lorna but not often. I sit on it. Sometimes send off a poem to my friend Brian Brett, but not for criticism, just to share what I'm doing, creating.

RT: Lorna Crozier, your companion, is, of course, a well-known Canadian poet. How have her responses to your finished products affected your work?

PL: In the early years of our relationship, 1978 to 1984 or 1985, I would show Lorna some of my new work and she would respond critically, but in the past fifteen years I show her perhaps one of ten poems I write. I do ask her to read my manuscripts when they're ready and I find her responses valuable. She's an excellent critic, a fine and close reader of poems. It's a delicate business mixing love and friendship with criticism. I trust her and value her criticism even though I don't always show her my work. Still, when she does read it her responses are valuable. I have never used an editor from a publishing house for poetry. For fiction I have, but I've selected the editor always. I've always been my own best critic. I never grew up with workshops and group poetry critics. I work solo. Lorna is my best friend and confidant. I trust her, but I use her rarely in the capacity of critic. Still, when she does it with complete manuscripts her response is very valuable.

RT: I have quite a few poems that I've been fiddling with for years now, and still don't feel I've got them right. Do you feel that poems are ever truly finished?

PL: No, not often. Some poems become finished pieces but I think that's up to readers, critics and academics. Poems get exhausted and then I move on to the next. At times the poem is satisfying in its completion, but I'm not often satisfied. *Winter* was satisfying (about half the poems in the collection), and the poems in *Mortal Remains*, the first half of the collection only. *Too Spare, Too Fierce*, some, but not all. The poem leads to the next poem, a long string of thematic urgencies that are rarely satisfied in me. Perhaps Auden was right in saying the poem is never finished. I think if I really thought a poem or poems "finished" then I could stop writing. Sometimes I think I know where the poem comes from but that knowing slips away when the new poem comes swelling out of the imagination. I think writing poetry a kind of madness, really. That leaves me in the heart of the Romantics, but I do think the utterance of poetry is inspired by something other than the mind, the logical and rational centres. There are times that I wish the poems would stop coming and leave me alone. It would be nice not to have them taking over my life.

RT: How has criticism of your work affected you or your poetry?

PL: Richard Ford told me an anecdote about being reviewed in *The New York Times* by a man he greatly respected. As Ford says, "The review broke my heart." After that, Ford never reads any of the reviews or articles about his writing. I think his has been a wise choice. I like good reviews and praising articles of my work. Hate the ones that don't like my work. In that, I'm the same as any fragile human being. I want people to love me, who wouldn't? Consequently, the former creates an inflated ego, the latter creates anger and despair. Either way I get fucked by it. I try not to read my reviews, tell my publishers not to send them to me. Friends will often phone to tell me of a bad review, why I don't know. They rarely phone about a good one. I never read a criticism of my work that ever helped me to write. If anything, most reviews are utterly destructive. I value a few close friends' responses to my writing. Other than that, the poems go out into the world like orphans in search of God and rarely ever find anything resembling a creator.

RT: Has it ever become impossible for you to write?

PL: Being unable to write is simply fear. Either fear that the poem will not live up to my expectations, or fear that I will not live up to the poem and its subject. I fear sentimentality, that failure of feeling. There have been times I haven't written, but I would never say there was a time when I found it impossible to write. Some days nothing good gets written, but I still work at it. Discipline, getting the words down on the page. This is good. The hardest thing to let go of is pride, ego, etc. I have to get naked and clean and honest; bring my craft to bear on what is needed to be said even if I don't necessarily want to write about it. I never adequately dealt with my father's death for twenty years but that didn't mean it was impossible to write about. I simply had to wait until I was ready emotionally, spiritually, aesthetically and finally old enough and, hopefully, wise enough to be true to what I felt about that tragedy which changed my life forever. Death is a great betrayer.

RT: I know there have been poets whose work has moved me onto pathways towards where I feel poetry can take a reader and/or writer of poems, and whom I've been very grateful for – yourself, Layton, Thompson and Page among Canadian poets; Blake, Yeats and Lawrence among the English and Irish; Roethke and Kinnell among the Americans; and a whole array of marvelous poets from other parts of the world. Can you say which poets have had the greatest effect and influence on you?

PL: This has changed over the last forty-five years. The great poets from 1850 to 1950 have always been a measure to me whether it was Browning, Wordsworth, Dickinson or Whitman. The great Modernists like Auden, Williams, Frost, Pound, Yeats (especially Yeats!), etc., were paramount in my formation as a writer. Post-World War II and Canadian, I would say Layton, Acorn, Purdy, Webb, Page and a few others, very few. Of the foreign writers, a significant anthology back in the sixties was *Modern European Poetry*, which I read carefully and deeply. The German poets were most influential, Rilke, Georg Trakl, Gottfried Benn, Ingeborg Bachman (I loved), Celan; the French hardly at all; Italians Eugenio Montale, Pier Paolo Pasolini, the Greek Cavafy (a major influence); Russians Sergei Yesenin, Akhmatova, Pasternak, Osip Mandelstam; and the Spanish – Machado, Jiménez, Vallejo (a major influence), Lorca, Neruda (a major influence). The Americans, post-Second War: Lowell and Bishop, Roethke and Jarrell, Charles Olson, James Dickey, Richard Hugo, Robert Creeley, John Ashberry, James Wright (important), Philip Levine, Anne Sexton (very important in the sixties), Gary Snyder. . . . Last ten years: Charles Wright, Robert Hass, Charles Simic, C.K. Williams, Louise Glück, Jack Gilbert, Stephen Dobyns, Stephen Dunn, to name a few. Don McKay, Tim Lilburn, Don Coles, Jan Zwicky and Don Domanski are all writing fine poetry and I read them carefully. All of the above influenced me formally in that they gave me possibilities of ways to express what I felt. They rarely, if ever, influenced me in terms of content. What I wanted from them was "how" a poem can be written, not "what" a poem is written about.

RT: What would you say the function of poetry is as opposed to the function of prose?

PL: Poetry is closer to the gods than prose. There are prosaic exceptions, of course, but such prose writers are really our epic poets: Lowry in *Under the Volcano* an example, Faulkner's *Go Down Moses* and *As I Lay Dying*, Hemingway's short fiction. I don't think there is some demarcation line between prose and poetry. It's all one. It's just that most prose is sloppy, flabby poetry at best. Most fine poetry works on lineation, rhyme, rhythm, metrics, etc. It pays attention! Prose mostly doesn't. There are always a few pages in Atwood and Ondaatje's novels that are poetry, but their novels are crammed with poor writing. They're among our best writers, but I'd rather they, like all the rest of the novelists, spent more time getting it right. Poets still pay attention to each word, you see. At least, the ones I love do.

RT: What role does suffering play in your poetry?

PL: Here we get into content and I feel uncomfortable here. Who doesn't suffer? Poets express suffering constantly and forever. Hass says: "All the new thinking is about loss. In this it resembles all the old thinking." I agree. Suffering is loss. The celebratory joy of Walt Whitman has no counterpart in the twentieth century. I have written love poems and think love is all that keeps me alive, love of my woman, friends, my cats, a grudging love for humanity, though ask me and on any given day and I'd agree with Jeffers: "I'd sooner, except the penalties, kill a man than a hawk." From my childhood on I witnessed nothing but suffering – at home, at work, in my marriage, my parents, brothers and sister, friends, peers, etc. – and early on I swore to myself that, as a writer, it was my duty to report back to people the daily suffering of men and women that I'd witnessed. There are times I find the world unbearably painful. Having tried suicide once, thought of it often, I think I survive in this living by the skin of my teeth. My alcoholism and other various addictions have all been to numb me in this daily world. That I chose depressants to avoid depression is another lovely irony in my life. I'm sober now almost a year and I find the "sober" world without depressants just as unbearable as it always was. Poetry has saved me more than once and given me reason to stay alive. I don't mean I contemplate killing myself every day with a knife, razor blade, pill or gun, but there are times I find it hard to live in the face of this new and terrible century. I'll be happy to be rid of it soon enough, given I'm sixty-two and am unlikely to live much past eighty. That sounds depressing, doesn't it? I think I'm simply being honest, if not pragmatic.

RT: You mention Irving Layton as being one of the Canadian poets who was important to you in your formation as a poet. When I was a teenaged neophyte, and on into my early twenties, I lived in Montreal and knew Layton. I remember he told me I should read your poems – which I did, with a real shock of pleasure. After, I followed everything you published. I've felt all along that there were several connections between your work and Layton's work (as between your work and no other Canadian poet, really). For one, a fascination with form. For another, what I feel is the presence of what Lorca called *duende*. Do you agree?

PL: Layton's early poetry affected me a great deal. His poem "A Tall Man Executes a Jig" became a kind of mantra to me. The spiritual transformation he speaks of in the poem touched a deep need in myself. My own struggle to achieve spiritual health has been a long one. That poem, more than any other has been the basis of much of my work. I owe him a great deal. "*Duende?*" That dark mistress of the soul blowing in from Africa? Lorca's definition holds good for me. How else describe where the words come from or where the heart of poetry lies? Not a muse, but a dark urgency, a brooding upon the heart of things.
       As to formal concerns, I have always believed that much of the poetry pub-

lished in the past fifty years has been formless prose broken up into lines in order to slow a reader down and make them pay attention to meaning. But poetry is much more than that. Rhythm, rhyme, repetition, metre, etc., have been much ignored. The heartfelt statement in prose is fine but it doesn't go where poetry wants to take you. There is, in the great poems, a song, an incantatory celebration of our deepest needs. I only have to go back to the beginnings of poetry to find it. The original peoples of this earth knew this of poetry and I don't just mean the Native peoples, but all people everywhere, the Irish as well as the Cree. If I have tried in my life to write poetry I have tried for that original song. Of course, I have failed many times, but I hope that, in some of the poems, I have succeeded.

RT: Your poem "Fathers and Sons" in *Mortal Remains* seems to me to be a great poem and the sort of piece a man must have lived intensely and almost a lifetime to be able to write. I wonder if this poem is as important for you as I feel it might be. Can you speak about what this poem means to you?

PL: "Fathers and Sons" along with the other family poems in *Mortal Remains* took a long time to write. I think I have been cursed to remember. As a child my brothers and I spent our early days after the war telling stories about our brief past. We were already fascinated by it, dwelt on it, celebrated it and mythicized it. The obsession never left me. When I wrote "Fathers and Sons" I wanted to end a lot of pain and bring my father and I back into a relationship we really never had. It was also an affirmation of my own manhood, a putting away of childish things. Rereading it I feel there is an acknowledgement of my own death, those last lines walking me to my own sweet grave. Beyond the personal, it's also a poem about being a man among men. I try not to think it might be in response to the so-called Men's Movement of Bly etc., but what's in the wind infects us all. To some degree the poem is an affirmation of men after thirty or forty years of the Women's Movement and the sometimes blunt criticism of the patriarchy, its power and its subjugation of women. Of course, I agree with much of that criticism, but in this past half-century men have struggled hard with the emotional and spiritual aspect of who they are. Hopefully my poem answers some of that.

RT: Is this what poetry offers an individual, then – spiritual transformation? And, thinking of your "Fathers and Sons" and what you say about the poem, I wonder if you'd say that spiritual transformation through poetry is the telling of the story that you must tell. I'm thinking of what you say about having to "get naked and clean and honest" and "bring [your] craft to bear on what is needed to be said"; I'm also thinking of what you say in one of your fairly recent prose pieces on poetry [from "Meditations," which will appear in a title forthcoming from McClelland & Stewart]: "What we must risk is our own truth." Would you like to comment further on spiritual transformation?

PL: The spiritual is always at hand, felt, and resonant in us. Of all binding human concerns the spiritual is the greatest because it strives to take us to the past and future of our mortality, that which lies beyond us. The transformation the poet reaches for rests in language and its ability (combined with his craft) to surround that mystery, not explaining it, but articulating its existence. When I say I have "to risk my own truth," then I have to allow the poem to speak to the issue of my deepest concern, that of both life and death. That's why Layton's "A Tall Man Executes a Jig" spoke so deeply to me. Those last words – "transforming all" – cutting right into my soul. In "Unborn Things" I write about how this might be done, "Folding my hands on my chest/ I will see the shadow of myself," and go on to invoke the "father" who "create[s] the birds and beasts of dreams." The same with "The Carpenter" poem, which ends with a spiritual transformation: "and alone lifts off into the wind/ beating his wings like nails into the sky." The greatest poetry takes us to that place: Wallace Stevens's "Man on the Dump," or "Ideas of Order at Key West," for example. P.K. Page's "Stories of Snow," is only another of a thousand examples.

RT: You characterize "much of the poetry published in the fifty years" as "formless prose broken up into lines." I read a piece by the late Primo Levi in which he says he found that in the death camps of the World War II, when people recited poems to each other, they recited fairly metrical and/or rhyming poems as opposed to more prose-like poems – not only because the poems were easier to draw out of their memories, but also because such poems were more deeply consoling. What would you say regarding Levi's observation?

PL: Of course, poems must by rhythmic. I think my poems are all rhythmic in the classic sense of what poetry has always been. Cadence, a measured line. Prose-like poems are flat and lack the incantatory chanting effect of a good poem. I've always striven for a rhythm in the poem that is an exact echo of the content it seeks to explore or expose. The traditional metric of the past has not been lost in this past century. It may not reveal itself in rhythms of such strict order as iambic pentameter, but it must have a syllabic beat. I've always counted syllables in my poems in order to achieve a rhythmic effect that the speaker of the poem can rely on. A poem is a musical score for voice. I hope that anyone who reads a poem of mine aloud will find that cadence I've built into the lines. At least I hope they do. As for much of what passes as poetry these days? It will pass, I think, into the obscurity it espouses in its forms and rhythms. It's not so much what we say, but how we say it, right? Levi is right. I carry fragments as well as whole poems from the twentieth century canon in my mind and can recite them at will. They are all poems with built-in rhythms and, of course, such rhythms are aids to memory.

RT: You say that in your "To the Outlaw" piece of thirty years ago, the "silence"
      you referred to spoke to your own "self-destructive desires as much as the
      poem." In one of your fairly recent prose pieces about poetry (one of your
      "Meditations"), you speak of "the immense silence" within "the emptiness of
      a great bell" as having to do with poetic "authority." I wonder if you'd like to
      say something about the more recent comment in the context of the statement
      you set down in the sixties.

PL: The "silence" I spoke of in the late sixties or early seventies was the silence of
      death à la George Steiner's essay on silence following the World War II and the
      camps, etc. I was hell-bent on self-destruction back then, both artistically and
      physically. There was a great self-loathing in me, which I sympathize with now
      if only out of a tender feeling toward the young man I was back then. The
      "silence" I would talk about now is exemplified in the poem "The Sound"
      where I liken it to "a great bell." I stood inside a huge bronze bell when I was
      in China in the early eighties. The pressure on my body and spirit was pro-
      found inside there. I've never felt anything like it before or since. I ran my
      hand along the inner bronze surface and the sound went right through my
      body into my bones. It was the only time I've heard my bones sing. That is
      what silence is.

RT: I suppose, in the end, I've never felt that poetry could be anything other than
      language that allows for a certain strange intimacy with the soul. I love that
      statement of Keats's: "The world is a vale of soul-making." Would you say, as
      Keats seems to have said, that poetry is an act of "soul-making"?

PL: Not "soul-making" but "soul-revealing." The poet or artist of any kind takes
      us through an object (and here I include objects in sound such as song or the
      spoken poem) into the mystery. It is why we are moved by Mozart or Dylan,
      Handel or Cohen, Van Gogh or Tom Thomson, Alden Nowlan or Jack Spicer.
      At their best, they reveal that which we know in ourselves. The object allows
      us to feel it again. The poet/artist lives with the weight of perception on a
      much more constant basis than most people. I don't say that egotistically,
      rather I say it with some humility.

Where Voice Meets Text

SHARON THESEN

Interviewed by Helen Humphreys

Sharon Thesen was born in Tisdale, Saskatchewan, and now lives in Vancouver, where she is an instructor at Capilano College. Her poetry collections include *A Pair of Scissors* (Anansi, 2000), the winner of the 2001 Pat Lowther Award; and *News & Smoke: Collected Poems* (Talonbooks, 1999).

Helen Humphreys is the author of two novels and four collections of poetry, the most recent of which is *Anthem* (Brick, 1999). She lives and writes in Kingston, Ontario.

HH: Do you have any explanation of where your own voice came from, of why you became a poet?

ST: Creative writing students are often enjoined to try to find their own voice. This seems to me to be inviting them to develop habits of articulation that may be successful in a creative writing class situation but which may come to haunt them later. Young poets should be interested in poetic diction, not their own voice. Their own voice already exists and will emerge naturally, but most often it is the weakest part of the equation.

 "Voice" is often what is most predictable in the work, most vulnerable to parody and, worse, to unconscious self-parody. I'm not saying writing should be anonymous or machine-like, the personality (sometimes called the voice) of the writer expunged completely, like a bad smell. In poetry I like, I'm always aware of a spirit or ghost or signature that is unique to that poet, but when I sense that voice becoming the dominating ego of the poem, I'm turned off. That thoughtless "I" also reveals itself in what Robin Blaser once referred to as "the 'I am' among the platitudes" – not, as far as I'm concerned, an interesting or worthwhile poetics. Voice has to be both there and not there, a phantom. It's where voice (as desire) meets text (as constraint) that the possibilities of something wonderful lie. But "discovering your own voice" too early in your brilliant career as a poet can be limiting. Maybe this is necessary for fiction writers, I don't know. Some poets are fiction writers or inspirational journalists in disguise: maybe they're the ones with the all-too-recognizable "voice."

 The actual physical voice of a poet is always fascinating to me. Often writing that fails to reach me from the page reaches me via the voice. Voice in that sense is a seduction. I feel I have not read a poet until I've heard him or her read aloud, been seduced by the voice. That auditory (and visual) experience changes everything; it's like falling in love. I know for myself that I have to be standing (rather than sitting) to read, I have to have room to move. The slight "conducting," which I do with my right hand (and I'm not even right-handed), is a way of digging into the rhythm of the line.

 The physical voice is fascinating, and unforgettable. I love the stories about someone phoning somebody twenty years after a brief fling and the person receiving the call recognizing the voice at once. I'm fascinated by people who deliberately change their voices – like the actress Lauren Bacall – to a much lower timbre. A voice stained by time, by patience, by experience and emotion – like Jeanne Moreau's, like Leonard Cohen's – is as precious as a species. When I think of writers who have died, like Roy Kiyooka, for instance, it's his voice I miss, the sound of him laughing. I think of death more as silence than absence.

HH: What drives a poem then, if not voice?

ST: What drives a poem for me, I think, is an intuition about language which moves along a stream of rhythm, narrative or image. By "language" I mean whatever is being generated in my mind as it meets or senses a sort of ghost-language that surrounds me. "Voice" here is really nothing but the management of the complications. I try as I'm writing to stay just ahead of the words I'm writing down, otherwise I get pulled into controlling, evaluating, etc., and at the same time I'm aware of the unspooling thought of the poem – but again, lightly aware. That is how it feels, anyway. The "voice" that I recognize as "mine" usually gets in the way or wants to do something it has already done. But at the same time it is necessary, I need it, because I want to push its intelligence, quite literally, push it toward what it knows. But this too mingles with, again a stream-like, watery way, the general "mutter" of words and language and other voices, maybe the "voice" of a poem I've just read. But it all has to happen at once. I can't collect phrases and put them in a poem at some later date, because the voice isn't the same as it is at that precise moment's necessity. I've often felt bad that I don't keep a notebook with me at all times and write down stuff I hear on the radio or what people say or notes from reading: seldom has that ever helped me. I'm alone with everything at that moment of the blank page. It all happens then or it doesn't.

I've also tended to avoid procedural writing and other interventions, even when their aim is to impress the reader with the marvels of what language can do more or less all on its own. It is indeed impressive. But I prefer playfulness to arise naturally, the way a cat will suddenly take a whack at your ankle as you're walking by. It's playful, but it's also not. If I haven't written for a long time (for me, a long time is a year or two), I've had to impose projects or structures on myself. For example, I'll decide to write a page "blind" (i.e., compose on my Selectric typewriter or on the computer with my eyes closed) for a month. But then I'll wind up doing it only for eight or ten days. My habits as a writer are mercurial.

HH: Louise Glück has said she writes each of her books to answer a specific question or problem she has posed herself. I tend to organize my books around a theme – *The Perils of Geography* around the notion of what constitutes landscape; *Anthem* around one's direct and covert relationship with language. What makes a book a book for you? I am particularly interested in the impetus behind the writing of *Aurora*, which I will confess is my favourite of your books.

ST: I recall Louise Glück saying she set herself a new task with each book, deliberately changing a habit of her line in the most recent book. This is a great idea because it obviates the problem of constantly repeating yourself. It's also a reminder that we can't ignore good old-fashioned "craft" problems. I admire the self-discipline involved in her projects. Then there was the Portuguese poet Fernando Pessoa's solution – if you can call it a solution. He "was" several different poets, with different names and different styles, and worked on many different books at the same time.

What makes a book for me I'm afraid isn't very complicated or theoretically charged . . . my books are simply collections of a lot of the poems that were written since the previous book came out. I've written only one sort of theme book and that was the poems for Malcolm Lowry (*Confabulations*). I do tend to write in sequences or series, though, and a book will often contain at least one set of these, e.g., the "Gala Roses" sequence in *Aurora* and the "A Pair of Scissors" sequence in the book with that title. Once I've amassed enough poems, I put together a manuscript (and I don't publish big books; I prefer smaller, shorter ones: to me, the ideal poetry book is a chapbook). Then the book eventually comes out. It has internal consistency only because of the time period the poems were written in. A period of time does leave an imprint on a poet's work, subtle or otherwise. The period of time the poems in *Aurora* were written was quite a long one, probably four years. Obviously, I'm not a prolific writer. Also, trauma tends to silence me. I suffered a catastrophic divorce during that period, quit my job, lived in practically a cave in the Slocan Valley for a while (but a beautiful cave), returned to Vancouver and moved house. I moved from the west side of town (rich-trendy) to the east side of town (poor-trendy). I went back to my job. The poems of the sequence "Gala Roses" were written after spending part of the summer listening to CDs of Orthodox liturgical chants. I was also reading Michele Leggott's poetry and drinking a lot of wine.

When I put the book together, I sent it to Coach House, who, apart from the selected poems with McClelland & Stewart, had been my main publisher for years. Michael Ondaatje was still a contributing editor for Coach House and he accepted the manuscript. I wanted an image of the goddess Aurora for the cover. My colleague Josephine Jungic, who teaches art history, told me of a beautiful painting depicting Aurora on a palazzo ceiling in Venice. We had to go through quite a rigmarole to get permission to reproduce the image. It wasn't too long after the book came out that Coach House more or less folded as it was and morphed into the Coach House of today. I feel fortunate to have had the book published by them almost at the last minute. There was an error, though, in the printing process and part of a "Gala Roses" poem was blanked out. So when I sign copies of the book I often write in the missing words – "yanked" and "off course." When Coach House folded, Talonbooks took over my list, which also included *The New Long Poem Anthology*. Talon published another selected poems, *News & Smoke*, which included poems from *Aurora*, since all my books, including *The Pangs of Sunday* (the McClelland & Stewart selected poems) were out of print and had been for quite a while. As well, Talon did a second edition of the long poem anthology. And House of Anansi published my most recent book of poems, *A Pair of Scissors*, a couple of years ago.

HH: How have your feelings about poetry, the reading and writing of it, changed since you were in your twenties?

ST: My feelings about poetry haven't changed much. Over twenty years, a lot of our notions of what poetry is, what it can do, have been through the old heave-ho of post-structuralism, and the field remains pretty much divided between the lyric poets and the language poets, with some "postmodern lyric" poets in between. Then we have geniuses like Lisa Robertson, one of the true poets of our time. The poetry world as I see it has become more fragmented but probably less polarized than it was ten or fifteen years ago. Today the divisions seem more between the haves and the have-nots, the celebrities and the pre- or post-celebrities, the famous and the obscure. I remember a time when just about all published poets were more or less equally infamous. They could behave badly, get into fistfights over poetics, drink too much, divorce too often, live in poverty, not teach creative writing. I miss those days. Poets, if they weren't braying jackasses, had a vulnerability which was quite beautiful.

Not just poetry but the whole of literary culture now seems to be mired in the machinery of marketing, promotion, prizes, awards and brand recognition. And not only is poetry the product, so is the poet. You can't be published even in an anthology anymore without a photograph being attached: this is fine if you're young, good-looking and photogenic, but really embarrassing if you're not. Especially if you're a woman. Having my photo taken is torture for me, and it looks it, too, in the result. I don't understand why every publication, announcement, advertisement, book and poster has to have photographs of the writers on it. Half of the time the photo doesn't even resemble the writer in person: it was taken twenty years ago, or through a smeared lens, or from above as the poet is lying on her back. But this too is part of the way marketing has taken over as the main purpose of a publisher. It's not even the publisher's fault: to survive, they have to compete in a marketplace more and more devoted to image.

I wrote a poem around 1982 called "Running into Other Poets at the Toronto Airport," about reading circuits then, and the high likelihood of seeing other poets at the Toronto Airport as they criss-crossed the country doing readings. Such a poem seems impossible now. The poets who do travel around seem to be handcuffed to agents and publicists. About the only thing that's the same is the reading fee: $200.

Another thing that hasn't changed is my uneasiness about "being" a poet. Unless a woman poet is possessed by the sexiness of celebrity status, her poetry writing can be the kiss of death socially. Want a conversation stopper? Try telling someone – the stranger, say, sitting next to you on the plane to Toronto – that you're a poet. Only in Europe and occasionally in Montreal have I not been embarrassed to admit that I write poems. Because poetry is still associated with emotionality, irrationality and the merely oppositional, the woman poet is thrice rewarded by devalued currency. In her book, *Words of*

Selves, the English poet, Denise Riley, recognizes the "linguistic unease" of the woman poet, the "sheepish" feeling of committing an undesired exhibitionism in the act of writing, the mistaken and presumptuous identity-making between the writer and the work. I recognize these dilemmas as a permanent part of my experience writing poetry and "being" (seen as) a poet. In fact this problem is sometimes a subject of my poems.

In Canada too it is expected that a poet will, or should, graduate into fiction writing. To continue writing poems becomes a stubbornness, a sort of unnecessary self-marginalization, even a refusal to get real and grow up. Some poets can and do write fiction and to do so is obviously more lucrative and respectable, in the sense of attention-worthy. But, at least so far, my own forays into fiction have been brief and disappointing. I would like someday to write a set of recollections, though, about being a sort of anarchist in the house of love. Poetry and my years teaching would be the context.

HH: Who or what are your influences as a poet?

ST: Influences in a strict sense must be what change your work in some way, move it onto a different course; or poetry itself, what you're reading at any particular time. It is hard to be uninfluenced, and one probably influences in one's turn. Sometimes I write in a state of near panic because I want something fresh to bubble up, a fresh writing experience. But as someone who by necessity must write out of or with inspiration, by the seat of my pants, in stolen minutes, seldom ever hours (this is a whole other story), I go by that thing of being seized or surprised by whatever daemon or grace has ever-so-recently visited. Influences, i.e., poetry, can be inspiring, powerful, maddening, intimidating – something you write with and for, but also at times in resistance to, against. These are poems of argument, of irritation. At times, especially in the late eighties, early nineties, I felt coerced to get with the program and embrace theory and write out of that. Well, I've never been a big fan of "theory." It feels too much like "being saved," that old evangelical trope for agreeing to see the light (and nothing but the light.) I understand its attractiveness but feel that there are many ways of being radical. All poetry worth reading is radical, i.e., rooted in a profound sanity. This probably has something to do with form. The enemy of poetry, and of the radical, is hysteria.

Modern and postmodern poetry and poetics are such a battleground because as text, poetry can do, and be, almost anything. Therefore, my poetics, *c'est moi*. One's poetics become a badge of one's ideological stance. For example, if you write lyric poems you're a patriarchal gynophobic egomaniac. Well, so what? Everybody inhabits their own little hell, one of the worst being inescapable mediocrity. And, what is a "lyric poem" anyway? To me, it's just another jar, another glaze. I can't get too exercised about seventies-style line breaks being fascistic. A bit lazy maybe, but if shag rug can come back, why can't line breaks? Why can't the word "I"? Bandwagons, ideas-du-jour conjured in the hothouses of neurotic English departments, the dictates of sour-faced puritanical bullies: to heck with them, I say. On the other hand, you have to take an interest. You have to read your contemporaries and know what's going on. And there's important work being done by younger poets connected with Smoking Lung, Pulp/Arsenal, Talonbooks, Brick Books, Gorse Press, New Star and magazines such as *West Coast Line*, *Raddle Moon*, *The Capilano Review*, and *The Malahat Review*. One could do worse as a writer than to live in British Columbia. Sometimes I think, if we weren't born here, we come here to die. Quite recently, a book of essays under the rubric "Anarcho-Modernism" was published by Talonbooks: I have a feeling this might define my own intellectual ground, if a moment of self-categorization has arrived.

As far as "influences" go, I think the ones you admire can be much more problematic than the ones you feel oppressed by. In an influence you recognize something of your own soul (and I do care about souls) but that writing is usually in a different location, one that's been earned by different linguistic experiences and influences in its turn. By allowing the influence to inflect one's writing out of enthusiasm can be to short-circuit one's own process. In the end, you'll wind up back where you were anyway. It's better to just take lines or stanzas from the influential one wholesale for the same reason Tchaikovsky did of passages by Beethoven: love. Also by "influences," I mean poetry, canonical or otherwise, that I've been energized by, that has made me happy, that has, essentially, restored my love of poetry, my sense of its beauty. But poetry can also be all the books that surround me as I'm writing and in relation to which I feel apologetic, as if to say, why add to an already over-burdened and unread genre? Who needs more of this? Why dump more bad writing into a world already choked with it?

HH: I'm interested to know who your original influences were.

ST: As far as that set of early books or writers who presumably set one's compass and to whom one returns as to a shrine, there were some I discovered on my own in the high school library and loved (John Newlove, Patrick Lane, Allen Ginsberg, T.S. Eliot, Louis MacNeice) and others whose work people I admired taught me to love, though I probably would have been attracted to their work on my own as well (Charles Olson, Jack Spicer, Robert Duncan, Edward Dorn, Denise Levertov). I was to find later, though, that I felt a greater affinity with the poetics of the New York School and some other west coast Americans like Duncan McNaughton and Diane di Prima. I've been fortunate to have been guided by extraordinarily gifted teacher-poets such as Robin Blaser, who remains a friend and mentor. And an enormous influence is Phyllis Webb, whose work I discovered with joy and a sense of companionship I'd never felt until then. I've also learned from the promptings from who-knows-where of my own teaching, heard as if from outside myself. Influence is the landscape you live in, the drive to work, the company you keep. Or apparently absolutely nothing but the shock of language and its infinite worlds.

I believe one of the biggest influences on my writing was growing up in a house where there was a lot of live music – the old standards of the twenties, thirties, and forties; the Ink Spots, the Mills Brothers, Hoagy Carmichael, Louis Armstrong. I come from long lines of musical hedonists on both sides. My father was a talented self-taught musician and entertainer. He was a terrific teller of jokes who especially admired the "timing" of Bob Hope. I studied piano, banging out Rachmaninoff pieces in twilit Prince George winter afternoons. All of this resides in the forms of my writing. And like most influences, music has been both a strength and a limitation. It keeps me from "doing things" with or to language that might move me out of rhythm, its pulsations, and its assumptions about reality. I mean this in terms of both what I write and of what I read, or rather enjoy or don't enjoy reading. My earliest influences in academic poetry, which I studied in a special program in Prince George in grade nine, as well as the major influences that persisted until I was well into my thirties, were male. And American. This has been an important fact for my writing, as well as for my life.

HH: What do you think is the public function of the poet?

ST: The restoration of joy and tenderness to the soul. Relief from bullshit. Beauty. Truth-as-laughter. Wholeness and connectedness, bite, intelligence. This is what poetry can achieve. As for the poet, well, I think some poets are better than others at being public intellectuals or social critics or laureate figures. Whether poets are public intellectuals writing on a range of social, psychological and political issues, or whether they are devoted solely to poetry, probably depends on temperament, but poets always have an aura of aloneness. I don't think poets have any particular public function as poets, however they may conduct themselves as writers, teachers, whatever. Poets are taken either too seriously, it seems to me, or not seriously enough. There's still a lot of ooga-booga around poetry, probably a remnant of the accurate intuition that poetry has something to do with magic.

And then you have to ask what is "the public" anyway? Is it an imaginary space? Is it a site of competing privacies and interests, the poet's among them? The poet's public role has historically been dramatic, either as playwright or bard – of the male sex, also, no doubt. I don't think there's ever been much of a public role for modern or postmodern poets, at least in North America. Poetry's value can probably be measured in inverse proportion against the amount of public "free" speech permitted in a society. But just because poetry can be valued as a genre doesn't necessarily mean it's worthwhile as writing.

But no matter what's going on, poetry is always anachronistic. This is part of its charm. This is why, in times of grave civic occasions, a few poets can be drummed up to write something memorable and unique. And more often than not, they rise to the occasion quite splendidly. I remember Lorna Crozier's poem about Pierre Trudeau at the time of his funeral: the image of Trudeau as a white fox on the shore of a lake was beautiful, consoling, and apt. Generally, poetry seems to belong to the realm of "feelings," and the poet to the role of unintelligible outsider, earnest emotional exhibitionist, or stand-up comedian. That so many readings now require seventeen poets to go on stage and read for five minutes each only encourages this tendency. A friend of mine once observed that a lot of poetry readings nowadays may as well be fart-lighting contests.

HH: I have recently become a little disillusioned with poetry. The poetic moment often seems to me a very static one – that small revelation as the geese fly overhead – and as I get older I am less convinced by the reflective moment. Poetry too often seems merely a way to name loss, but it cannot accompany one on the necessary journey of loss, which is life itself. What do you think is wrong with poetry? What are its limitations?

ST: Its marginality. At least as perceived from outside. But poetry is a subject and an activity; a way of perceiving, a making. That's what *poeisis* is, a making. I feel that there is at once too much poetry and not enough poetry. Poetry gets saddled with a lot more programs for its improvement (and, by extension, for the improvement of society) than prose does. Poetry seems always to be down at the police station confessing its crimes and promising to behave better in the future. Poetry has to bear so much of the puritanical and positivist impulses that continuously worry at North American culture, encouraged by institutions, therapies and administrations. This is not to say poetry (or any art) is immune from the corruptions of history and power relations. But surely it is just as mistaken to see poetry as little but the transmitter of exploitive power relations or the key to unwinding them. Poetry has about it some of the same mystery and surprise as love. Eros is its true muse, especially in its appositive – "the bitter sweet" as translated by Anne Carson – and in its work of connecting, relating and feeling.

It is much easier for poetry to be a hobby than prose; for poetry to be unintelligible, incommunicative, boring to the point of torture; for poetry to be presented as self-performance and therefore to be, by definition, beyond comment. At the same time, I wonder what a self-performative, incommunicative, torturing, hobby poetry would actually be like! Maybe great! Look at Artaud, look at Dickinson, look at Wallace Stevens!

So, we get back to the fact, or rather the hope, that poetry cannot be contained, defined or coerced. In this sense it is a bit identical with human consciousness. There seems to be a *tremendum* about poetry that causes people to act silly around it, as if it carried a taboo. For certain, to be a poet is to be somehow associated with morbidity, death, melancholy, tragedy. This is all too often a reality in the poet's life, and can lead to social as well as artistic marginalization.

HH: How important have reviews, awards, other honours been to your feelings about your work? Is competition healthy or unhealthy for a poet?

ST: Prizes are great, especially if they come with enough money to enable you to take a few years off from work, or put a down payment on a relatively inexpensive townhouse outside of Brampton. Major prizes now can drive poets into major careers, especially as prose writers. The problem is, there either aren't enough prizes to go around to properly recognize deserving poets or the few prizes that are awarded are – and who could possibly be surprised by this? – compromised by procedural, institutional, fashionable or political machinations. Everybody knows this, and so the official line is that the whole system of awards, grants, and prizes in Canada is "a lottery."

I like to think of literary prizes as gifts, wonderful surprises coming out of nowhere – not a writing goal. I think, for a while, the Governor General's Awards were like that. But not anymore. A lot of publicity for both the poet and the publisher can be won or lost by a nomination. Although a plethora of prizes attends prose writing, until last year there really was only one major national prize for poetry in Canada, and that was the Governor General's. Now there is the more lucrative and more glamorous Griffin Prize. All these prizes are welcome because they bestow importance and varying amounts of cash on a larger number of writers. The problem is when a few prizes and awards become the only alternative to obscurity, penury and a sense of failure. What writers and poets could really use are more, and more generous, private, institutional and corporate endowments and grants – genius grants, residencies, patronage appointments, retreats, travel and teaching opportunities, fellowships and so on. And if the Canada Council focused on a more generous grants-to-publishers program, smaller publishers could afford to give a decent advance to a writer to complete a book. The prize system would then just be gravy.

Writers and publishers shouldn't have to live or die according to the whims of juries who all too often are either inexperienced or over-experienced. In the end, a jury is often really awarding itself by choosing the standard-bearer of its collective taste, or by forestalling the negative judgments of posterity. Also, a jury must come to consensus, which casts its own shadow over the proceedings: one member can dominate or the winner can be the result of compromise.

Winning important awards and prizes can also hamstring poets, thrusting them into public space burdened by an importance they must henceforth live (or write) "up to." You would never again have the freedom to publish a shitty book because you were trying to do something you don't usually do. A grant, on the other hand, is based on faith in what you can do, rather than a rather random and noisy anointing of something you've already done.

Despite evidence of increased book sales, I'm not sure poetry books are really all that well served by awards. Awards and prizes may give the book more publicity, more visibility, but as a reader I've many times avoided buying, even looking through, an award-winning book. It has ceased to be a discoverable world; it has become an artifact, a trophy. Its official seal of approval and subsequent ascension into what Charles Bernstein calls "official verse culture" even anticipates the wording of the poet's obituary. A precious morbidity attaches to award-winning books of poetry, which I find repellent. Even so, I'm thrilled when someone whose work I think is deserving wins a big fat prize – but that's not because of the big gold seal that gets glued to the book but because of the time and freedom to work that the prize money brings to the poet.

HH: In your poems you are often an observer of disparate phenomena. What's going on in the world around you enters into the poem itself and, to a large extent, becomes the poem. No content precedes the form. How do you consciously order the world into poetic form? And to what end is the poem the world?

ST: This question intrigues me; it's perceptive of you to notice this. I don't feel I order the world into anything but that that order is there to be discovered in and through the writing. It's not an ultimate order, it's simply the order of a moment. That's why I depend completely on the moment, why the poems I try to write in a procedural, researched or predetermined way never have the same presence, or literally speaking, immediacy as the poems which depend on the moment. I have to concentrate on the feeling of a simultaneity of phenomena both internal and external, and a simultaneity of time, and hold it through the whole of the composing process. It is sort of like the blank canvas approach, I guess, and it can be taxing, and it fails much of the time.

What I worry about is triviality. I despise the trivial-for-its-own-sake and for a poet whose major characteristic as described by critics is the exaltation of the mundane details of everyday life, the drift into the trivial is a real worry. Besides, I don't intend to exalt the mundane details of everyday life. They are mundane, they are awful, they are soul-destroying even. These are the things that can bury us, and most often do. I think most of what we have to live in and with day by day is atrocious! If I exalt anything, it's the way we so determinedly, and sometimes gracefully, put up with it. Jeff Derksen's work critiques this space in a very effective way, I think. My work is much less ideologically informed, but that doesn't mean anything. I still believe in individual genius, or, etymologically speaking, idiosyncrasy. I'm inclined in certain directions; I have to follow my inclinations . . . but the moment I sense a dead end, I'm out of there. "My" inclinations can also be those of the Zeitgeist, or fashion. These enthusiasms are all too apparent as mistakes in my work.

To whatever end the poem is the world is the degree to which some fresh new thing is shaped by the language and rhythm of the poem. You know how some very competently written work can just sit there on the page lifelessly? I don't know why, or how, but when a poem "is" a world, it is alive. It is as alive as any natural thing. Charles Olson wrote, "art is the only twin life has, its only valid metaphysic." That could be my motto.

Kingdom: The Darkening Forests
and Hockey Rinks of Don Coles

DON COLES

Interviewed by Stephanie Bolster

Don Coles has published a number of books of poetry in Canada including the winner of the 1993 Governor General's Award, *Forests of the Medieval World* (Porcupine's Quill, 1993), and *Kurgan* (Porcupine's Quill), the winner of the Trillium Prize for 2000. He is presently writing a novel.

Stephanie Bolster has published three books of poetry: *White Stone: The Alice Poems* (Governor General's Award and Gerald Lampert Award, Signal/Véhicule, 1998), *Two Bowls of Milk* (Archibald Lampman Award, McClelland & Stewart, 1999) and *Pavilion* (M&S, 2002). Born and raised in Vancouver, she teaches creative writing at Concordia University in Montreal.

SB: In your discussion of Edvard Munch, whose life and work inspired poems in *Forests of the Medieval World*, you write that the artist "returned obsessively throughout his long working life to a very few themes from childhood or early manhood – these include the death of his mother when he was four, the death of his sister Sophie, his love for 'Fru H.,' his loneliness." Your own writing pivots around a few, not all that different, themes. I'll begin with where I see myself most in your poetry, and that's in its acute awareness of the passing of time. I call this awareness in myself a nostalgia for the present. Joan Didion calls it a "presentiment of loss." What do you call it? Would you say this is a quality of your temperament, or of your poetic temperament?

DC: "Nostalgia for the present" and "presentiment of loss" are both good (without being identical they are very similar) and I find myself easily in either. Both, of course, are seamlessly linked to memory. The feeling, this "nostalgia" or "presentiment of loss," can be overpowering, even paralyzing: at its most positive, though, it's as close to the centre and source of art, of poetry, as anything. That's not strong enough: it *is*, for me, the principal source of poetry. To respond to your question, I would think it's a "quality" of both personal and poetic temperament. One can be struck by its power in obvious ways, e.g. watching one's child in a particularly moving moment, knowing that this child is even now growing away from this moment – also, though, in less obvious ways, in any moment at all in which the thought of transience occurs to one. And it's entirely clear to me that the power would be either less or altogether absent were "time," its passing, not an essential part of it, of this image one is watching. It can seem intolerable that it will not endure, the physical, living, reality and beauty of this moment ("Stay, stay, thou art so fair!" as Faust cries out). If this unendurable feeling is indeed what I'm calling it, i.e. "unendurable," then I must do something about it or else, I suppose, in one sense or another, metaphorically or literally, die. That's no overstatement (I *do* say "metaphorically"!).

        Out of this, then, comes a poem. A good or a bad poem, of course. In either case it's a response to this near-oceanic feeling. If the poem doesn't meet the feeling, then it fails in every sense, the "life" and the "art" sense, and one is left feeling confused, alienated or impotently sad. If the poem rises to the occasion, then nothing becomes more tolerable, really, but one becomes, in a real sense, part of the image, one has somehow (luck and skill are both involved here) wiped out or healed a great deal of, maybe almost all of, the distance from this receding image that one was feeling, was suffering from, was finding unendurable. One has caught it before it fades "into the forest dim." The sadness, or "sense of loss," or "nostalgia" remains but it has been acknowledged, and this is such a privileged and marvelous (and also mysterious) feeling that one knows it to be a kind of blessing, a benison. Nothing to do, by the way, those last two nouns, with anything that I want to call religious.

SB: Have you been aware of any changes to this attitude over the years?

DC: Yes. Very much so. As one grows older (and older) one becomes, of necessity, more of an observer and less of a central actor in, you'll pardon the phrase, life's drama. This isn't all bad news. If art relies upon memory, which in a quite exact and detailed sense it does, then one can say that memory, in its turn, owes huge debts to observation. And if observing has become more central to the events of one's day, and ego-strivings have faded a little or a lot, this can obviously be of interest. It's unlikely to mean a flowering or up-rush of a powerfully "new" level of poetry, though it seems to have done this here and there, but it does make for change. Leafing, just now, *Kurgan*'s pages, I find many poems which I think relate to this "change in attitude": from the title poem to "Kingdom" to the Caspar David Friedrich poem to the Beckett poem . . . and more. None of these would, I think, feel at home in my first collections. That last sentence is harder on the early books than is really needful. There are a number of soft-centred and thinly original poems in those early books, especially in *Sometimes All Over*, but a number of the poems in *Anniversaries* (my second book) remain among my favourites.

SB: How have those moments you've captured, and the act of capturing them, affected your sense of self? In "Someone Has Stayed in Stockholm," you write: "Although you can fall into places deeper than language,/ can't you? Yes. He has." Obviously you have, too. What is deeper than language, for a writer? And – the key question, I think – what is insufficient about language?

DC: I think that almost anything we think about closely is deeper than language. Both the world and our thoughts flows/flow outside and beyond our language capabilities. Language tries to keep up, and its success can appear huge (in art, in good writing, etc.) – huge in that it *does* do something, it slows the flow, it stops at least small parts of that flow and allows us to watch it or wade into it, stand in it. But it fails, inevitably, in terms of the totality of any moment. Camus says in his journals that true "realism" in literature is impossible: the myriad of impressions any mind has (if a writer were describing the motions of a mind) would overflow the margins of every page that has ever been published. If this feeling of failure becomes oppressive it's bad news. Failure can be seen in different ways. It can be the artist's certainty that he/she has failed in whatever the aim was; or it can, crassly, arrive out of continuous rejections of one's work. (I'm sure you know how omnipresent this is! – you publish, I publish, but all God's chillun do *not* publish, though they send out their manuscripts in hapless swarms every year.)

        "Deeper than language," though, means many things. It can make the so-called artist (poet, etc.) aware in every step of what he's doing that it's at best a simulacrum of the reality he senses, notices, fails to rival. It can on the other hand intensify his commitment, because the knowledge of that gap stimulates the desire to bridge it. And of course, finally (well, probably not "finally" – what can be "final" about this?), I haven't even touched the other argument, which loiters hereabouts keeping its mouth shut but knowing what it knows: and which is, of course, the certainty that language can lead us beyond the speechless world and deeper than formless thought. Which seems to undercut all that I've been on at up above. Well, that's the way it is. Elusive, paradoxical, colliding with itself, endless.

SB: After what you've said about the inadequacies of language – and, yes, its successes, too – why write?

DC: I believe that I write because I have learned that out of this event, which is composed of (1)my own unhurried ruminations and (2)language and (3)the greater or lesser "formatting" (the chosen shape) of a poem, can come sentences, words, understandings, that interest me much more than any other way I have come upon to bring thoughts to the surface. Once that has been said, I must go on to say that sharing these thoughts/words, knowing that whether they are read or not I am at least giving them the chance to be read, is very important to me. So important that, as the old conundrum regarding the fall of a tree in the forest asks, if I could absolutely know that there would never be a reader for this or that poem, I would not work further on it. I make no assumptions as to how valuable or otherwise any potential reader will find the poem: but that it will have a chance to be read, this matters totally. The possibility that somewhere outside my window someone or several or even many persons exist who will one day read this piece that I'm working on, is in a very unstated way moving and exciting. Perhaps this is partly because, if it comes about, if those readings do happen, it/they will justify and more than justify the solitary and unwatched hours one is now in the middle of going through.

SB: In his poem "The Dead Poet," Al Purdy, speculating on the origins of his poetry, asks "how else explain myself to myself/ where does the song come from?" There's an interesting parallel here to your "To An Older Brother Born Dead," as Purdy's suggesting that his voice came from his brother, who died in the womb just before Purdy was born. Do you have any explanation of where your voice came from, of why you became a poet?

DC: Where does the "voice" come from? From all the experiences of one's life. My mother's voice is in it: she was the one who gave me the books in my early and adolescent years, not pedantically, just putting them in my way. That voice didn't tell me what to think. What it did, uniquely in my experience, was to provide an unfailingly intelligent space in which my own arriving voice could – how slowly! with how many false and still-continuing starts! – become audible. Some of my teachers are there. My own family, of course, all three of them, closer than anyone, speaking out of their varying ages, I mean out of their early lives and their present lives, our first meeting and our latest meeting, unaware, any of us, of the emotion that will build around those multiple voices.

"Foreign" languages are there. I can read French and German and Italian (sort of, that last one) and Swedish and Norwegian and Danish, and I speak the first two of those quite decently. I think this awareness matters very much to one's growing sense of words and their sounds. Mostly, certainly, what are there are the "voices," rhythms, words, of a few thousand books. And among these, since I became of age, some writers very particularly, some on grounds of a style I liked and tried, briefly or at more length, to emulate, some for content, for maturity – for wisdom, let's say. Among the former, heavy on lyricism and romantic longings and shaky everywhere else, but valuable to me in important emerging stages of myself and hence not to be shown my back now or ever, Cyril Connolly, Scott Fitzgerald, to a much lesser degree a writer like Lawrence Durrell; among the latter, Shakespeare, all on his own; later, Tolstoy, Chekhov, George Eliot, Trollope, Flaubert, Camus, Constant, Heinrich Böll, Goethe, Rilke, Söderberg, Leopardi, Italo Svevo. And, among near-contemporaries, Iris Murdoch, three or four of whose many novels mattered a lot to me. Among poets, Philip Larkin, Geoffrey Hill, and Thomas Hardy. And Keats. And Mandelstam. And lately, Tomas Tranströmer. Mandelstam I can read only in translation, but even there he's unique and deeply affecting. Tranströmer I have myself translated and now correspond with.

And reading good journalism, which in my case has meant English journalism: *The Observer*, for many years, and then, since its sad decline, *The Guardian* and *The London Review of Books*. The last-named was the first UK journal to publish poems of mine, which it has gone on doing. Bless it. Both these are so far above most of the journalism published in this country, in terms of subtlety and learning and trusting-the-reader, that it's an embarrassment. (I do not say 'all' of our journalism, and of course I'm far from alone in knowing this about the general and pitiable *niveau* of our literary comings and goings. Writers and poet/critics such as, to risk a not-so-brief list, Marchand and Metcalf and Taylor (Kate) and Solecki and Sarah and Moritz and Keith and Fulford and Sherman and Wiseman and Rigelhof and Starnino, all these seem to know most or all of what I know about this quality-gulf and in some cases, probably more. And increasingly often, it seems to me, they are saying and writing what they know, doing this more bluntly than I am in the habit of doing it, often to their cost. Bless them, too.)

But this level of public discourse is also, I think, not irrelevant to the choice of the UK as a whole-or-part-time place of residence for so many US and Canadian authors, the ones who can afford it (and who usually, surely for domestic reasons, seem to keep quiet about this choice). Gertrude Stein wrote that "America will be a good place for writers someday, but not yet." Many years have gone by since then and there is still room for improvement, sea to shining sea. But that's another book-length discussion, one we needn't have.

SB: Your influences are far more international than those of most Canadian writers. Obviously the following isn't an either/or question, though for simplicity's sake I'll put it as one: did the influence of someone like Tomas Tranströmer creep into you because you lived in Scandinavia, or did you choose to live in Scandinavia because of an innate affinity for the region and its writers? (What is it about the North calling to the North? A visit to an exhibition of Scandinavian art in Buffalo is cited as a major influence on members of the Group of Seven.) Did *The Globe and Mail*'s Val Ross have a point when she wrote in 1993 about your "Northern melancholy"?

DC: Yes, there's an affinity, I'm sure. But there's a huge difference, too, between the experience of living in Sweden and living here – between being a Swede and being a Canadian – and, at its simplest, it is (or seemed to me to be) that the Swede who walks into one of his or her great forests can, if he is so inclined, feel he's in touch with the past of his family, of his culture, even unto the very dim prehistory of all that; which we here cannot feel. Canada geologically is as old as Sweden, needless to say, but culturally the line into the far-back just isn't there. People walked in our forests, of course, but culturally they were not my forbears and they left few testaments, few hints. It makes for a difference, a very real one. I went into some of those great Swedish forests north of Upsala, by myself (as many Swedes do, orienteering has its origin in these parts), and although I'm sure some of what I felt was sheer exoticism, I think there's also a colouring of something else – there *is* a literature and a history there which even if my own direct forbears had no part of, culturally I can readily relate to.

      You don't need to be an "artist" to need, to benefit greatly from, a connection with the distant past. Of course we can all do that, too, even us New Worlders can do that, through reading and travel; but it's closer to one's daily life if one actually lives in that other sort of place (whether Sweden or Britain or, plenty who choose this, Greece – although I'd best add here that Greece never meant half so much to me when I was there as "the North" did; or as the UK did and does). There's a poem in *Landslides* called "I Long for People Through Whom the Past . . ." (a quote from Rilke) which relates very directly to this.

SB: To talk not specifically of the North but simply of temperament – and this is a question that's been asked of me, and probably of many writers – do you think the poet, particularly if he or she hasn't suffered the kind of dramatic loss or other trauma that many people think is required to become a writer, has, one might say, a responsibility to be unhappy?

DC: Complicated matter, with, of course, a long history. I think of several things off the top here: one is a memory of Irving Layton spouting off about how he envied Mandelstam and other Soviet citizens for being harassed as they were

– it must have driven them towards greatness, Irving more or less said. Having been an idolater of Mandelstam for (I bet) longer than Irving was, and more seriously too, I found and find this asinine. Mandelstam was as you know killed by Stalin, starved to death probably, in Siberia – a young man still. Or I think, quite a lot more positively, of Marie-Claire Blais, who when she was asked after a reading if she had experienced in her own life the same awful-nesses that her novel described, replied that she had "always thought that what was central to the act of writing was imagination."

On the other hand I'm sure that I would never have known what the hell was going on in a book like, say, *I Never Promised You a Rose Garden*, or in many other stories of unreason and madness, if I hadn't experimented with drugs and lived through at least a few (modest, no doubt) "trips"; until then I believe I was the most "secure," unflappable human being in history. Was this, as a learning experience, a good thing? Dunno. You pay somewhere for any-thing you do. And you lose somewhere for things you do not do. The problem is of course beset with this (hidden agenda) aspect: those who seek unhappi-ness, or at least, I'll say, risky experiences of the mind, don't always come back to witness to what they did. Those who survive tell us about it and all seems pretty much on the plus side. The other witnesses, the lost ones, might scare the life out of us if they could make it back and could still talk.

Your query relates, as you know, to the *obiter dicta* of the Rimbauds and, at an absurdly lower level, the Ginsbergs of this world, slogans such as "the true artist must experience everything." With which, for reasons just implied, I totally disagree. I have to believe that we can integrate into our understand-ing of life many, many wisdom-fragments from art, from history, from reading and listening and walking about in the wider world. We don't have to enact everything with our bodies.

SB: Unlike many Canadian writers (the two you've just mentioned being quite rare exceptions, though both Blais and Layton are still better known at home than abroad), you have a significant profile outside of Canada – most of your serial publications are non-Canadian – and obviously it's occurred to you that your career might have developed differently had you continued living in Europe, during those years you talked about earlier. "Someone Has Stayed in Stockholm" is clearly a key poem in this regard. I know you still spend a good bit of time in Cambridge, so I'm wondering how you think you would have fared full-time in England, for example? And, if this isn't getting too personal, how did you feel when you read, in W.J. Keith's piece in *Essays on Canadian Writing* (#55), that some well-known Canadian poet ("who ought to have known better," as Keith says) remarked that you shouldn't be seen as a Canadian poet because you, according to this anonymous person, write "almost exclusively about Europe"?

DC: Starting with Bill Keith's comment – no, chauvinism isn't an elusive thing to identify, and remarks emanating from it have never bothered me. I remember seeing on TV a bunch of Canadian establishment figures: Layton, Berton, Betty Kennedy of *Front Page Challenge* (before your time), Farley Mowat (he of the suspect claims to have lived for X years with the Inuit) . . . and Mordecai Richler, who of course has always been accused of betraying his roots in favour of all those years in London. Richler tried, three or four times (I was counting) to put in a word or two about just this topic, about home-and-abroad and the writer, and each time he was cut off by the braying of Berton, or Layton, or Mowat, or some even dimmer individual; finally he looked at the camera (at us watchers) and shrugged, and then sat back and didn't speak another word all night.

Good on you, Mordecai, thought I. I am grateful to have been born where I was (Woodstock, Ontario) and to have benefited from Canada's prosperity, to have enjoyed a vigorous health and made extensive use of this during all the years in Europe (about sixteen, altogether – that's counting sabbaticals from my job at York); grateful, also, to have had parents who were as tolerant of my trite (as some observers must quite reasonably have thought) dreams as any long-established Euro-family could have been; and grateful, also, to teachers in Toronto (Frye, McLuhan, Underhill) who were miles brighter and more committed than any teacher I met at Cambridge during the two years of my studies there. But it remains true, for me, that any inhabitant of the New World has to do what she or he can to privately make up for that newness.

Having mentioned Richler a minute ago, here's a private little lament, if we have space for it. I lament that I never got to meet him, a feeling I have about no other Canadian writer. I have not a shred of proof that this would have mattered to anyone but me, and of course he had a more than ample number of pals – but here's the thing. It's not just his novels, although these are of course my chief route to what I know of him; it's three other things that I know he was knowledgeable about, that he liked a great deal, and which I may be just about as uselessly knowing about and like not a whit less. London, for one: he lived there for lots of years, I for only five (I had another ten on the continent, to compensate) but I'm certain we'd have a few preferred places in common, streets and parks and pubs and theatres; we must, for sure, have seen some of the same football games and sat about in one or two of the same cafes at uncoinciding times; and have subscribed to the same newspapers.

For a second thing, hockey – I remember reading his dispatches from Scandinavia when he was covering the world juniors for *Maclean's*, and his attachment to the Habs is well-documented; as for my own credentials, I watched Canada, possibly the Trail Smoke Eaters, possibly not, beat Sweden 10–0 in Stockholm one night in the late 1950s, remember seeing our goalie, I think it was Seth Martin, flat on his back in the crease with seconds to go in the game, probably two Canadians in the penalty box, the last Swedish shot just lifting past him – and he reaches up a hand from his prone position and catches the thing; and ten thousand *svenskor* just gasp and then roar, finally deciding they might as well enjoy their team's humiliation. Those were the days, I imagine myself concluding this anecdote with, although it'd be nice if I'd found a fresher line, and I catch an ironic but perhaps compassionate glance from this companion I missed out on.

And finally, snooker: he admired Cliff Thorburn as I did, we certainly could have shared a lot of remembered dramas involving Hurricane Higgins and Steve Davis and Dennis Taylor and Jimmy 'Whirlwind' White. He had a room built for his regulation-size table out there in the Townships; I inherited my father's Brunswick-Balke-Collender 8' x 12' table and his cues and score-keeping spools and have all these in my not-purpose-built basement room. And I read somewhere that his son Daniel regularly beat him at the game and my son Luke leads me about forty-six games to six (but who's counting). In spite of that I'll bet that neither of us thought or thinks he was or is all that bad.

SB: While we're on the subject of the past, of going home or not, how have your feelings about poetry, the reading and writing of it, changed since you were in your twenties? In particular, I'm thinking of something you told *The Globe and Mail* in 1993: "In my thirties, I guess my writing tended to be wordy and ornate. But I stripped it down and got rid of that. The best craft is transparent." I'm coming to a similar realization myself – I used to be drawn more to obviously displayed linguistic skill, while now I'm more impressed by a writer's insights first, and how they're displayed second. (Though of course, as you're probably thinking, in good poetry the two are inseparable.) Do you remember how you came around to this realization that the work needed to be stripped down? And since you mention your thirties – what were you writing in your twenties?

DC: I would guess that either the decorated prose was simply bursting-with-uncritical-energy youthfulness or, maybe, the effect of the heroes of the time. During my time in Cambridge Dylan Thomas came and "read" to the English Club and everybody who hadn't already signed onto that boat decided that this was the way to write poetry; and Christopher Fry was the flavour of the decade as far as theatre went – verse drama, *The Lady's Not for Burning*, *A Sleep of Prisoners* and four or five more. I wasn't drawn to poetry but I did write three full-length, three-act (prose) plays while I was at C. – none of them of the least interest to me or anyone else now, but writing them was a better use of my time, I still think, than drowsing through the all-style-no-content hours in the Mill Street lecture rooms.

Come to think of it, this playwriting probably had more to do with impressing, astonishingly briefly, a girl who was in the undergraduate Amateur Dramatic Company than with Christopher Fry. I also did, though, write a Fry-influenced verse play which I still have around somewhere, the cleverness and wit of which isn't half bad, if you ask me. I sent it in to a contest for verse drama held by the Tower Theatre in London (since vanished, I believe) and got a note back saying they would mount a production of it (several nights' performances only) if I could come up with a hundred pounds to "assist in costs." A hundred pounds was major money then, or so I felt, and I indignantly declined the offer. End of a career. Also of the ADC connection.

The above may seem and perhaps is more frivolous than you and I, Stephanie, are for the most part being here, but it has some small relevance to your question. Mostly, though, the "stripping-down" which you refer to happened as a result of an erratic but never quite abandoned reading programme which I hung in with during all of those years away. If you think of (and I sometimes did think of, because I had almost a year in Paris during which I immersed myself in some of the irreplaceable, really, pages available to readers in that language) Gustave Flaubert, who for years forbade himself even the reading of, e.g. the local newspapers, because he felt that all of his senses, *all* of them, should be (forever if possible) trained upon "the best that was ever thought or said" (to quote Arnold, I suppose), then although you will not have any accurate idea of what my readings did for me, you may have, at least, a sense of the ideal I was trying to keep before me.

I don't mention this to impress, I who read the sports pages before anything else in the morning paper wherever I am living and have never varied in that commitment – but in matters of *books*, yes, I was usually keeping in touch with things. And have kept that up. Not because of a belief in the "rightness" of such a program, but just because I had made it to the other shore, the one where, once you're there, mediocre writing is boring within seconds, somewhere halfway down page one.

SB: In his lengthy review of *Little Bird* in *The Fiddlehead* (#173), Christopher Wiseman brings up the fact that you use rhyme but don't appear to use metre in your work. First, is this a valid observation? (It seems in general valid to me, but I may not be reading closely enough in this case.) And, if this question is on the mark, could you explain the preference for rhyme over metre?

DC: I'm not altogether clear what it means to say one "doesn't appear to use metre"; not unless "metre" means a *regular* sound pattern, an established and henceforth adhered-to pattern (which of course in this case Chris Wiseman does mean). A degree of regularity does appear in some of my poems, e.g. the Ivor Gurney poem "Gone Out is Part of Sanity." These tend to involve also rhyme, regular stanza-length, etc. But a meaningful use of metre, as far as I am concerned, is always critical and is, I hope and think, at least always attempted in every one of my poems. That is, metre, stressed and unstressed syllables following one another in a far-from-random or unconscious way, is something I am (and here again I must say: "I hope") always aware of and at work on. But the adherence to a predetermined sound/stress pattern will always, in my case, be discontinued, be obliterated I would like to say, by the arising requirements of the poem, of the line: thus a quite "other" metre will be noticeable at a given point in a poem if it serves the poem; the poem will not be allowed to lose its self-discovering way in the service of the above-mentioned adherence. I've read a few thousand poems (and have stopped halfway through a lot more) where the regularity of metre just crushes my attention to what I will call "the poem." It points my thoughts towards the conscious involvement of the poet in his/her poem, rather than the poem itself. Which latter is surely the only thing anyone's interested in.

SB: I suspect this has something to do with the colloquial force of your poetry, but isn't rhyme even more intrusive (i.e. less "natural") than metre in this case? (Particularly since so much of our speech is, or at least is said to be, naturally iambic.)

DC: Yes, it can certainly be more intrusive. But it need not be. If it's done as it must be done, then it serves the poem rather than dominating it. It pleases and lifts the reader's attentiveness without shouting its presence. The thing about rhyme that interests me in a positive way is something quite other than all that. I'd never have guessed this unless I had written poems myself, and had done enough of it (in this rhyming mode) to realize the absolute (for me) truth of what I'm about to say: which is, that the search for rhyme, once one has established that this feels appropriate to the poem one is working on, need not – not at all – limit or constrict the freedom of the poem to grow in its own pro-foundest direction.

No, what it does, instead, is to force the creating mind beyond a solution to a line's requirement which might (in the absence of the need for a rhyme) have come readily to that mind and might have been thought acceptable, ade-quate. But now, because that easier, more accessible solution doesn't "rhyme," the writer can't persuade or trick himself into finding it acceptable; he has to keep at it, has to probe further, has to think and assay and then think and assay again, who knows how often . . . a process which can be annoying, awk-ward, time-consuming . . . but which, I've found time and time (and time) again, can, improbable as it may have seemed (for an hour or several days), lead the entire poem into a stratum deeper and richer than the writer could have guessed had he not been forced back into it, not been compelled to reopen his mind to what might happen here. How often have I been just filled with gratitude (yes! though it does sound overdramatic to say so) to the rhyme scheme of a poem, once the crisis is over and the solution (or "a" solution) has been found and I've realized just how much richer the whole enterprise has become.

SB: The time has come to talk about reputation. Michael Harris, with whom I know you worked on *K. in Love* and *Little Bird* when he was editing Signal

Editions, told me once that he believes that you can write what you want, because you've paid your dues – you've been "capped," as he put it. In one of his poems, Mark Sinnett writes, "Today I revisit poems of Don Coles . . . I am reeled when reading again *Sometimes All Over.*" W.J. Keith writes, "To those attuned to such subtleties, Coles is obviously one of the most technically sophisticated poets writing in Canada today, perhaps anywhere in the English-speaking world." Do you feel, yourself, the assurance – not necessarily when you write, but when you publish – that others project onto you? Do you feel the respect accorded to you?

DC: Regarding being "capped"! There's something valedictory about that which I would happily sidle away from. Still, I know what is meant, and I don't think it's meant unkindly. The honest answer is, I suppose, that yes, I feel something of this; I feel I've been treated decently by reviewers and critics, sometimes much more than decently, sometimes I've been just about floored by praise from people I admire a great deal (they're usually not poets, I've noticed, although there are exceptions to that too); and I must not pretend that I'm anything other than pleased (too small a word there) when some of the much-younger poets in this country have let me know that they like what I've been on at.

     So, basically, yes, it feels good. I was, after all, a late starter: my first book didn't appear until I was well past, good God I hardly realized this, forty. So I wasn't exactly spoiled with recognition (and therefore with confidence, *qua* poet) in my pre-prime years. But I wasn't, either, particularly insecure. On the third or fourth hand, though, there have always been poets around who I knew, and know, were writing poems which I guessed (sometimes felt totally sure) were better than mine, than all of mine or certainly than most of mine. There were times in my writing life when some of these were Canadian (Atwood, chiefly – her early poems, as in "The Animals in That Country," knocked me out when I first began reconnecting with literature in these parts – about 1965 this would be), but although I admire the work of seven or eight established poets in this country, and feel that there are a clutch of very young poets (some of whom I am in touch with, and am happy that this is so) who may do wonderful things, I can't say I feel I've much to learn from them at this point.

     In the wider world the near-contemporary names I have paid most attention to are Larkin and Roethke and then, later, Heaney and a few more – not many more but a couple. I don't think there are too many other poets who have recently risen up to the level of these. And having said this I should add that of these unmissably great ones, some seem lately to have lost their self-critical apparatus. They've been drowned or at least waterlogged with awards and applause and are now publishing indifferent work, work I have no interest in. This would apply to Heaney, who has fifteen or twenty altogether beautiful, dazzling poems scattered among his first five books, poems I admire immeasurably, but whose most recent three or four books are pretty thin. (His essays always make good reading.) Of course there are also a very few poets, unnamed so far, whose work lives at a level nobody else even aspires to: Osip Mandelstam, already mentioned here, may be just about alone up there, as far as the twentieth century goes. But I don't think you were asking me for an assessment of the world's poems, were you?

SB: In a broader sense, how important have reviews, awards, other honours – the Governor General's in 1993, for instance – been to your feelings about your work?

DC: These things have mattered, for sure: I don't go about giving readings anymore (I did plenty of those in past decades, or so I feel – Harbourfront numerous times, almost every university in Ontario and also in most of the other provinces; have declined invitations from the odd starry place abroad too, some of which declinations I rue), so these other things have helped sell books, probably helped placate my publishers, who in general have taken this behaviour on my part very well. But this is not what you're asking, which is: have awards etc. altered my feelings about my work? – to which I think I must answer, yes, they have, to the degree that I know that what I want published will be published. The effect (of knowing this) can be good or ill: either you bring a heightened seriousness to the work, knowing that it will soon leave you and enter upon its public life – this is good; or else you (as implied above) think you've become so infallibly halo'd that your slightest effort will always merit publication – this is not good.

SB: Is competition healthy or unhealthy for a poet?

DC: Mostly the latter, I think. Competition is fine for people all of whom want to run the 100-metres faster than anyone else, but a poet wants to do something quite different from that which anyone else, e.g. another poet, wants to do – he wants to write a different poem than the poem which anyone else wants to write. So there is, in a very real sense, no competition going on here at all, and the illusion that there *is* such a competition, or the behaviour that such an illusion fosters, is surely of no help to anybody. I suppose that no one will claim not to be aware that X or Y has, last year or this year, won an award which every right-thinking juror should have known that A or B (just A, really: A being meself) deserved to have won; but this has nothing to do with poetry, only with vanity and ego. One of the fine things about all art is surely that in spite of all that ego/vanity stuff, which the human being cannot forego, the artist can feel something like pure disinterested joy reading a really fine new poem, looking at a painting, listening to a piece of music, by someone else, known or unknown. This happens as often as that fine new piece of art comes to one's attention, and as soul-affecting events go it's the best thing around.

The "new piece of art" has to be really, really fine though, and there aren't many of those, not this year or any year. Anything less and the other parts of the machinery start to clank into gear. Pity, really.

SB: When I studied with you at Banff in '94, you were the first person to ask me directly what I meant by a particular line or phrase. Your queries forced me to look past surface lyricism in my work to find the confusion, vacuity, or – when there really was something worthwhile in there – insight beneath. You speak often about your frustrations with most contemporary poets. What is the problem?

DC: I'm amazed, really, that nobody asked you "directly" what a line or phrase "meant." Not amazed that people in general don't do that, that's no surprise: people in general are intimidated by "poetry" and don't wish to appear naive, they fear that it will be seen as gauche to ask a "prosaic" question like that. But other poets, other teachers? *Porca miseria*. Poetry, in spite of MacLeish, can "mean" as well as "be," by God. The licence to merely "be" is one that a lot of egregious poets have carried around their entire lives, avoiding "meaning" and posturing self-indulgently among words which, apparently, nobody ever calls them on. How totally lovely it would be, at a poetry reading given by one of these apes, if someone, just once, would cry out something along the line of "what the bleedin' hell does that *mean*?"

SB: How did you deal with such issues while teaching at York? Was your approach to my poetry typical of your teaching approach?

DC: I think that, yes, my approach to your poetry was, if not "typical," similar to that I took in my workshops at York or elsewhere. Of course there are boxes inside boxes when it comes to any art or craft, aren't there? So there's a limit to what one can demand of people in an undergraduate workshop – there you're looking for freshness in the use of language, your sights are lower, but the general drift has to be the same: has to do with honesty, with a close attention to the image at hand, with an awareness of fustian and bombast and cliché and *idées reçues*, all that. With the poem as search engine (a phrase I've never used before, as it happens) rather than as a mere putting-on-paper of thoughts held and images and metaphors taken note of before the search began.

SB: Do you see any hope for change?

DC: I think so, yes. I think the influence of Philip Larkin and Seamus Heaney and Theodore Roethke and a few, not many, more, is an influence in the direction of plain utterance rather than obfuscation. This does not, though, repeat *not*, mean that their poetry aims any less high or deep, or that their metaphors are any less striking, that a potent imagination is in any shorter supply, that there is any less true energy-crackle audible in their poems, than in the superficially noisier and more exotic poets of the several decades before them.

SB: How have teaching and writing fit together in your life? Do you find that, since retiring, you have been writing more often? Have you been completing more poems, or does each poem just take more time, now that you have that time?

DC: Teaching and writing fit together pretty well for me, as far as I can judge. That is, I taught, and enjoyed most of that, and wrote a fair bit, and had much pleasure and some success with what I wrote. I cannot judge how much better or worse the writing would have been had I not been using 75 percent of my energy and time for teaching. Since I retired (from teaching) I'm constantly surprised, amazed even, at how much more focused I can be, and all year, not merely summers or on sabbaticals, as far as "writing" goes. On the other hand much of what I taught I also learned from. Would I have discovered Osip Mandelstam, who now means so much to me, had I not been teaching and reading widely in the furtherance of that teaching?

SB: In *Kurgan*, you've included a fair number of earlier poems – revised, though not extensively so. This isn't something done all that often outside of a self-declared "new and selected," and when it's done, it seems to me, most writers leave the poems as is, or else rewrite them drastically. It's illuminating, in terms of your craft, to see the changes – particularly to lineation – that you've made to each poem, and in terms of your career as a whole, to see poems from different collections shuffled together. Was this reader-insight a primary reason for republishing the poems? Given your tendency to recurring themes, why not just write new poems on similar subjects?

DC: The rewritten, recycled poems are in *Kurgan* for the most mundane of reasons: because my publisher wanted a thicker book than I'd have had without those poems. Granted that they were going to appear in this book, naturally (I find it natural, anyhow) they were going to appear as strongly, as effectively, as they could manage. I don't think this meant I was merely sanitizing them, ridding them of perceived flaws, bringing some allegedly more mature wisdom to bear on them, in any case I hope not: but I did sometimes come upon a line which could, I felt, enter the poem at a different angle, or disappear in the name of assisting some remaining image to glow out more urgently – and when I found this to be so, I made the change. I don't think one is always right in these latter-day changes, but it's a chance I'll always take.

SB: Of all the things you've written, what are you most proud of? A book, a poem, a line, even – what one thing do you come back to in those moments of discouragement and reassure yourself by thinking, "I wrote that"?

DC: A very good question – I'd love to be able to ask it of, say, Larkin, or Mandelstam, or Edward Thomas (a poet I haven't mentioned here at all, but whom, along with Thomas Hardy, I reread more than any other poet, ancient or modern). I think a poem called "Recluse," which first appeared in a collection called *Anniversaries* published in 1979, is the one I'd be slowest to hand over if I was at gunpoint. Or "Kingdom," a recent poem about a darkening hockey rink and a Zamboni driver. Or a section in a multi-section poem called *Landslides*, in a book called *The Prinzhorn Collection* (and it reappeared as the title poem in a "selected poems" a few years later). The section is numbered "IX," and like all the sections of that poem it's about my mother, who is pictured here in her early childhood in the Eastern Townships in Quebec, in winter, skating. It tells the reader how she "Sped on the neighbour's rink/ Under the blue bulb swinging/ At early dusk on its cord . . ."

A Matter of Focus

ROO BORSON

Interviewed by Julie Bruck

Roo Borson is a poet, essayist and a member of the group Pain Not Bread, whose *Introduction to the Introduction to Wang Wei* was published by Brick in 2000. Her new collection, *Short Journey Upriver Toward Oishida*, will be published in 2004.

Julie Bruck is the author of two books of poetry: *The End of Travel* (Brick, 1999) and *The Woman Downstairs* (Brick, 1993). A former Montrealer, she now lives in San Francisco.

JB: Your earliest books were made of relatively compressed lyric meditations, and
       you often used repeated images (rain, moon, light, stars, the progression from
       day to night), as a kind of formal structure for both the poems, and for the
       book as a whole. Over time, your work includes more and more of the chaotic
       human world, and your formal strategies seem to expand in response. How do
       you think your work has changed from the writing you did in your twenties?
       How have your feelings about poetry in general – the reading and writing of it
       – changed?

RB: A friend once told me that I reinvent myself with every book. But different
       forms, different styles, rhythms and ways of speaking, actually allow you to
       say different things. Whatever you want to focus on, whatever you're curious
       about, has to find a form in which it can live. Really it's the urge to explore.
       We all have a broad range of experiences in life, but in writing, to expand the
       range of what is expressible your technical fluency has to grow in new direc-
       tions.
           Partway through any book it becomes clear to me what it is that I'm
       trying to tackle . . . over time it becomes necessary to incorporate more and
       more into the writing. So, as you say, incorporating cityscapes into land-
       scapes, or a broader range of social relationships into the lyric. It's all been
       done before in one way or another, but each writer still has to learn how to
       go about it. At another point, I was interested in rhetoric, not in the sense
       of persuading by the use of rhetorical devices, but simply in terms of what
       moods are created by certain rhetorical structures. This might all sound
       deliberate, but that's only in retrospect. What I'm doing only becomes clear
       after I've been doing it for some time. More recently, in a long poem, I've
       focused on a visceral sense of music, and, in some other pieces, on sim-
       plicity of speech. These are in my new collection, which is still in
       preparation.
           I wouldn't say that my feelings about the reading and writing of poetry
       have changed, but simply that my poetry has changed. It's clear that the work
       I did in my twenties embodies a more youthful way of seeing than my current
       mode. So the art goes along with the life, or at least my art goes along with
       my life.

JB: In *Intent, or the Weight of the World* (1989), you describe the heart as a shovel,
       ". . . always digging up old ground, always wanting to give things a decent bur-
       ial." You moved to Canada in the mid-seventies, and yet so many poems walk
       your readers through your original northern California landscape, "the smooth
       green hills where writing comes from." Over time the homesickness becomes
       a sharper, more specific pain, as the poems mourn the deaths of parents and
       friends, and as your childhood home is lost to a wildfire. But your work never
       loses that sense of longing for the essential piece of ground (in Spain, I think
       they call it the "querencia").

Here's an early example, from "East" (*In the Smoky Light of the Fields*, 1980):

> I left you as you were,
> owner of that hour of the day
> when the coast's sails fill with purple light.
> Here it is night already,
> and all that was to come has passed.

How has leaving that landscape – both literally and metaphorically – influenced your work?

RB: When I lived there all those years ago, all I wanted was to get away and see new places. Places inhabit me as much as I inhabit them. But I guess that first place, the place where you're born or grow up, where you first learn the world, is special in that it very early becomes identified with, or as, the world, or so it was for me. The longing is not for what actually was, but for what lodges in the memory.

It's impossible to say how my writing would have been different had I stayed in California; my life would have been different, I would have seen other things. I don't know whether or not I would have experienced the same sort of longing: it's possible, since the California of those days only partly exists in the present California. It's a very different place. Still, watching television I can always guess when a scene has been filmed in coastal California: the light, even captured on film and transmitted electronically, is recognizable, and it makes me want to fly there immediately. It's a reflex.

JB: Which writers have been most important to you? I'm guessing that Robert Creeley (another Californian) might be among them? Who else?

RB: Although this is a simple-sounding question, it's an impossible one for me to fully answer. There have been so many works that have affected me strongly as a person, and therefore as a writer. So, yes, Creeley, though Black Mountain, if it's anywhere, is in the east, but something like the wind of Bodega Bay blows through his writing. Like many other people, I feel a strong sympathy with the (very Californian!) work of Robert Hass. By "sympathy" I mean something indirect but important, maybe a kind of tenderness, a feeling of intimacy with both the landscapes and the trajectory of the work. And of course I admire what he's able to do. I'm unable to emulate any of the writers I admire. Kim Maltman's work has been enormously important to me in several ways, and he is the writer from whom I've learned the most, though I can't write anything like him. M.F.K. Fisher (another Californian); Peter Handke in Ralph Manheim's translations; Tanizaki, Kawabata, Tranströmer . . . Lately I've tracked down as many works by Donald Richie as I could find.

And in libraries there are many out-of-the-way books that no one seems to know or talk about, books that are as good as anything ever published, but which never made a splash in public, or at least not where I live. But this sort of list could proliferate indefinitely, and it's no doubt best to keep it short but suggestive. I keep stumbling across works that are mesmerizing. The written world is a huge world.

JB:　How important have reviews, awards, other honours been to your feelings about your work? Is competition healthy or unhealthy for a poet?

RB:　Competition among poets is literally absurd. No one actually writes quite like anyone else. And Canada has plenty of good writers, so that in any given period of time there is no single "best" book. For the Governor General's Award, for instance, in a given year there are always several "best" books, and quite often not one of the ones I'd put in that category makes the short list. I'd say the politics of the literary scene are unhealthy for just about everyone, and yet unavoidable. For me, reviews, awards and the like affect how I feel about myself as a person within the society, at least in the short term. The question is whether the work is valued or not, and there are very few indicators of that, and the indicators that exist are faulty. The writing itself, however, exists in a zone that remains more pure, more free. So there's a conflict. Writing and publishing are social acts, public acts. Unfortunately the ants and the bees have no use for our writing.

JB:　Unlike many writers who depend on teaching jobs for their livelihood, you've spent most of your writing life outside the universities. What effect do you think that's had on your work?

RB:　Again, it's hard to say what effect something I haven't done may have had. But actually I spend large amounts of time at universities, reading in the libraries, sitting in on the occasional course. And then there are also occasional readings, workshops, or residencies that I'm involved in. Hands-on work of that kind is stimulating in the long run, rather than draining. I didn't train in literature, so a regular academic job teaching in an English department would have been beyond my scope. Instead I followed my nose, which led to writing, the life of an artisan or practitioner. What I've learned I've learned by trial and error, and by reading, and from certain teachers. I've also learned from every job I've ever had, including those completely outside of writing. If I'd been employed by a university I would have learned other things, no doubt.

　　Some of the changes in universities over the last ten years or so seem to be to nobody's benefit. I'm a little surprised that students haven't risen up against their demotion to "clients" or even "consumers of education." The terminology bespeaks a disdain, a disrespect, for the disciplines being taught, as well as for the people who teach and the people who learn. In some quarters there's still a feeble sense that the "consumer" is empowered, but in fact the individual consumer is helpless to affect the range of goods on offer. There is terror at the spectacle of a world composed only of manufacturers and consumers, and it's showing itself on a grander scale in the rather inchoate protests against globalization and the economic irrationalism that has gripped our society.

JB: In *Water Memory*, a poem called "Coast Road," strikes me as emblematic of your writing. It's a redemptive piece that follows a series of poems about loss. It describes your most loved and intimate landscape – and adds, "If before I'm burned, they want my citizenship, just give them this place, and the time." It's a Borsonian *Leaves of Grass*. Where Whitman, with characteristic grandiosity, instructs us to look for the poem's speaker "under your bootsoles," your speaker says, "just say on my behalf, 'the present,' and look at your shoes."

This insistence on the plain, unembellished, yet luminous things of the world is one of the many pleasures of your work. The stained cookbook, the resolute shoe, all deeply imbued with human presence. You've written: "If to record is to love the world, let this be an entry." Do these objects work as entries in another sense for you, and for your readers? Are they portals to feeling? Or maybe, containers that make the feeling manageable for the writer, even as they amplify those feelings in the reader?

RB: I can't speak for readers, but I like your double play on "entries." The doors of perception, as they used to say. For me, writing is communication, but it is communication of things that are largely non-verbal. It is, in part, communication of images. Without material things, there is no world. Feelings, manageable or unmanageable, don't seem to reside within the objects, but among them, maybe like the old concept of ether. But this is only one way of looking at it. I was relieved to read a book called *Descartes' Error*, written by a brain researcher, that, without setting out to do so, "debunks" some of the ridiculous statements made in recent years by literary people who seem to have convinced themselves that "thinking" occurs only in language. What a weird idea that's been, with still-incalculable consequences.

Writing is a two-way street. On the one hand, words can be used to try to communicate images that haunt one; and on the other hand, words create all kinds of things that were unforeseen, and which can be far more interesting than whatever was foreseen, including imagery. To go only one direction along that two-way street would be terribly limiting, to either try to excise whatever actually matters to you emotionally and intellectually, or to keep yourself from learning from the new combinations that words arouse. But back to your question. What's important to me is daily life, the daily life of seeing and feeling. The actual things and happenings that surround us and haunt us and make us aware of being alive in the moment.

JB: As a less prolific writer, I'm very curious about how you keep that level of openness. You've written many fine poems with the drowsy, Keatsian kind of attention that comes on the edges of sleep or waking, or from absolute stillness. Those are receptive states that seem harder and harder to maintain in urban cultures, or at least, outside of actual meditative practices. I now live fifteen miles from the Berkeley Hills where you grew up. This morning, I was thinking of your poems as I walked through Golden Gate Park and noticed the flowering bushes were alive with wind. I looked again. Were they, in fact, alive with homeless people? I looked harder. It *was* the wind. But as I pushed my little girl's stroller home, I'd pulled down an internal shade. The meander was gone from our walk. Maybe all I'm saying is that attention is often painful, and that ain't news. But when you describe yourself as a practitioner, I wonder about how much mindful practice comes before the poem is begun?

RB: I don't do anything to intentionally prepare for writing, so writing just comes along of its own accord. I've been doing it for a long time, so to some extent the "openness" is habitual, or learned. A friend of mine who used to do a lot of photography talked about Ansel Adams saying that the point is to be there with the camera when the picture occurs in front of you. The stance of readiness, or in fact receptivity to what's going on around us, is the way we live anyway: the trick may be to accept what actually occurs.

You have phrased very beautifully the experience which led to this question. The meander, and then the shade being pulled. That sort of contrast provokes a question, and writing is one way to explore that contrast or confusion. It's the way I've chosen. But what sort of writing? You can go in any direction. But you have to start where you actually are, with the faculties you already have. As long as the question remains active, it will force you to try different perspectives, or forms, or styles, until you can accommodate it.

I don't think of myself as prolific. Temperamentally, and within the limitations of what I'm able to do, I'm a perfectionist. I have to be; I write down a lot that just isn't any good. A great deal gets crossed out. There are lots of false starts and premature endings. The process of writing any given piece is so slow, so accretive, that it could be described as belonging to a kind of practice, though for myself I don't quite categorize it in that way; that is, I don't set writing apart from other things I do. Very often I have to wait to finish a piece until something happens in life that provides some kind of provisional end, or answer, or further question, to the question the piece is exploring. And I revise until I'm in danger of destroying the piece, all as part of that same exploration. (I realize that the "question" would rarely be obvious to a reader, but at the heart of every piece there's something I've been curious or confused about.)

I've found it's okay to live inside many different frames of mind. It's okay to trust the discipline. Purely from an emotionally practical point of view, since I finish things so slowly, it's useful to be working on several things at once:

that way, when one of them is closed to me, another might be open. But we all work differently. I follow my interests of the moment. I like the "making" of written things; I like the procedures and kinds of attention that writing and revising require, but just liking these things isn't enough. There has to be something propelling the piece. It has to feel somehow "pertinent."

JB: You've written collaborative books with both your partner, Kim Maltman, and with the performance group, Pain Not Bread (Borson, Maltman and Patton). Can you describe how these collaborations work?

RB: Working with other people, when you're not inhibited, is exactly like working with yourself, only more so. You have other people's gifts to draw on, talents and facilities which you lack; and you have to find a way to argue against what you see as their blind spots, shortcomings, temporary insanities, chronic errors of judgment, bullheadedness. But it's still like revising your own work, only within a broader spectrum. It's a very special pleasure, working really closely with other people. People in some of the other arts must feel this more often, in the theater, or in dance.

    Kim and I have consulted with one another since before the publication of our first books, and that collaborative aspect has grown stronger all along. The book we did together contains poems by each of us, but while they were jointly edited, and some structural echoes were created deliberately as part of the process of writing the book, the poems can't be said to be jointly authored, though of course the book as a whole is jointly authored. Pain Not Bread, on the other hand, *is* an author, whose work is unlike that of any of the three of us individually. Or you could say it's like all of us yet isn't any one of us. One musician in a group can't make a sound like the group sound, which is the sound the group is identified with in the ears of listeners. Kim and I in fact have increasingly collaborated on one another's work even in the pieces that are "singly authored"; the rewriting process is very intense, and often collaborative to one degree or another. What remains the work of a single author is somehow the "vision" or "texture," the "intent." There's no accurate word for what I'm trying to say.

JB: The poems in *Introduction to the Introduction to Wang Wei* (2000) are variations (in the widest sense of that term) on poems from the Tang dynasty. Has that project opened up new directions for you in the work we've yet to see?

RB: In fact, only a very few of the poems in the book are variations in any strict sense. Those few will be instantly recognizable to those familiar with the most famous poems from the Tang Dynasty, and for anyone unfamiliar with that history, the true "variations" are listed in the material at the back of the book. More often the poems were written straight from head to hand to paper, or rather from three heads to three hands to paper, and then argued over. It's very much like writing one's own poetry, except that, even beyond having three instead of one of us, we also had a vocabulary from a long tradition both inside and outside of our own language.

Working in that way with Kim and Andy made me despair of my own limitations as a writer. I had to get over that, which took some time. I missed that dimension, being able to be in a friendship which was also, to some extent, an aesthetic fusion. We are of course all still the best of friends, and having had that experience together no doubt deepened it in unexpected ways. It was truly a deep literary friendship which produced those poems, that book. It's fitting, given the importance of the idea of friendship, and literary friendship, in the Tang Dynasty. My current work is a continuation, and I hope deepening, of things I've been doing all along. But it's impossible to disentangle what might have opened up in my work due to Pain Not Bread from what has opened up in response to other experiences.

JB: When you write about the texture of grief – particularly the kind that attends the deaths of parents – you do it nakedly, and boldly. Could the title poem in *Water Memory* also describe the process that brings your elegiac poems into being? I'm thinking of how your speaker exhorts the reader,

> No one made this world, there's no need
> to feel ashamed. Be water,
> find a lower place, go there.

RB: In a word, yes. The event that crystallized that poem was seeing a live kidney, in a small cold-box, on the counter in front of me at the Albuquerque airport. It had just been removed from the donor's body and was being shipped immediately elsewhere to be placed inside another person. Such moments feel exceedingly real. Life and death stand naked before you, as they do whenever someone dies. You asked about objects before: that box was a primal object. It's a matter of focus. Instead of holding up large bundles of feelings (shame, hope, anxiety), if you allow yourself to sink like water, then the ground will hold you up. This is true all of the time, not just in dire situations. But it's the death of someone close that brings most people to an enforced or involuntary focus of this kind. You spoke about "mindfulness" before, or "mindful practice." I've never been quite sure what these terms mean, but I do know what this kind of focus feels like, and probably they're related.

JB: How would you describe the difference between the impulse to poetry and the impulse to fiction? I ask this in reaction to a growing assumption (particularly in Canada, perhaps?), that poets "grow up" to become novelists.

RB: I'm very curious about the impulse to fiction, as it's an impulse I don't have.

In fact I've spent some time privately "interviewing" fiction writers about this very matter. Some fiction, of course, is just a variation on the truth, a variation on events the writer has experienced personally or vicariously, and in this way is no different from most poetry. Maybe at base all writing is just that. But among fiction writers there are those who venture further into what seem to be imaginative constructs than others, and this is what interests me, as I have no internal sense of how (or exactly why) they do it.

One time, a fiction writer and I were finding the bathroom in someone's house. We had to go through the bedroom to reach it, and afterwards she said, in a deliciously conspiratorial voice, "Wasn't that bedroom fascinating?" I'd noticed an object or two, not because they were fascinating but just because they were there, while for her a character was already assembling itself out of the "suggestive" objects she'd seen at a glance. Another time a fiction writer told me that a stranger would be walking down the street toward him, and already he'd be hearing that person talking away, with a whole life behind him. Someone else said that without even thinking he'd composed elaborate lies every time he opened his mouth as a kid, and didn't everybody do that? I told him not everybody did.

Still, I think the writer is always evident inside the writing, no matter how imaginatively far-flung the work seems to be. Evident in the style, that is, and in the concerns, and in that sense all writing is highly personal. Yet there's not necessarily any direct correspondence between the words on the page and events in the writer's life. And whether something appears "made up" or not is very much a matter of the point of view and experience of the reader. Readers, especially of poetry, are often fooled by the use of personal pronouns, as if "I" means I, and as if "he" means he. But in writing, the use of personal pronouns is like the use of tenses: each sheds a particular kind of light, or mood, upon the scene. Each allows you to say different things. So the way in which writing is "personal" is far more subtle than is usually supposed.

Anyway, it seems that the impulse to at least a certain kind of fiction may arise out of a different set of interests than those which give rise to lyric poetry. But there are so many variations: narrative poetry, fictionalized memoir, lyric or "poetic" novels, narrative fiction, lyric poetry . . . and there are important technical differences in the writing of each of them. Over the last decade or two a few verse novels have been unusually popular (for poetry) partly because they go on long enough, and are suspenseful, driven either by an energetic plot or by a kind of "soap-operatic" interest in the ongoing lives of the characters. Most people in our culture who read, read very fast these days, so fast that it's possible to miss all of the subtleties, which in the case of lyric poetry or highly indirect prose means that everything of importance might be missed. The reasons for writing in any of these forms could be either aesthetic or practical, having to do with the "material" finding its proper form, with the writer wanting a new challenge, or with trying to make a living.

As for poets "growing up" into novelists, I agree that it is particularly in

Canada that there's this new assumption. In the US, who would expect Robert Hass to write a novel to prove his worth? It would seem that poets are not taken seriously (as "adults"), even by some publishers, because their work is not highly saleable. The rare exceptions to this include poetry written by successful novelists or songwriters, or (even more rare) Canadian poetry that is highly regarded in the US (a larger "market," and one with a more developed and respected infrastructure of reviewing, which Canada lacks). Both a livelihood and "sufficient" recognition for one's work are now at least possible in fiction; in poetry, they're still lacking for all but the luckiest.

This leads me to a question for you. I came into a world, first in the US, later in Canada, in which poetry, while not wildly saleable, had a great deal of respect, and in which literature in general was valued. The writer was there, but in the background. Now it seems that the figure-ground relation has been reversed, as though the vital statistics (including sales volume) of the writer are of more interest and value than the writing itself. Not universally of course, but predominantly. My impression is that apart from a few exceptions (Brick Books springs to mind), among publishers the perceived worth of a book has to do almost entirely with projected profit. Publishing is an industry, and writers are now "export products," so this isn't news.

The hard thing is that really fantastic books go completely unrewarded, and simply disappear. It seems to me that a sense of dignity around literature has been eroded, but I can't know whether this feeling has more to do with my age and particular experience than with shared realities. Maybe younger writers are able to bond with the writing culture, and each other, in new ways. So I wonder what kind of a world (in terms of writing) you feel you've come into, in Canada and now in the US?

JB: Sure, sometimes being a poet feels like an anachronism – close in social standing to a shepherd. But I didn't come to writing with expectations of it being any other way. Poetry was valued in my childhood home and I've always known people who wrote and cared passionately about writing. Shepherds, all.

For me, writing (without going nuts) means distinguishing between the publishing or media worlds and the writing culture. Big publishers do think in sales, and even smaller ones have to account to the agencies that grant them budgets to publish and promote their books. I worked as a book publicist for over a decade and know the drill all too well. Maybe I'm a realist when it comes to the limitations of underfunded public broadcasters and daily newspapers that have had their arts pages cut to nearly nothing. Maybe I began publishing at a time when poets had diminished expectations of the kind of critical attention their books might receive. Is the public's new interest in the author a reflection of the media's "packaging" and all the tired language that attends it? Undoubtedly. But what if it gets poetry into the reader's hands, and one or two or however many more readers has the experience of "what is found there"?

The "writing culture," it seems to me, is made of the people who care deeply about poetry and its possibilities. There is a blessed, small audience of true readers, and of course, poets. In Montreal, I had the good luck to join a group who've met twice a month for years to roll up their sleeves and look deeply and rigorously at each other's drafts, share exciting work they'd discovered in their reading, etc. I've met people of similar ilk in California, and elsewhere in the States, though I'm much less involved in anything that could remotely be called a "scene" here. Also, organizations like the League of Canadian Poets and the Writers' Union have made it easier for Canadian writers to connect with their audiences across the country. Whether that still happens, what with diminished funding for writers to tour or to attend AGM's and such – is another matter. I felt very lucky to live and publish in Canada, with that kind of infrastructure in place. The potential readership for poetry may be larger here, but the sea of indifference feels correspondingly vast, and there's no CBC to give even an illusion that the whole country has just stopped breathing along with you to hear the end of that poem from a young writer in Regina, or Dennis Lee or Roo Borson. I miss that more than I can say.

RB: I think poets of my half-generation didn't have expectations of their books doing well in the marketplace either; certainly nobody ever expected much money or fame. (When I took poetry workshops I didn't expect I'd ever be able to have even one poem in a magazine.) But what I'm responding to is what seems like a diminishment over time of what "worth" constitutes in the writing and publishing world as well as in the academic world. I hope I am wrong about this. But I guess part of my experience may also reflect changed circumstances, or maybe it's just the people I meet! For instance, young people wanting to go to certain M.F.A. writing programs *because* of the possibility of making contacts that will then lead to publishing, etc. . . . I can't think of anyone I knew in my "early days" in Vancouver and Toronto (and even before that, in Vermont) who would have even considered this. The focus was almost *all* on the art itself – though one exception springs to mind, and of course there were the usual jealousies, feelings of competition etc. – it's just that usually these didn't lead to the kind of strategic planning I've encountered fairly often in both younger and older writers in more recent times. And the non-monetary sense of value in art does indeed still exist: it just seems harder to find these days. But I may be quite wrong about this! Maybe the "savvy" can coexist with the other thing.

JB: In his poem "The Dead Poet," Al Purdy, speculating on the origins of his poetry, asks "how else explain myself to myself/ where does the song come from?" If you don't recall the poem, Purdy suggests that his voice came from his brother who died in the womb just before him. Do you have any explanation of where your own voice came from, of why you became a poet?

RB: Purdy's is a nice symbolic story. Neruda had one too, something about gifts passed beneath a fence by people who can't see each other. I don't have a singular story like that, but if I were to choose an episode from my life, it might involve a set of famous lines I heard over and over as a child:

> Sweet are the uses of adversity,
> Which, like the toad, ugly and venomous,
> Wears yet a precious jewel in his head . . . .

What's important about that jewel is that it exists simultaneously in the world and in language. That mysterious jewel, for me as a child, was in poetry as well as just outside the door. I've read somewhere that Shakespeare was probably talking about a particular kind of toad that has a red fleshy lump on its forehead, but for me as a child, the jewel in my mind's eye looked something like a ruby, and at the same time that jewel in the head was poetry. There's something important in those lines about the mystery of the relation between beauty and ugliness. Throughout the Second World War my father carried a book with him, a small leather-bound volume of Shakespeare's collected works on very thin tough paper. He was born with a photographic memory, so of course could quote all kinds of things at will. In fact he talked much more about science than anything else. But a feeling of delight, in poetry and in the world, was communicated directly to me in his voice. I didn't know it at the time, but I was lucky in that way, to have had such a teacher very early, before I went to school. Especially since, for me, almost until university, school was nearly all unmitigated dread. It's rare for someone to possess, and be able to communicate, such delight and curiosity, which is at the base of all learning.

There Is No Place That Does Not See You

JAN ZWICKY

Interviewed by Anne Simpson

Jan Zwicky is the author of six books, including *Songs for Relinquishing the Earth* (Brick, 1998) and *Twenty-One Small Songs* (Barbarian Press, 2000). *Wisdom and Metaphor* is forthcoming from Gaspereau Press in 2003.

Anne Simpson is a writer and artist living in northeastern Nova Scotia. Her poetry collection *Light Falls Through You* was published by McClelland & Stewart in 2000. Her novel *Canterbury Beach* was published by Penguin in 2001.

AS: In his poem "The Dead Poet," Al Purdy, speculating on the origins of his poetry, asks "how else explain myself to myself/ where does the song come from?" When did you know you had to write poetry, Jan?

JZ: I've never known this. It's one among a bunch of things I happen to do. My experience, talking to other folks, is that everybody writes poetry as an adolescent. So maybe the question is, why didn't I quit? I guess because my sense that it was a way to get at truth outweighed my sense of frustration with its difficulties. When did I know I had to get at truth (by whatever means available)? Pretty early on, I'd say – from the time I was a child.

AS: Why do you think you chose poetry (rather than, say, prose)? I ask this because I find that the ideas inherent in my poetry often work their way into my fiction: poetry remains a touchstone for all other writing I do.

JZ: This question, I think, is assuming that poetry and prose are closely related species of the same genus, viz. writing. I'm not sure they are. I think poetry may be a species of non-linguistic thought, whose peculiarity is that it gets expressed in language. Anyway, I'm really bad at extended fiction and fiction-like writing and it feels like it has something to do with the way I think. I don't, for the most part, think in language – at least not when I'm trying to figure out how stuff hangs together. So expressing myself linguistically always involves an act of translation. I find that the thinking doesn't get as mangled when I translate into genres that are generally regarded as "poetic" – I'd include aphoristic prose here, too, though.

AS: Which poets have had the greatest influence on your work?

JZ: Early on, it was a schizy combination of John Donne and Alden Nowlan. We didn't have many volumes of contemporary poetry in the house, but my mother was fond of Nowlan, so we had most of his stuff. His poems moved me deeply, and the first attempts I made at free verse tried to imitate his emotional directness. But I wrote an awful lot (as in lot of awful) sonnets, too. Later, when I discovered him, I was very drawn to Larkin – the grief, the concision, the extraordinary combination of emotional truth and technical virtuosity. His work is still a kind of touchstone for me, and there's no question it was a formative influence.

          In the last fifteen years, I've also been influenced by my friends – or rather, have tried, not always consciously and usually without succeeding, to echo what has most excited me in their work.

AS: How might a poem begin for you: could it start with something tangible like a phrase of music or light falling into a poppy in the backyard, or does a poem begin with an idea and develop from it?

JZ: A couple of ways. Sometimes a rhythmic phrase, without words but with an emotional/tonal "pitch" or colour, will announce itself in relation to something. Occasionally it will come with actual words, too, but usually not and then I have to find the rest of the poem. (Usually, it's a phrase or line close to the end, the turn into the poem's final cadence.) Other times, I'll just become obsessed with something – yes, a poppy, for example, or a piece of music – and wander around hoping eventually that it'll speak to me in English. More often than not it does and I have learned I can abet the process by throwing words at the obsession and seeing what sticks. But on a few occasions, I've carried the thing around for years and never found its verbal shape.

AS: Do you work quickly or slowly?

JZ: It varies. The poems that start by announcing themselves with a rhythmic pattern or a line or two can sometimes come very quickly. The ones that start with an obsession can take years, and fill whole filing cabinets with drafts.

AS: And to what extent do you edit your work?

JZ: Extensively. And often I edit in response to comments from friends.

AS: The way we approach poetry from one stage in our lives to another can shift dramatically. How would you say your feelings about poetry, the reading and writing of it, have changed since you were in your twenties?

JZ: In my twenties, I was confident I knew what poetry was (and wasn't). I'd had very little formal schooling in English, having refused to take it after grade eleven. (Those were the days when you could still get out of high school by passing a set of provincial examinations, no coursework strings attached.) So, apart from liking Nowlan's directness, I had no conception of the forces that had shaped free verse in the twentieth century. In my third year of university, I took a workshop in writing poetry from Christopher Wiseman, which opened my eyes to the importance of editing. I had always had, and still do have, a great fondness for Donne, Marvell, Sidney – the English metaphysicals, I guess – but I didn't begin to read extensively in contemporary poetry, in English and English translation, until after my first book was published and I actually began meeting other poets. I think I'm still feeling out the effects of that encounter. In particular, I've come to feel quite sharply the tension between the postwar rejection of the high rhetorical line and a gut instinct that the genesis of poetry is musical not verbal.

      For some poets, I think, the poem starts with an image; but I usually don't feel I've got the image until I hear the music. Anyway, I'm a music junky – and sometimes what I find most musically satisfying turns out to be in emotional bad taste: "dim lands of peace," etc. I'm instinctively drawn to the idea that poetry is memorable speech. But in – rightly, I think – depriving ourselves of certain rhetorical stances, what we are now able to make is more like memorable image or memorable thought. (That last not in some abstract sense, but in a sense fully compatible with William Carlos Williams's dictum.) So, the upshot is that I'm much less confident I could actually say what poetry is. But also, partly as a result of a lot of experience editing other people's work, I find I don't really care anymore. What's important, and moving, is the imprint of the unsayable on what is said – and there's enormous range in the ways the unsayable manifests itself.

AS: Yes, and there's an intense pressure of the unsayable on the sayable. Very little may be said, as in Paul Celan's work, but the pressure upon those words is immense. Sometimes you experiment with more than one voice in a poem, such as the haunting "Mourning Song" in *The New Room*, which calls out to be read aloud. Is this braiding of voices a way of approximating polyphony? And if so, what interest do you have in poetry that allows for more than one voice?

JZ: Robert Bringhurst and I have had an extensive correspondence since the mid-eighties. For some time, he has been very interested in verbal polyphony and the construction of multi-voiced poems. I have not been convinced that it could be done the way he wants to do it. "Mourning Song" was my attempt to experiment with double voicing in a way that demanded less literally simultaneous semantic overlay. So it's a compromise with homophony, in a way that Bringhurst's "New World Suite, No. 3," say, isn't. It's a compromise that I think you have to make, because the semantic density of language adds a dimension that can overwhelm the whole and thwart its attempts to be comprehensible. I've discussed polyphony in more detail in an open letter to Robert in *Canadian Literature* No. 156 (Spring 1998).

AS: The seven elegies in the last section of *The New Room*, which include "Mourning Song," are deeply poignant, perhaps because of the acuity of vision. I know it's a bit like trying to put an ocean into a plastic bucket, but could you comment on the role of elegy in poetry?

JZ: Hmm. You could write a book on this one. Roughly, briefly: lyric aims to reside in the dimensionless present, which, as beings of time and language, we can't make our home. We'd like to, though – or at least the lyric artists and thinkers among us would – since it's the moment in which we're fully unseparated from the world. And so, lyric art is essentially celebratory/elegiac. There are some (but surprisingly few, when you start looking closely) lyric poems that are purely celebratory – that manage to relive that fused moment of joy without contextualizing it in any way – but as soon as you get context, you've got loss. Hence, the preponderance of the elegiac tone. This is one of the themes of *Lyric Philosophy*.

AS: Could you say more about *Lyric Philosophy*? Did it guide you to a deeper understanding of your own poetics?

JZ: *Lyric Philosophy* was indeed – at least in part – an attempt to write the poetics for *Wittgenstein Elegies*. But it's also part of an extended conversation with Don McKay who once said, jokingly, "What decent poet cares about rationality?" I realized that he was pointing to something important, and that nevertheless I did care. That was the beginning of the book. (Amazing trouble you can get yourself into when you don't get a joke.)

AS: Jan, let me move to something I've been wondering about for some time. We tend to think about metaphor as something embedded in the poem, or as something ornamental, but lately I've been thinking about it differently. Metaphor is not just something added on. Would you say that metaphor is a way of knowing?

JZ: Yes. It's *the* way of knowing. A real metaphor (as opposed to some clever bit of verbal play) discerns a homology or an isomorphism between things – it's a form of seeing-as. But although metaphor discerns a resonant connection between things, it also insists on their separateness: not one, not two, as the Buddhists would have it. And that live metaphorical relation – in which individual things are themselves and, simultaneously, reflections of the resonant structure of the world – that lived paradox, just is the meaning of what-is.

AS: Could you go back to that idea of metaphor being "not one, not two"? If metaphor depends on the separateness and wholeness of two distinct things, can it ever suggest something else besides: perhaps a third thing?

JZ: I'm not sure I've grasped the question. Are you asking after the nature of the relation between separateness and wholeness as these are embraced by metaphor? That relation, I think, is importantly non-hypostatizable: there's no "thing" or "stuff" or "idea" that it corresponds to. That was what I was trying to get at by calling the relation "live": you move back and forth between two complete but incompatible gestalts, like in those reversible figure drawings (face/chalice, cube-projecting-up/-projecting-down). There is no third thing those drawings "really" are: they are two incompatible things simultaneously, and to comprehend them is to experience the movement back and forth. The same thing is going on when we understand a metaphor.

AS: It's that oscillation between two things that's important, then. And you mentioned paradox before. Would you say that it's part of the fabric of things?

JZ: Sort of. But because even the faintest whiff of idealism (current variant: poststructuralism) makes me skittish, let me clarify: It seems to me that what-is presents itself to critters with our capacities for linguistic thought in a way that requires those critters to use paradoxical expressions if they want to talk about what-is using language. All good metaphors are paradoxes, yes. But paradox is the result of linguistically inflected thinking trying to comprehend the world.

AS: Yes, it's true that language can't help but involve paradox. And as a result, poetry is something of a hall of mirrors. But it's a hall of mirrors in which we can see ourselves – or the world around us – more clearly. In writing many of my poems I suppose I wanted to speak for those who might be voiceless, whether I was entirely aware of doing that or not. In an essay – "Bringhurst's PreSocratics: Lyric and Ecology" – that you wrote in *Poetry and Knowing: Speculative Essays and Interviews* (1995), you quote from Rilke: ". . . there is no place/ that does not see you. You must/ change your life" (trans. Snow). Is this true for you: would you say the poet has a responsibility to the world?

JZ: The lyric artist's gift is the capacity for ontological attention. I wish this translated into political conscience, but I don't think it does: politics is the art of compromising our capacity for ontological attention by exercising our capacity for systematic (criterial, justification-supplying) thought. Not everybody who has the capacity for ontological attention has the capacity for systematic thought; not everybody who has both has the discipline to live the compromise.

AS: In your case, though, a concern for the environment – or what has been called the current crisis of ecocide – is evident in *Songs for Relinquishing the Earth*. Is poetry, for you, a way of meditatively attending to the world and also a way of remembering or bearing witness?

JZ: Yes. That's another way of saying that lyric art is the material trace of ontological attention.

AS: In *Songs for Relinquishing the Earth*, the poems are grounded by sorrow and also by a teasing wit. What's the importance of humour in your work?

JZ: It's that metaphor thing again: when you get the connection right, when you get the constellation of a thing laid over the constellation of another thing just so, you get a release of energy. Sometimes that release is comic. (Gassing aside: it's a sorry truth about me that I'm a sucker for a good joke. No, I take that back: I'm a sucker for any kind of joke . . .)

AS: And the praise songs you've been working on – are they representative of a shift in your thinking?

JZ: I don't think so, not really. They are praise songs, yes, but almost none of 'em manage to do it without some gesture to context. (One friend recently advised me not to publish them in a pack because their elegiac tone was too pervasive.) But I guess because of the praise song aspect they do mark a different approach: same house, different door?

AS: So what you're saying is that praise and elegy may not be so very far removed?

JZ: Right. They're sides of the same coin. Praise says: "This is here, now!" Elegy says: "This is here – now." Some of my favourite lyric poems actually flip back and forth throughout between these two tones of perception.

AS: How important have reviews, awards, other honours been to your feelings about your work? Is competition healthy or unhealthy for a poet?

JZ: I'd like to say that awards haven't mattered at all, but I don't think that's true. I really don't think awards are a good indicator that a person's work is of exceptional quality – as we all know, some poets are superb but insufficiently recognized while others are lauded beyond their talents. But if you are consistently shut out of award nominations, and consistently get bad, or few, or no reviews, you have to have enormous strength of character not to wonder if the neglect isn't deserved. And if you wonder long enough whether it's deserved, it can mess your head up. (On the other hand, a certain amount of neglect, especially early on, is good for discerning vocation and commitment, and can give a person time really to find their voice.) Anyway, awards betoken a measure of acceptance by the community. It's like being in high school: you don't necessarily want to be the most popular girl in the school (I mean, look at their stupid haircuts) but you want very much not to be regarded as a hopeless geek. Being nominated for, or winning, awards has not made me confident I'm a good poet – I know I'm not as good as I want to be – but it has relieved me of the concern that I might be a really atrocious one.

In general, though, I don't think competition is good for poets; and if the concern about geekdom can be relieved some other way, then that's much to be preferred. Competition is not good precisely because, often enough, the best don't win, and confusingly, sometimes they do. But I don't know what the answer is, because at the most basic level I suspect each of us (unless we're a megalomaniac) needs some measure of acceptance. I've seen promising voices derailed by the easy laugh, and by the rigours of political correctness – the poet stops listening to the world and starts trying to impress an audience. It's very difficult not to do this because acceptance is such a powerful instrument of socialization. (Notice that we use it to train dogs as well as children.) A few alpha males, with their eye on the patriarchal prize, can turn ostracism into an affirmation of their own powerful individuality, but most of us can't. No matter what we do, because we're a social species, poets will hope for acceptance from readers and from their peers. Even if we eliminated every prize and drew straws for Canada Council grants, the problem – writing to an audience, rather than listening for the work – would remain. Maybe the answer is better toilet training, but I'm not going to hold my breath.

AS: And finally, Jan, would you say there is a place where poetry, philosophy and ecology converge?

JZ: Lyric and philosophy converge where thought is governed by a twinned eros, when it seeks clarity and coherence simultaneously. All ecologies are coherent to some degree or another, and the world as a whole is an ecology. In the desire to understand clearly the nature of what-is, lyric, philosophy and ecology converge.

"Sprawl, Twiddle and Ache"

DENNIS LEE

Interviewed by Brian Bartlett

Dennis Lee was born in Toronto, where he is currently the city's first poet laureate. His most recent books are *Nightwatch: New and Selected Poems* (McClelland & Stewart, 1996), a book of essays entitled *Body Music* (Anansi, 1998) and *The Cat and the Wizard* (Key Porter, 2001), a children's book.

Brian Bartlett is a Halifax poet whose most recent books are *The Afterlife of Trees* (McGill-Queen's, 2002) and *Granite Erratics* (Ekstasis, 1997). He is currently editing a book on Don McKay, and completing both a novel and a collection of assorted prose pieces about poetry.

BB: We could kick off with Canadian nationalism, your key terms "cadence" and "polyphony," your sources of inspiration such as Hölderlin, George Grant, Mother Goose, Al Purdy. But maybe there's a more basic place to start: the poem on the page. Denise Levertov says on the back of your book of essays, *Body Music*, that your poems matter to her "because, more consistently than those of anyone else whose work I know, they manifest a full awareness of the poem as a form of musical score." What do you think Levertov meant by that?

DL: It touched me that another poet got what was going on in my stuff – that she was on its wavelength. And I'd enjoy zeroing in on the nitty-gritty technical things that are involved in the poem as a form of musical score. That's where some of the most intimate aspects of a poem happen. Okay, I think Denise was talking about *rhythm*. And about the craft of *scoring* rhythm on the page – which is a foreign medium for it, after all. We experience rhythm directly with our bodies, but now you're trying to convey it by means of words on a flat piece of paper. You're reaching for a layout or scoring that will activate your kinaesthetic sense, and configure your mind and your heart. And for that, you have to rely on the resources of the eye and the ear simultaneously. (There's a phrase in the essay "Body Music," about how in free verse you have to "hear the poem out loud on the page.") I think Denise recognized this preoccupation with how a poem enacts, in its rhythmic moves, a whole way of our being in the world. In fact if you're lucky, it enacts a way the world goes about being itself. Or at least it tries to.

BB: But how does poetry "enact," rather than just reflect, those ways of "being in the world"? Or ways the world has of "going about being itself"?

DL: For me, it means you don't just give a description of objects and events, tricked out with some edifying thoughts and feelings. It's a whole different gig. I sense the world as a polyrhythmic process – a dance of simultaneous energies. And the poem has to mime that process – not by describing it, but by reenacting its simultaneous sprawl and twiddle and ache. Right in the way it moves, its rhythmic trek. That's what a poem is really "about" – the under-music it enacts. So when Denise spoke of the poem as a musical score, I think she was pointing to this dimension of scribbling. How the way you orchestrate words on the page manifests your deepest cosmological hunches – your sense of the vocabulary of coherence that obtains in the world.

Of course, it's much more groping and instinctive than that implies. You don't start off with a general formula for "how the world coheres." You just fiddle around with a run of lines till they feel right. And the craft of how you do that, the specific technical moves, is what embodies your body sense of grace and cacophony in the world. Which is almost a form of worship, to score the poem with that full attending.

BB: Could we talk a little about "specific technical moves"? For centuries most English language poets were faithful to the left-hand margin as the starting point of each line – with some exceptions like Herbert's "Easter-wings" and "The Altar," or the regularized indents (like every second line) used by many poets as far back as Spenser. But in the second decade of the twentieth century, something opened up. Lines could begin anywhere on the page – or they might be broken vertically, staggered, dragged down, tugged rightward. But there are still lots of poets – including some of our most prodigiously inventive – who maintain that reliance on the left-hand margin and aren't especially interested in placing unpredictable gaps on the page. I'd say your poetry often *is*, visually, a poetry of unpredictable gaps. What's the link between how a poem is visually designed and how we read it, silently or aloud? How much do a poem's visual features, including line breaks, guide us in figuring out where to pause, where to slow down or hurry up? Or how much is a poem's visual character something for the eye, not so much the ear?

DL: It's for both. Meaning that you have to absorb it with both senses at once – the visual and the auditory. Or as I'd rather say, the visual and the audio/kinaesthetic. Nobody is *obliged* to get into this kind of open scoring, of course. Using the "gaps" you spoke of. We're talking about poetry in free verse, and the basic way of pacing free verse is with the line breaks – playing them off against the syntax, the phrasing of sentences. So the speed and emphases of the poem are created by that syncopation – of line break against syntax. And as you say, lots of free-verse poets write wonderfully without going any further than that; they rely on the left-hand margin throughout. Which is perfectly cool.

Even then, though, you can see what I'm talking about. Suppose you're going to say "I came to Halifax" – a memorable line, right? And suppose you're going to stick to the left-hand margin. You could set up the four words as one line, or as four lines, or as various versions in between – there are five more possibilities, if I'm not mistaken. And if you write them all out, which is actually a worthwhile exercise, you find that each one choreographs the movement and emphasis in a slightly different way (most of them of no great interest). But (hang on; I believe I'm getting to the point, some point, any point) when you read them out loud, no matter where the breaks fall you can't reproduce that tiny hesitation, and then extra stress, that the line break creates on the page. Not unless you give an exaggerated pause – which falsifies the subtle effect. To experience the resonance of the line break on its own terms, you have to simultaneously see the words on the page (including the line break) and hear the flow with your inner ear – you have to absorb the kinaesthetic movement with your whole body English. You have to "hear it out loud on the page."

Most poets have a signature way of controlling the pace through the line breaks. My own first impulse with the Halifax line, for instance, would be to break it once, after "to." Another poet would gravitate to something else – treating it as a single line, say; or breaking it after "came." In this regard, I think a specific poet's "signature" depends on how often he ends a line where the sense pauses (which gives a slower, measured pace), and how often he breaks after a word like "to" or "the" – which pulls you ahead, so it speeds up the pace. I was knocked out when I saw how fluently Al Purdy moved between those two kinds of break in a poem. That's when I first realized there was a serious craft involved, and it was something you could learn in a concrete, hands-on way. Anyway, after I'd written *Civil Elegies*, which does hug the left margin, I got intrigued with a more open, limber way of moving. So I started playing with indents as well – with staggered margins. That creates a further way of syncopating against the natural phrasing of the sentences, because the eye has to travel back a varying distance each time to the start of the next line.

Staggering the margins is strictly a matter of trial and error, for me at least. I found it intimidating at first. But you start to discover a concrete, technical craft for orchestrating the movement. I mean the actual strategy of where the lines fall on the page. For instance, I set up a series of tab indents, each four characters beyond the previous one, then I let the lines dance around among them, back and forth all the way down the page. Improvising draft by draft till the moves felt right. Sometimes I'd use only two or three of those margins in a poem, sometimes up to eight. It was a way to latch onto some structure in the apparent flux. Mind you, this is all in aid of coaxing your rhythmic intuitions into words. It's not just a batch of portable techniques to use at random; it's how you do justice to what's claiming you, what you're trying to mime. The pre-verbal tumble I call "cadence."

BB: Recently it struck me as odd that we say "line *breaks*," as if something was broken, or torn, or incomplete. Does the potentially negative ring in "break" weaken the term? ("Enjambment" may be the more highfalutin' word, but I like it because it's got the French for "leg" tucked into it – as if hinting how one line *steps down* the page to another line.) Likewise, maybe I shouldn't have called you a poet of "unpredictable gaps," because "gap" too suggests something missing. "Space" is probably the more accurate word.

DL: "Line break" doesn't bother me. I did flinch a bit when you spoke of "gaps," because if you do this stuff right, the white spaces play their own positive part in the overall rhythm. It's not a matter of leaving anything out; if you *didn't* include the spaces, you'd be leaving something out.

BB: I was asking about the visual vs. the oral because with some poems by William Carlos Williams and Marianne Moore it seems impossible to take all line endings as signals for pausing aloud. If you read Moore's "The Fish" and emphasize the line endings at all, the pauses seem tortuous and conversationally very unnatural. In a poem like that, the shape and look of the poem on the page – and the delightfully eccentric syllabic-count patterns she set up – seem to be what determines where lines end. My impression is that in your poems the staggered lines, while visually intriguing, *are* guides for reading the poems both silently and aloud.

DL: Now you're cooking! And you're right about my stuff. The layout, the scoring, is all about trying to let the poem dance in kinaesthetic space. Whereas in Moore's poetry, a line break simply means that the line has reached the full syllable count she assigned it – in the second line, say, or the seventh, of each stanza. That's partly why my body feels so un-revved when I read most of her work. Sometimes she did get a kind of grave, meticulous rhythm going, but the line breaks play very little part in it. Which is simply to say that she was writing syllabic verse, not free verse.

I'm not sure what you mean about Williams, though. To me, he's a shining example of what I'm talking about. There's an extraordinary rhythmic aplomb in the way he moves through a poem – think of that little one about the cat stutter-stepping through the pantry. The poem exists to let us *feel* that preternatural fluidity of movement. "Look! This is one possibility – one way creatures can go about being themselves. With an exploratory yet sure-footed grace." And he brings that possibility to life right on the page, in the medium of words on paper. Which he could never have done without choreographing the line endings (though in this poem, not the margins), scoring them precisely the way he does:

> As the cat
> climbed over
> the top of
>
> the jamcloset
> first the right
> forefoot
>
> carefully
> then the hind
> stepped down
>
> into the pit of
> the empty
> flowerpot

BB: Perversely, I was thinking of the few (atypical) Williams poems in which the line endings don't always signal significant pauses. Some sections of the sequence "Pictures from Brueghel" seem tricky to read aloud without ignoring some of the line – er – breaks (for example, "two/ helpers one in a red/ coat

a spoon in his hatband"). The "preternatural fluidity" of Williams's lines –
thanks for that, Dennis. The cat poem (just called "Poem") is a hard-to-shake-
off, quietly comic example, and another is that other short one, "The Term,"
about a big sheet of brown paper rolling down the street in a wind. Who before
Williams had the guts to revolve a poem around a sheet of brown paper blow-
ing down a street? (In English, that is – I suppose Japanese haiku masters had
done that sort of thing many moons earlier.) Not to downplay your indebted-
ness to Purdy, but going further back, would you say that Williams and Pound,
more than Eliot or Stevens or Moore, gave you guidance in finding ways to
steer your poems across and down the page (or to let them steer you)?

DL : Definitely. And there were also people who blew the doors wide open, gave a
sense of great freedom, even when I didn't particularly connect with the uses
they were putting the freedom to. Cummings, for instance, or much of Olson.
By the way, let me go back to those lines of Williams you quoted: "two/
helpers one in a red/ coat a spoon in his hatband." I agree that if you're read-
ing them out loud, you have to minimize the line break – I mean, not create
an unnatural pause – or it'll just sound mannered. But that confirms what I
was saying before, doesn't it? The break there, with the tiny hesitation which
the eye picks up, is part of that general sense Williams's stuff conveys, of the
mind and heart constantly probing to get an exact, discriminating point artic-
ulated, as they interact – *here!* and *here!* and *here!* – with the world around
him. (That's not evident if you look just at these lines, but it connects with a
gazillion other instances in Williams.) And what conveys that sense of prob-
ing *is* the line breaks – which is a matter for the eye alone, when you
encounter the poem "out loud on the page." That's the "on-the-page" half of
it, the eye's share. So Williams is capitalizing on the page resources of free
verse, which inevitably get screened out in a purely oral reading . . . .

Maybe this is how it is. When you read free verse out loud, the only way
to indicate a line break is with a pause – a quarter-second's silence. But when
you're reading it "out loud on the page" – with the eye, the inner ear and the
kinaesthetic sense all engaged simultaneously – then the line break doesn't
signal that kind of literal pause in the first place. It alerts us to something
entirely different: a shift of equilibrium in the poet's attention, or a tightening
of focus – something on the mental/emotional front comparable to cocking
your head, squinting to see better, or relaxing slightly before you pounce. You
know? It has virtually nothing to do with a literal pause in the speech flow.
But these are things that come through only when you're responding to the
scoring on the page – silently, but with all your faculties ticking. That's how
the kinaesthetics of free verse unfold. And they configure tiny movements of
the heart and intelligence.

BB: Some poets say a poem reaches its full being only when performed aloud
(often they mention the origins of verse in oral traditions). So I'm cheered to
hear you defend the unique qualities of the poem on the page – as I was to

read these bits from "Body Music": "When you read a free poem out loud, it's often difficult to translate the spatial notation into physical sound . . . It [the pointing] is fully accessible only in the original, spatio-temporal medium, where the notation can be seen." Of course, you then note: "there are new resources when you read the poem aloud, such as volume and pitch." Something's lost, but something's gained? Maybe we should resist arguments for the superiority of poetry projected physically from a mouth *and* arguments for the superiority of poetry savoured in silence. Instead, the best thing to do is celebrate that a poem can have two homes, as it were – two lives.

DL: I like that. Though with the proviso that "savouring a poem in silence" means, to me at least, that you do *hear* its aural dimension with your inner ear; and you do *feel* its kinaesthetic rhythms with your body sense – what I call your kintuition.

BB: Right. And sometimes it's more than the "inner ear," isn't it? Didn't McLuhan write about how centuries ago reading was always done, even in solitude, with the lips moving? So monks found it very alien when they started reading without moving their lips. Some of us find ourselves literally mumbling or mouthing as we read poetry closely – or at least we feel faint clenches and flexes in our throats. Too bad in a way that kids are told from a young age not to move their lips when they read – somehow that's considered immature or even shameful.

DL: That's right. And in fact I feel my whole musculature being stimulated when I read poetry, not just my lips. That's how I *hear* it. And if there's no such bodily reaction, I get bored; the poem may be very intelligent, very articulate, but it's got no music.
      So I'd make a distinction between two kinds of poetry. With one kind, the native medium is the page; when you read it out loud, you're translating it into a second medium – which is closely related, but not identical. Like French and Italian, say. All free verse is of this kind (and certainly all my stuff). The other kind of poetry starts off in the oral dimension as its home medium – and when it's set down on the page, *that* is a translation into a related yet foreign medium. All traditional oral poetry is of the second kind, of course; it usually loses a huge amount of its original power in the translation to print, the same way most song lyrics do. A lot of Ginsberg's later work is of this second kind. Sound poetry is another extreme example – have you seen transcriptions of the Four Horsemen? Bringhurst thinks of his own poetry in these terms too. Putting it down on the page is a necessary evil, but it's always a reduction of the richer original. Robert and I sort of meet in the middle when it comes to scoring on the page; often we overlap, but we're coming from opposite directions.

BB: We've not yet touched on the influence of jazz, blues and other kinds of music on your poetry. You said in a 1993 comment in your book of essays that jazz – bebop especially – had "had as much effect on my recent poetry as anything I read." Does that still hold, or was the bebop influence at its height with *Riffs*?

DL: *Riffs* is far and away the boppiest thing I've written. But you're right to point in this direction. A lot of the rhythmic juice I feel out there isn't in poetry at all. It's in various kinds of music – jazz, obviously, but also in blues, rock, Bach, country and so forth. Plus many of the abstract expressionists. Your body feels what's possible in these other media and you just itch to do the same thing in words.

BB: The itch is there – but you can't really do "the same thing in words," can you?

DL: You can sometimes fail into poetry.

BB: You wrote an M.A. thesis on Pound, which I hardly need to tell *you*. Some day a good reader should do an in-depth exploration of relationships between some Canadian poets and the poets they wrestled with most in graduate school (if they went that far) – Lee and Pound, Birney and Chaucer, Atwood and, what was it, some Victorians? McKay and Dylan Thomas. Did your thesis on Pound emphasize poetics, and what did it do for your own poetry – even in a very delayed way?

DL: This tells you quite a bit about where I came from. At the time, around 1964-65, I was a thriving young critic and a crappy young poet. So what I wrestled with in the thesis was stuff I could analyze with those resources and those limitations. I was interested in Pound's formal intuitions, in the new structural methods he'd worked out to link disparate chunks of material. I connected it with the crisis that Poe was the first to articulate – that the traditional frameworks for linking epiphanies or intense moments into a coherent whole, a cosmology, had eroded. I wanted to track a similarity between Pound's innovations and the formal intuitions of field physics, relativity in particular. (That was too ambitious, though, so I ended up doing only the Pound half.)

I argued that he was writing in what I called "ekstatic form" – the stuff that used to be called vorticism, the new way of organizing discrete fragments into a coherent whole; or what Pound at least believed was coherent. But the truth is, I now think that is the least useful part of Pound: it's where his titanism came out right in his craft. I won't go into detail here; it's along the lines that the moment of aesthetic insight, when the poem produces in the reader a perception of analogy between discrete chunks – as in "In a Station of the Metro" – is in itself self-certifying. It produces a formal "ek-stasis," a standing-beyond the sequential logic that's indigenous to literature. So once you have that formal epiphany produced by reading the poem, you can do without the validating framework once supplied by traditional world views, and also without the connectives people once accepted as intrinsic to long poems. But trying to make that strategy the basis for finding coherence in everything that exists becomes an exercise in megalomania. The poet's consciousness, as embodied say in *The Cantos*, is supposed to be our sole true guide and guarantor of a universe that makes sense. Which is solipsistic bullshit, or so I believe.

Anyway, that's what my thesis was about. Whereas the groundbreaking stuff Pound did that was permanently important seems to me now to have been at the micro level, in the new prosody he devised: I mean free verse. But at the time, I was too gridlocked in my own rhythmic sense to come to terms with free prosody. I still heard things metrically, and even though I was in awe of a lot of what Pound could do rhythmically, I was three or four years away from connecting with any of that in my own stuff. In fact, I had to get out of the academy altogether before I could.

BB: Yesterday I was reading the newest issue of *Brick* (Spring 2001). It includes an interview with Sharon Olds, in which she comes up with a memorable image of her stanza-less, single-block poems as being like "whirling dervishes." Esta Spalding asks her, "Why no stanzas?" Olds answers: "Looks like art" – pejoratively meant, it seems. She almost always sets aside one of the major tools for free-verse pacing and spacing – not as a temporary measure, but as something *habitual*. Could you be happy with abandoning stanzas – not as one of many options, but as a rule for nearly all your poems?

DL: In principle I would, if that's what the music I was listening to called for all the time. In practice, that doesn't seem very likely – certainly I'd never adopt it in advance, as a one-size-fits-all general rule. But it's kind of weird that you ask. I'm working on two manuscripts right now, and both of them have taken an abrupt turn away from many of the things I talked about above. Neither of them does much with staggered margins; they tend to hug the left. And in one of them, which has very short pieces (quarrying down into individual words and syllables), there are very few stanza breaks. For whatever reason, it's coming through on another wavelength right now. But I'm working in the dark; it's purely catch-as-catch-can. No general rules.

BB: I have to admit that, despite the other powers of her poems, the near-stanza-lessness of Olds's world ends up making me feel aesthetically deprived. And why say "Looks like art" of stanzas, when you could as easily say it of line breaks, which Olds exploits all the time? Well, we could talk about the poem on the page all day – all month. To move on . . . how important have reviews, awards, other honours been to your feelings about your work? Is competition healthy or unhealthy for a poet? And I might add, did being one of the first three judges for the new, much-ballyhooed Griffin Prizes force you to think more than usual about such matters?

DL: With awards and such, I've tried to learn something that doesn't come naturally to me: to savour the honour for a few days, and then forget about it. (The second comes naturally, but not the first.) As far as competition goes, I think competing with other poets – the agon – is great. I don't mean competition for recognition, but in the quality of what you write. It teaches you where the bar is really set. Competing for advancement or favourable reviews is bush-league. (Which is not to say we don't all have bush-league impulses at times. But we don't have to act on them.)

BB: What things about being a Griffin judge did you find most satisfying?

DL: Discovering some wonderful poets who were new to me. Observing a certain malign ratio emerging across hundreds of books: the worse the poetry, the more extravagant the jacket blurbs. And working with Carolyn Forché and Paul Muldoon, who were thoroughbreds. They took the whole thing with consummate seriousness.

BB: Let's retire to a more private sphere again. The vocabulary you use trying to get a handle on poetry is sometimes poetically charged itself – such as your "simultaneous sprawl and twiddle and ache" above. Add to that phrases from your essay "Cadence, Country, Silence": "surging and thudding and pausing," "judder and carom and chug." From "Body Music": "move with a quicksilver stutter and glide," "parasyntactic whirl and crossfire." In your '93 interview with Donna Bennett and Russell Brown, in talking about *Riffs*, there's "honks and bleats and weird unofficial music," "bizarre crackle and pop."

    There's a tremendous amount compacted into those words – from the jazz-sax allusions of "honks and bleats" to the contrast between "sprawl" and "chug," or between "stutter" and "glide." I'd love to ask you to gloss all of those terms individually – but I won't be that cruel. How conscious are you of building up a fresh vocabulary for discussing how poems – including your own – work and play?

DL: It's true, I get revved up when I talk about all these livewire species of cadence I sense. It's a love affair; that lingo just pops out unprompted. The more technical language I've developed for it – cadence, polyphony, enacting a trajectory of meditation, body music, cosmophony – that's the result of a more conscious mulling on my experience of how poems "work and play," to use your nifty expression.

BB: Another question about influences. In your and Tim Lilburn's work, despite many differences, there are some clear similarities – long, margin-teasing lines, a mix of zingily down-to-earth diction and religion-tinged language, a passion for large forms, a desire to expand on your poetry in prose pieces, a development of what you just called "technical language" mostly (but not only) for your prose. Readers know from bits of printed biography that the two of you were raised in Protestant families, yet early on – and independently – you both started responding strongly to something in early Christian (Catholic) sources, like Meister Eckhart and *The Cloud of Unknowing*. Lilburn entered the Jesuit order for eight years. How would you describe the dialogue between the two of you?

DL: It's intriguing. Tim and I go back about ten years, but as far as I know, we found our way to this degree of overlap completely independently. I was startled when I came across those big-muscle poems of his, which I loved. And I didn't know that any other poet in English Canada was at home in the tradition of negative contemplation – Saint-Denys Garneau was the only one I'd found here. So it was moving to discover someone else with similar obsessions. And of course there are also resonances with what Robert Bringhurst is up to, and Don McKay, and Jan Zwicky. But these are very different and very independent poets and thinkers; it's a matter of mutual respect and stimulus, not direct influence.

BB: In your essay "Poetry and Unknowing," you wrote: "I sometimes think I'm an idolater of voice," and you go on to say: "voice embodies being." How hard is it to say what "voice" means in poetry?

DL: Extremely . . . Okay, I'll try. I mean by "voice" everything I said up above about rhythm. And on top of that, I mean the feints and twiddles and full-tilt crescendos you get when the *level* of diction keeps dancing around. The vocal register, you could call it. If you span street slang and ontology within a couple of words, for instance, that embodies a certain athletic reach in the consciousness of the poem, an on-your-toes readiness to encounter the world in sundry dimensions at once. Polyphonically. In many timbres, many vocal modes. So "voice" includes register as well as rhythm.

       Hmmm – I don't think I've ever said that out loud before. Now I'll have to figure out if I agree.

BB: In his poem "The Dead Poet," Al Purdy, speculating on the origins of his poetry, asks "how else explain myself to myself/ where does the song come from?" Do you have any explanation of where your voice came from, of why you became a poet?

DL: Nope. Sorry.

BB: Okay. Let's approach "voice" from another angle. In the last few months, your wife, Susan Perly, has published a novel, *Love Street*, spun out in the bebop-ping, bluesy voice of a New Orleans radio DJ. Reviews are already saying that the novel's glories are very much in its "voice." Any comment on what you and Perly might share in dealing with voice in poetry and fiction – and its rela-tion to music, especially jazz and blues?

DL: I guess the first thing is simply that we *do* share that obsession. It's not some-thing you try to sell anybody else on, talk them into caring about; either it mesmerizes you or it doesn't. And of course there's gorgeous poetry and fic-tion that excels in other ways. But once it does get its hooks into you – that's it, you're a goner. Susan is far more adventurous than me – I can't believe some of the vocal high-boards she pitches herself off. It's not that she doesn't know if the pool is deep enough; she doesn't know if there's water down there at all. But off she goes, and man, what an arc! I remember when she showed me the manuscript of *Love Street* a couple of years ago – I wanted to wring her neck. I'm not putting my own stuff down when I say this, Brian. Whatever you're claimed by, that's what you've got to live by. My job is not to sound like somebody else, even my own wife. It's hard enough to follow the indis-tinct, magisterial music you *do* get given. You're lucky to get nabbed in the first place.

BB: Your language here is interesting: "mesmerizes you," "whatever you're claimed by," "follow the . . . music," "get given," "get nabbed." Near the end of your poem "Cadence," there's also the phrase "what claimed me," and vari-ations of it pop up in the last sentence of "Body Music" and twice in your preface to the book. Such phrases emphasize a passivity, some sort of yielding to other forces. But your reputation for active rethinking, rewording, reshap-ing – all those drafts over many years to complete *Riffs* – is almost legendary. (I've even been warned about this interview: "He'll never stop revising!")

DL: Moi? Revise? Never!

BB: Right, Dennis . . . and birds don't fly. But how do you hold together the need for "following the music" and the need for consciously making the music?

DL: With difficulty. But one thing is, my first drafts are often way too laborious, full of mental *ahem*s and over-explanatory side alleys. That's one reason I hate them so much. It's only by revising that I start to find a clean line through, which usually feels a whole lot more spontaneous . . . Of course out the other end, you often reach a point where you've got the thing right, it feels as if it just fell out of your pen onto the page in one go – but you can't stop yourself, you go on revising through another half-dozen drafts before you realize it's getting all gussied up again. That's when you have to be the tough cop, drag yourself off the poor thing and go back however many drafts, till you find the point where you started to over-elaborate it. And for the time being, at least, that's your fair copy.

BB: Glad to see you speaking of first drafts as "laborious" and later drafts as feeling "more spontaneous." I get tired of hearing about the supposed duality of first drafts as inspired/improvised/unconscious and revisions as tinkering/laborious/conscious. That split is a myth. You seem to imply that the improvised – the "inspired" – can be as much a product of a tenth draft as of a first draft. But then, right, we've got to recognize the stage when revision gets counterproductive – like when a hockey player tries too hard and trips up, loses his rhythm. Do you save earlier drafts so you can return to them, in case things get too encrusted with rethinking? And do you have any tips about how to recognize that moment of encrustation?

DL: I do save my drafts, yeah. About a year ago I cleared the paper out of my study, and there were forty-five cartons. That was a few years' worth, mind you. How do you recognize when you've gone too far? I don't think there's any magic way – I don't know it, at least. The best thing I know is to set the poem aside for a few days or weeks, and monitor what happens when you come back to it: is there a sense of letdown, that it doesn't have the crackle or urgency or newness that you sensed before? But of course that's pretty useless advice, because when you're hot on the trail, setting it aside for a week is the last thing you're gonna do. It happens most readily when circumstances drag me away. I've gone on holiday a few times, and reread what I was doing previously when I got back – and had this real downer epiphany: "Oh shit! Everything I did in the last two months was just meat-grinding. I've gotta set 90 percent of it aside, and try to get back to where I was before." Of course there's still a certain elation in that, because at least you've recognized it in time.

BB: Do you find that the imminence of publication – knowing you've only got so many days left before the thing is fixed in stone for an upcoming printing – sharpens your editorial eye and ear, and makes your glitch-detector perform faster and better than normal?

DL: Yup. It's like that quote from Dr. Johnson, which I don't recall exactly – how knowing you're going to be executed in half an hour concentrates the mind wonderfully. Mind you, I like to think the opposite: that I'd write exactly the same thing with or without a deadline. But it's not true.

BB: I've been looking at an early version of your poem "The Gods," published as a chapbook in 1978, and comparing it to the later version in *Nightwatch*. Some of the changes seem to be for greater accuracy – "inhabit the godforce" becomes "channel the godforce," "Men lived in such a space" becomes "We lived in such a space," "civilizations grow/ flaccid" becomes "technology/ happened." In the third passage there, did you feel any loss in giving up "flaccid," which has such an appropriately deflating sound at the start of its line? A sort of sheep-like bleating in the vowel sound: "flaaaaa-cid." Plus, there's the wit of suspending "civilizations grow" at the line end, only to reveal in the next line that the growth wasn't healthy. "Technology / happened" doesn't have the purely sonic ring of the earlier draft, but it's arguably more precise. I'm trying to imagine your thoughts and feelings in making the change.

DL: I hadn't remembered that I wrote "civilizations grow/ flaccid" in the 1978 version, so this is all conjectural. But my retro-guess is this. "Civilizations grow/ flaccid" tells us something nobody could disagree with; it's pretty sententious. My mind says, "Sure, that's true enough," but that's the extent of it; no other part of me is engaged. I suspect I was looking for something that would ambush you more, drag you into a different *way* of experiencing what the lines are going on about. If I'm not mistaken, you get a slightly weird effect when you start a clause by saying, "Technology . . ." – we expect it to continue along the lines of "Technology is evil," or "Technology has liberated the human race," or whatever – and then, after the line break, career straight into ". . . happened." "Technology" changes its nature abruptly, right before your eyes, or right inside your nervous system; suddenly it's not a large abstraction, it's something like a rainstorm or the outbreak of a war. It *occurs*, dynamically. I think it was that volatile shift of perspective that I was trying to drag the poem, and the reader, through. Where a set of reading assumptions suddenly caves in. Miming, I guess, the onset of the historical change.

BB: In an earlier interview [Bennett and Brown], you discussed the great differences between *Riffs* and your earlier books – especially its movement away from "heavy-duty content" to poetry where there's often "no paraphrasable content," where the "music itself makes the real declaration." Is it right to suspect that in working on *Riffs* your *ear* was more engaged than ever before (though sounds always been vitally important to your poems)? In writing (and endlessly revising) *Riffs*, the wedding and clashing and slip-sliding of words must've often overwhelmed anything the sequence was "saying."

DL: Well that's right. In fact, it was so much that way that the pure babblement didn't really "overwhelm" what the sequence was trying to say. Initially, all there *was* was the babblement. I thought it was gonna be a sequence of pure music. And when it turned out that nobody could read it without nodding off, myself included, I couldn't figure out for the longest time what the sequence could "say," what it could be "about," that wouldn't just be glued on from the outside. It was only when I came up with that incredibly avant-garde breakthrough, a storyline, that the music started to work in a relaxed way.

BB: Your years of writing children's poems must've fed the playfulness – the garbagey delights – of *Riffs*.

DL: I think that's right. For years I wanted to do *Alligator Pie* and *Civil Elegies* in the same poem. And *Riffs* was the first time it happened.

BB: In *Body Music* you mention emotional restraints that can result from being of WASP stock, and much of your poetry reads like a breaking free from such restraints. One of your kids' poems I've memorized and recited to my son, "Mrs. Mitchell's Underwear," is first of all just a funny poem about women's underwear drying out on a clothesline on a windy day. The first two stanzas:

> Mrs. Mitchell's underwear
> Is dancing on the line;
> Mrs. Mitchell's underwear
> Has never looked so fine.
>
> Mrs. Mitchell hates to dance –
> She says it's not refined,
> But Mrs. Mitchell's underwear
> Is prancing on the line.

Last spring when your cancelled flight and late arrival from Fredericton made your Halifax reading start forty-five minutes late, that gave me a great chance to read your kids' poems aloud to the audience. I said that some of your poetry is like Mrs. Mitchell's underwear – dancing and prancing on the line, acting contrary to any prissiness and excessive piety readers might harbour somewhere within themselves. Poetry as dancing underwear.

DL: The lunge of the louche lingerie. Secrets, doing the twist . . . .

BB: Going back to "The Gods": that poem is surely *the* Canadian poem expressing a contemporary version of something that stretches back at least to the Victorians – agnostic meditations on the loss of faith in traditional gods, combined with a need to keep open to something ineffable.

DL: That's heartening. And if you want to revisit some of that stuff a decade or two later, you could go to "Hunger" in the "Nightwatch" sequence. That's one that tries to make its home in the condition of craving without answers – of hunger, or eros, which is keyed to not trying to possess. It's the discipline of the *Cloud*.

BB: Yes, "Hunger" is another poem I love – for its unfashionableness, its long breaths, its listing of names for divinities, its unique phrases ("nerve-end purr," "catgut hosannas," "arterial stammer"), its vernacular ("My mind still yacks and fidgets," "mooch in the nearness"), and its powerful expression of how "hunger hungers." A more passionate poem than some poems of religious certitude. Your poems aren't afraid to use words like "holy," "awe," "luminous," "tremendum." (In a review of *Nightwatch*, one of your big fans, Don Coles, has in fact courteously questioned your use of them.) Have you felt any hesitation in bringing such diction into your poems?

DL: Fair question. When you go right to the core of things, I have no names for what compels my sense of awe – no words that don't reduce it, reify it, turn it into something that my rational mind immediately starts quarrelling with. (Even referring to it as "it" is a falsification.) But that sense of awe is one of the irreducibles in my life, and I'm a poet, so I have no choice but to go on worshipping with words. I hope that some of the weirder coinages and rhythmic moves in my stuff enact that persuasively, convey the experience of being coaxed or riveted by – shit, what do I say? The sacred? The numinous? Joe Blow? But every so often you do need a shorthand way of referring to what you're drawn by. And you can't always turn around immediately and say, "No, no, that's not it; the word I used is just a verbal counter." But it's true; when I use the kind of terms you mentioned, I get a twinge. That's when I wish I was working with music or paint. Words do refer, denote, whether we like it or not. Sometimes that's a bitch.

BB: How have your feelings about poetry, the reading and writing of it, changed since you were in your twenties?

DL: Well, I felt like an absolute beginner then, but I had a lot of head-knowledge about poetry. I still feel like an absolute beginner. But whatever I've learned in the last thirty-five years is concentrated now in my reflexes, my instincts. So that's what I work from. Even though I'm always hoping for it to get blown out of the water – to get stopped dead again, find myself panic-stricken, discover I have to learn new reflexes from scratch, if I'm going to do justice to the new thing that's trying to get written. If that ever stops happening, the panic, I hope I'll have the good sense to stop writing.

BB: Maybe some day we should do another interview – just about children's poetry, or Canadian poetry of the 1960s, or being an editor, or music. Above all, it would be intriguing to hear you talk about more of your own poems.

DL: I think the best way to talk about poetry is when you forget about trying to ease into it, to make "poetry" palatable, and just talk turkey about things that matter.

Seeing Distance: Lorna Crozier's Art of Paradox

LORNA CROZIER

Interviewed by Elizabeth Philips

Lorna Crozier's poetry books have won the country's major literary awards, including the Governor General's Award and two Pat Lowther Awards. Her latest book is *Apocrypha of Light* (McClelland & Stewart, 2002). She teaches writing at the University of Victoria.

Elizabeth Philips has published three collections of poetry, including *A Blue with Blood In It* (Coteau, 2000). She has taught creative writing at the Banff Centre of the Arts (the WiredBanff Program) and in the Sage Hill Writing Experience in Saskatchewan. She is editor of *Grain* magazine.

EP: When did you first have the urge to write?

LC: You're going to like my answer – it started with a dog. In grade one, I wrote a poem as an assignment. I don't remember the exact nature of what we were supposed to do, but the poem I came up with was about my dog Tiny, whom I loved dearly and whom I suffered over almost daily. My parents were farm people who didn't know much about the care of dogs, especially small city dogs. They fed her scraps, including chicken and turkey bones, which splintered, and when they went through her digestive system they'd tear something. And so she was constantly – I thought – dying. I had this special praying spot at the top of stairs where I'd beg God to heal her. Since we had chicken every Sunday night, I was up there on my knees at least once a week, promising to be a better child if only Tiny would live.

        Probably everything I know about poetry I knew in my bones when I was in grade one. Intuitively, I wrote about what I cared deeply about; I used my imagination; I lied; I took a feeling that was true to me and ran with it. The poem was even musical – it was built around the refrain, "And we shall meet in heaven, by and by." You can imagine how bad it was! Anyway, my grade one teacher tacked it on the bulletin board and everybody started to commiserate with me because of my dead dog. And I didn't dare tell them that she was still alive. I felt like I'd done something wrong, I'd deceived them. But I also knew the thrill and the rightness of lying for the sake of a poem. The dog had to die to make the poem work.

        I clearly remember the deliciousness of the praise from my teacher and my classmates. And the wonder of how words could move off the page and live in someone besides me. Maybe that early pat on the head explains why I thought I could be a poet even though I came from a bookless family. I scribbled little rhyming things all through elementary school and moved onto unrequited love poems as a teenager. In university I had Simon and Garfunkel's "I am a rock, I am an island," taped on my wall. I knew I loved words but my reading and writing was indiscriminate and naive.

        That's chapter one. Chapter two was meeting Ken Mitchell, who was then one of the editors of *Grain*. He read some of my poems when I was in my mid-twenties and teaching high school English, and he suggested I go to the Saskatchewan Summer School of the Arts. I'd had one poem accepted by *Grain*. Remember how important that first publication was? *Grain* has been the first outlet for so many poets – it's always open to new writers. The editors are never snobby, and they often see promise in a writer before others do. When I went to the Summer School in 1976, I met people as obsessed with words as I was, and I found my niche. Found the people I love. Danced writing, drank writing, made love to writing. I discovered that this is what I'd been looking for, what I wanted to do for the rest of my life.

EP: In his poem "The Dead Poet," Al Purdy, speculating on the origins of his poetry, asks, "how else to explain myself to myself/ where does the song come from?" Do you have an explanation of where your voice came from or why you became a poet?

LC: Many of us who write poetry are driven to put something into language that we haven't found there before. For me, the drive to write has a lot to with where I grew up, in a lost small city in Saskatchewan, and the kind of poverty I came from. My dad never got on his feet after he lost the farm, partly because of his drinking, but partly because he was a labourer. Before and after freeze-up, he worked in the oil fields, but when winter came he was unemployed.

EP: He was an itinerant labourer . . . .

LC: That's right. He had little schooling and was good with his hands, and manual labour was the only kind of work he could get. When he had to take time off in his early fifties to get treatment for throat cancer, since he didn't belong to a union and there was no workman's compensation, he and Mom were without a steady income for the six months of treatment and recovery. It was a hard, hard time for them. I hadn't seen that kind of situation and that kind of man – I'll use my father as a symbol here – in literature. He was this laconic, wounded, macho westerner, who was representative of a lot of his generation. Because I didn't meet him between the covers of a book, I sensed this need to put him there, to get him into lines of poetry, not only for myself, but because there was this absence. There were gaps in the language, in the literature. Of course he's not all I write about so this is only a partial answer, but he's emblematic of what I'm trying to get at. I think that everyone who's a poet feels there's a silence they must break or fill. One day walking along the street, scuffing leaves, feeling the last of the autumn sun on your face, you know there's something around you that needs to get said, something you want to hang onto with a word, at least momentarily.

EP: It's as if you vibrate, like a tuning fork, to something around you.

LC: That's a good way of putting it. We're walking around with a dowser, a water-witcher's wand, and suddenly it dips down, and we can't see the dark underground stream it's pointing to, but we want to write about it because we know it's there – there's that vibration in the air. We work our way through what we see to what we don't see and that invisibility keeps us intrigued and searching for words to bring it to light. I would guess every poet feels this way. I don't know about prose writers, but I think we can generalize that about poets, don't you?

EP: You've anticipated one of my later questions, which I'll ask you now. In your book *Inventing the Hawk*, I noticed several images involving doors. Doors that let in a magical creature, a door that would not open . . . You had a difficult childhood at times, and you've written about that, about the poverty of your childhood. Do you think the poverty of your childhood continues to affect your work?

LC: It continues to affect my life, that's for sure. I feel pissed off at rich people; I know that's immature but I carry a chip on my shoulder. The anger I feel about how my parents had to live, what they had to live without, still affects me. The shame and fear. I don't think anything goes away. As I get older I realize more and more that you don't lose anything from the past. In fact, things become more solidified – for better or for worse. When I visit my mom in Swift Current, I can still see the rental house we moved into when I was nine. My parents got a new house about five years after I left home at eighteen, and my mom's been living there for thirty-five years now. But that old wrecked house is two blocks away, though it's now unoccupied and probably condemned. When my mom and her relatively new friend go for a walk as they do every morning, and the woman says, "Isn't that a dumpy little house?" as they pass by, my mom doesn't say anything. She confesses to me, "I never tell anyone that we lived there." The concrete signs of my family's poverty still exist in my hometown. They're alive materially and in my imagination. How can I possibly leave them behind? Why would I want to? We shouldn't forget where we come from.

EP: You were telling me about asking your aunt for her diaries, especially of the thirties, which was a time of great poverty. You were probably looking for poetic material, as well as just being curious, so that must be there.

LC: The great archetypal story of hardship and despair in the place where you and I grew up took place in the Dirty Thirties. Though I wasn't born until 1948, I felt that I was actually around in that earlier decade because I was surrounded by those stories.

EP: And by all the people who were formed by that experience.

LC: That's right. Even though my mother and father didn't have very much when my brother and I were kids, they thought they had a lot in comparison to what they possessed when they were married in the thirties. And times didn't get better fast. In the early forties, after they'd left the farm, they lived in an abandoned railroad cook car in the town of Success.

EP: And we've seen that cook car in your poems.

LC: Yes, we have, haven't we? And the Chinese cook – my mother went to the back door of his restaurant every night and he gave her a bowl of chop suey because he knew she was pregnant and she wasn't getting enough food at home – my brother was born in 1941. I mean those stories have certainly shaped me; they've influenced my way of seeing the world. The harshness of those bad times sits alongside such acts of selfless generosity.

EP: In *Inventing the Hawk,* a lot of the poems deal with parallel worlds. With worlds that run alongside the "real world," or worlds within worlds. Such as in "The Brief History of the Horse," "The Brain, "The Consolation of Horses," and your poems about angels.

LC: That's interesting . . . .

EP: Is this a kind of myth making do you think? The invention of a personal mythology?

LC: I guess so, but who'd ever think of it that way during the act of writing. It's hard to answer some of these questions because it involves such a self-consciousness about my own poetry. And you know, more than anyone, that in our poems we tap something we aren't aware of in the ordinary course of our days. Our poems keep surprising us. If they didn't, we wouldn't keep writing them. Personal myth making. That sounds so ambitious, doesn't it?

EP: Admitting that it's a subconscious thing, an impulse to reinvent, or to retell . . .

LC: Definitely to reinvent and retell. As well as wanting to make room for my place and my people in poetry, part of my revisioning comes from a feminist stance. In most of the old stories, there's no room for women. For instance in the Abraham and Isaac story from the Old Testament, there's no mention of Isaac's mother, Sarah. What was she doing when God commanded her husband to kill their son? I want to put her there by that altar. When women are part of the story sometimes terrible things happen to them, but these incidents are treated like asides and are deleted from the usual-version story. Right now I'm rewriting some of Genesis. I thought I knew its chapters well, but I was shocked when I reread it. What most of us remember, for instance, in the story about Lot, is his wife turning into salt when she disobeys and looks back at Sodom and Gomorrah. But when you read that story again, you discover there's so much more to it. Do you remember what happens to Lot's daughters? (The wife and daughters, by the way, are never named. They belong to Lot.) Before the cities are destroyed, the people from Sodom and Gomorrah charge Lot's door, demanding that he give them the two strangers he brought home from the gates of the city. To save his guests, who the crowd doesn't know are angels, Lot says he'll send out his two virgin daughters instead. The crowd can do anything they want with them. This amazing part of the story gets ignored or left out in the usual references to the tale.

EP: We get the *Reader's Digest* condensed version.

LC: Exactly. The version we hear is not necessarily the one in the Bible. It's been bowdlerized. When I went back to the King James Version, I'd say to Patrick [Lane], "Do you remember what's in here?" and read the verses aloud. I want to draw attention to what's been excised, erased from sermons or Sunday school teachings or the rants of TV evangelists. The desire to resist erasure is part of the desire to retell. You and I – well, all poets – are never satisfied with the surface of things. We want to know what's behind the story. No matter who's telling it, we know there's another narrative that deserves to be heard. And then another. These rich, buried versions sit alongside what we think we already know. They challenge our thinking and understanding of what we thought was the "truth."

EP: You are peeling back the layers, like an onion.

LC: That's why you see so many of my poems written in parts. I love poetic sequences, like the ones I wrote on penises, vegetables, Icarus, etc. You can say, well here's one way of doing it, one way of seeing it, and here's another, and another. And if you push and go a little deeper, you surprise yourself and find yet another version, the one buried deepest underground – and all of them are possible at the same time.

EP: And that's why the poetic sequence helps you get around the narrative problems, like transition, when you are trying to do something more literal as a prose writer would. If you try and do it in a prosy way there are all these awkward transitions.

LC: A poetic sequence can use a number to indicate a transition, or a bullet, or a space on the page. Which is more interesting to poets, I think; it creates a kind of mosaic patterning, instead of a narrative unfolding. And prosaic phrasing like "two days later," or "on the other hand," can go.

EP: And yet you tell a lot of story in your work, as I am doing more and more.

LC: Yes, you've done that a lot in the last few years..

EP: But it doesn't seem to be the same narrative impulse that fiction writers have, though it's related somehow . . . .

LC: Again I think the story in poetry is centred more on language. There's still character, but the character is so condensed that we are just seeing the essence – rather than the colour of the hair, the eyes and the name of their breakfast cereal or what they're reading in the newspaper (although sometimes that's there). We see character at the very heart of a moment, all things stripped away. Sometimes there's just the character "I" observing something in the world that resonates with meaning. In some of the finest poems, beyond what "I" is seeing or hearing and the tone of the poem, we know nothing of the person. When there's a story in the poem, we bring people and incidents alive in condensed flashes, don't you think? Through image and music rather than through plot. Though there's often the skeleton of a plot and a turn, a climax.

EP: That condensation is like a funnelling toward an image or two, rather than the fictional opening out into many.

LC: The opening out into many is the kind of thing you and I love reading in fiction. That's what Margaret Drabble does so adeptly in her novels. There's so much freedom to build and build and move around. And you were saying that the American writer Alice Adams is similar to Drabble. They build this tree that branches and branches . . . .

EP: It's dendritic almost, like nerve endings.

LC: If they write about a forest and its inhabitants, we write about one tree, one plant, one flower.

EP: The life of the leaf.

LC: The poetic space is so short and so charged that we're after the kind of meaning in a narrative that isn't stated or shown through plot development. So we use image and metaphor and music to tell the story. And what doesn't get said, withholding, becomes as important as what's included. The lyricism, the tropes, the working of the lines – they're as important as the anecdote.

EP: This is an inevitable question. You use a lot of imagery from the natural world, and more specifically, of wild and sometimes domestic animals. Is this, in some ways, the mark of a writer of place, who is interested in the animals of that place? In other words, do you understand why you have to defend the skunks?

LC: No, but I do think I've been put on Earth to defend skunks. And cats and shrews and spotted owls . . . I don't know why. Do you know why you write about the natural world? Maybe it's because I see animals as pure beings, unsullied. We're smudged and they're clear about who they are. I think that's my attraction. And it doesn't mean that they have a lesser intelligence – I've never believed that. And it doesn't mean they have a lesser communication system. I think it is stupid to say a chimpanzee has the intelligence of a five-year-old human. Well, a five-year-old chimp has the intelligence of a five-year-old chimp. There are things they know that we don't. In terms of your earlier open-door question, animals can open the door to a parallel world, which sometimes – very, very few times in my life – I've entered. Caught a sniff or glimpse of what's behind that door. On the most mundane level, it's like sitting outside with my two cats, and I don't think there's anything but them and me in the yard, but if I follow their eyes, I see there's a squirrel hidden in the tree. They make me aware of a world that's invisible to my lesser senses.

EP: Do you think that paying such attention to animals may be a way through to the voicelessness that we, as poets, are trying to translate into words?

LC: Oh, that's terrific. I think what we admire about their voicelessness is that they don't need to gab like we do all the time. It's paradoxical. We revel in the deer's silence, and yet at the same time we want to translate it. We want to be like them, and not have to do all this talking, in our writing and in our daily lives. And so we write to get to their silence; we use words to do away with our obsession for words. Go figure!

EP: In a way we are trying to go from silence into words, and then back into silence again.

LC: And animals are our best model for that.

EP: In my case, it's gardens and plants.

LC: You started listening to grass at one point, the most basic plant form, you found a voice for . . . .

EP: . . . the working class of the plant world.

LC: You've become their spokesperson! I've always had animals around from the time I was a little kid. My first memory is of lying with my cheek on the cold kitchen linoleum and watching my puppy drink from a bowl, her pink tongue lapping milk. It was exquisite. I'd never seen anything so beautiful. The other admirable thing about animals is that they are very clear about what they want and need.

EP: If they are confused, it lasts for a very short time. Then they go one way or the other.

LC: Yes, there isn't this fuzziness around it.

EP: Going back to the narrative impulse in poetry. I'm interested in *A Saving Grace* – you've done, essentially, a verse translation of a novel. What led you, initially, to undertake that? I know that *As For Me and My House* was a very important novel for you.

LC: It was the first novel I read that came from my place, from my heartland, and from the stories my parents told me. There they were in a book – they were worthy of literature. I must have identified somehow spiritually with Mrs. Bentley. What's easy to miss in the novel – because it's so depressing, she's depressing, her marriage is depressing, the thirties are depressing – is her love of the prairies. There are passages of pure lyrical beauty about southwestern Saskatchewan, even though the novel's set in the middle of a dreadful decade when nothing grows. Her description of the land, of the sunset, of the wind, is right on, and is full of praise. That hooked me into being interested in her character. Also, she mirrors the landscape; she and he husband are spiritually dry. That's a familiar condition of this last century, one that has fascinated poets since *The Waste Land*.

As well, I hadn't written before about my marriage and its end. I identified with Mrs. Bentley's feelings about her husband. The opening poem in *A Saving Grace* is about two people lying in bed, pretending they're asleep and trying not to touch. Anyone who has gone through a breakup would recognize that horrible dissembling and distancing. The novel itself resonates with what is not said and so does a marriage when it's about to fall apart. I wanted to capture that quality of dreadful silence between two people, and the silence this land can impose on those who live here.

EP: The drought in the land parallels the drought in the marriage.

LC: Yes, and that's what Ross captured so brilliantly. The inner and outer drought. I definitely wrote the poems as a complement to the novel and a compliment to him. Yet obviously I felt, again, that something more could be said about Mrs. Bentley.

EP: There was another world within the world of *As For Me and My House*.

LC: It's my parents' world, and the world of my marriage. I lived with my husband on a house we built in the middle of a wheat field. He wanted to plant a shelterbelt, and we ended up doing it, but I didn't want any trees around. I wanted that stark, clear, openness, perhaps because it represents something inside me.

EP: That does bring me back to regionalism – or writers of place – quite swiftly.

In the poem, "Mrs. Bentley," you describe her left eye as "her prairie eye." What does your "prairie eye" see that other writers from other regions of the country maybe don't see?

LC: Well – light and the beauty of openness. Here I am doing another book with "light" in the title [*Apocrypha of Light*]. I just can't seem to get away from it. It infuses everything. Even the word itself has become almost a cliché for me. I can't get away from thinking about how light falls on things and changes them. It forces us to see what was in darkness and then it moves on. I was thinking about this when I was riding the bus, once, on the way to see my mom in Swift Current. I managed to sit in the very front seat just behind the big windshield. And I was trying to think what it was about the space we have here, the openness, that is so essential to my writing and my inspiration. I finally came to the conclusion that it's not empty space that we're seeing. A lot of people think of it that way, because it's made up of so many absences. But the openness of the prairies feels like space just before something's about to happen, to announce itself. It could be a hawk, it could be an angel. It could be a thunderstorm, or the clouds we were watching build and shift outside the monastery the other day. I always have the feeling of waiting for something to show itself or to speak – all of my senses are on full alert. Remember when we went to look for the owl the other evening, and I said, "I just love the thought that there's an owl presence here"? I think that's what this place makes you feel: there's a presence, almost palpable, but it's a mystery, it's ineffable. And it makes us keep on writing again and again. What is it? It's not Tree, it's not Mountain, it's not Ocean. What is it?

EP: There's such possibility here.

LC: We actually *see distance*. When you live on the raincoast you don't *see distance* unless you make a special trip to the ocean itself. Inland, everything you see is close up – Douglas fir, cedar, undergrowth. Here we *see the distance* and we're not sure what it means. We know it's not our future, it's not even a destination in the physical sense, it's not the place we'll end up, but it takes us out of ourselves in a funny way.

EP: It's an escape from the claustrophobia of the self!

LC: Yes, certainly it is. But what does it mean that you see *distance*? What kind of character/poet does that make you?

EP: I know that I feel claustrophobic in places . . . And when I'm in the mountains, or even in northern Saskatchewan in the trees, I start to feel uncomfortable pretty quickly.

LC: So do I, I want to break out of them, into the light.

EP: It's like I can't see what's coming. I grew up by the lake, of course, Lake Winnipeg.

LC: But you grew up in the trees by the lake, didn't you?

EP: There are trees, yes, but they are in the background. There were no more trees than in your average yard. We lived a street and a laneway away from the lake. We could see the lake from our front window.

LC: On the prairies we live in a great nothing that is something, and we arrive at meaning through absence rather than through presence. I'm not sure I know what that implies, but I know it's essential to my writing.

EP: I'm writing a sequence about Lake Winnipeg and my "boyhood." (I was a serious tomboy.)

LC: I started writing about my childhood in *Inventing the Hawk*, when I was forty. I think a reckoning begins in your forties, more so than in your thirties, when you can still allow yourself to be a kid.

EP: Yes, and I'm thirty-nine now. You still think things are open-ended in your thirties.

LC: And in your forties they aren't anymore. You start to think of who you are, and that means where you come from. Who you were . . . .

EP: You and I have talked recently about how we gravitate toward writers of place. Who are some of Canada's best regionalist writers?

LC: Al Pittman from Newfoundland and Alden Nowlan come immediately to mind. But I don't know what being a regionalist means anymore, to tell you the truth. I don't see how anyone can write about anything else other than the place that shapes them even though imagination also shapes that place into more than the literal.

EP: But there are poets who aren't as rooted in place . . . .

LC: Yes, maybe that's a better way to put it. Regionalist has always a derogatory term in Canadian letters. It means you write about grain elevators and old aunts who speak in dialect.

EP: And you're anecdotal . . . .

LC: And no one is interested in reading you because your writing isn't "universal."
       It's better to say "rooted in place."

EP: Rather than rooted in language, or formalism or ideology. Place is the driving
       force.

LC: That's a workable distinction. Your poems, of course, are so place-centred that
       I think you'll be naming each grain of dust next! You've done grass, where can
       you go now? But who are the poets of place? Patrick [Lane] of course. Who
       would you think of?

EP: I think of American writers whose work I love. Robert Hass, and James Galvin,
       of course, who writes out of Wyoming.

LC: Al Purdy was a poet of place but his place varied, sometimes it was
       Ameliasburgh, sometimes it was northern Canada, sometimes the land of the
       Etruscans. But when you read his poems, you always know where the poet
       is. And I like that about his work. He takes that small place where he is stand-
       ing and then he leaps to the galaxy. That was his greatest skill, to be able to
       tie together here and where his mind could take him. You always felt it was
       Al Purdy talking to you in the poems but he was also Everyman, a Dorset
       carver from a thousand years ago, or even someone riding the stars of the
       future.

EP: What about Gwendolyn MacEwen?

LC: No, I don't think so . . . .

EP: Her work is rooted in the imagination . . . .

LC: And in an elaborate imagination. Although she sets her poems in Egypt and
       Greece, and Franklin's expedition in Canada's north, the places become mag-
       ical and mythic.

EP: The mythic place comes first, whereas you make a mythical place out of this
       place.

LC: That's an interesting distinction. You'll rarely see a bird named in MacEwen's
       work, or a plant. Jan Zwicky is rooted in place and Tim Lilburn, definitely. He
       takes a small square of land and makes from it the world, and a locus for all
       his philosophic meanderings – the Moosewood Sandhills, or the South
       Saskatchewan River.

EP: You don't consider yourself part of any different school, do you?

LC: I think it's the critic who puts you there. And they often label you wrongly.

EP: Do you think there are poets who think of themselves in any one school, as postmodernists say?

LC: Again, I think it is the academic that categorizes us.

EP: There are camps, of a sort, but that's more at the "party level," at the drinking level. Or jostling for prizes, or employment, or on juries. That's in the career arena.

LC: Yes, the University of Calgary Creative Writing Department is bent in one direction, Concordia maybe in another, that sort of thing. But surely the working poet doesn't think that way: I'm going to sit down today and write a postmodern poem. Even the distinction "performance poet" doesn't work very well.

EP: Some poets are good performers while others aren't.

LC: We were at a reading the other night from Ken Howe and it was a performance, but he doesn't fit into the "performance poet" category as that label has come to be used.

EP: This goes back to place again. In a sense, you are a poet in exile. You haven't lived in Saskatchewan for many years, yet I think a lot of people still consider you a Saskatchewan writer. Has your physical distance from this landscape changed the way you write about the prairie, or affected your writing in other ways?

LC: I have no idea . . . I can't answer that. The obvious answer is that now there are some sea images in my poems, but they were there before I moved to the coast. Also, I do keep coming back here, to St. Peter's, to colonies, every summer.

EP: So you don't feel exiled?

LC: Not in language. I felt physically exiled when I first moved away, in the beginning, but I think a great deal of poetry comes from memory. Perhaps when you lose your "first place," as Eli Mandel called it, you rely on memory or imagination more. The images get transmuted.

EP: There seems to be a trend in your work, following a long arc, from the more spirtual – even *Inside is the Sky*, a spiritualism of place, you might say – now all the way to *Apocrypha of Light*, which is a reworking of Genesis. Do you think spirituality, or even religiosity, is the natural province of the poet?

LC: It was John Berger who I first heard say that poetry is closer to prayer than it is to prose. And I think he's right on. In poetry we are always addressing someone, but not a particular lover (although it sometimes sounds like it) or an ideal audience. As in prayer, we're addressing the invisible, someone who doesn't answer back. We try to speak the ineffable. Which, again, is what prayer does. As well, as in any ritualized language poetry convinces and moves us through its music, its repetitions. At the heart of poetry is something very primitive and close to magic. I believe that poetry really does change things, or at least hold onto things that would otherwise disappear. Often I write because I don't want to let something go. I don't want to let it die.

EP: It's almost an incantation.

LC: If I can find the right incantation, or spell, then maybe that thing or moment will last. The poem casts a spell. "Spell" is a great word, isn't it, when you think of writing. Obviously I can't make anything immortal, but in a primitive sense I believe words can make things come alive again. Robert Hass speaks of the Chinese poets' belief that writing poetry is like being alive, twice.

EP: It's a paradox, a stay against death that accepts death.

LC: Poetry is the art form of paradox. I write about common things to get at the uncommon, the spiritual. For me it's finding the numinous in the actual, in the material. For instance we had a big snowstorm on the coast a few years ago, an unusual occurrence. Some of the goldfish in our pond died and Patrick had to scoop them out. He put a goldfish on the snow – this small orange goldfish against the white. The image vibrated. The closest I could come to describing it was through a metaphor – it was a candle flame broken from the wick. I say it better than that in the poem, I hope, but I couldn't nail it down. There was something shimmering there, something profound but at the same time it was just a dead goldfish on the snow. That's what I'm interested in. The nexus between what you know and what you'll never know, something coming close to you and then dancing away. The poem flickers in the middle of those two movements. Sometimes what's holy is how the light falls on the tomato sitting on your windowsill. It's that small and that fleeting. That simple and that complex.

　　　　When I'm retelling these Biblical stories, a lot of the time they take place – in my head at least – on the prairie, even though I may not use prairie imagery in the poem. When I see the movie reel of the poem in my head it's this place I see. It's interesting that the stories in the Bible took place in the desert.

EP: And we are getting closer all the time.

LC: Yes, sadly, we're getting closer all the time. I feel at home in the imagined land-scape, that biblical landscape, probably because of the desert here, and the metaphorical one in Ross's book.

EP: There's an uncluttered austerity here that allows for more.

LC: You just defined a poem perfectly. And don't you feel sometimes that you'd like to say less and less, pare the poem down to a couplet maybe?

EP: Or to the noun itself, "the cup," "the table." In the poems, I've written about a dying woman, I use those kinds of "first order nouns."

LC: That's interesting. To bring resonance to these common, ordinary, plain words. Like that wonderful word, "plainsong."

EP: Re-infusing spirit back into the things that have been worn out through com-mon usage.

LC: There's that passage in Rilke, in the *Duino Elegies*, where he says, maybe we're here, just to say . . . and he lists a number of objects, like "gate," "house," but to say them in such a way that the words mean more than they ever imagined they would. I'm paraphrasing of course, but he encapsulates what we're trying to do in our poetry. That's why it's single-word based, not sentence-based. And it's image-based. We look at a word like "cup," (let alone a word like "love") and try to make it come alive again, after all the years of its misuse and disuse. How do you make it shimmer in the line again?

EP: I like to distinguish in my own mind between my work, the writing of poems, and my *career* as a poet: publication, employment, recognition. Do you make this distinction too?

LC: To talk of the career of a poet is laughable; there really is no such thing. Publishing books gives you some money, but it's such a small amount. We give readings, do workshops, as you have these last few years. And that's our big career. Then we have to get a job to pay the bills. If you're writing with a career in mind, then be a novelist or better yet, a TV scriptwriter.

EP: How important have awards, reviews and other honours been to your feelings about your work? Is competition healthy or unhealthy for a poet, or a bit of both?

LC: Only one person wins the prize, which means that six thousand other people feel lousy, right? Prizes are good for the winners, and awful for everyone else. And there are so few awards in Canada, sometimes it feels like there are a million people after a heel of bread. Especially in poetry. Of course that doesn't mean I wasn't thrilled when I won the Governor General's Award and the Pat Lowther Award, etc. Because it means my peers said that those books deserve attention. But there are hundreds of other books that don't get recognized and should.

EP: But really it's a business thing. It helps the booksellers promote books, it helps the general public make decisions about what books to buy. Awards funnel buyers toward the product.

LC: And it's got nothing to do with your writing. Nothing to do with how you feel when you go into your room and you confront the blank page, the blank computer screen staring back at you. Winning awards doesn't make the writing of poetry any easier.

EP: And it can be destructive.

LC: Especially if you win when you're too young, and you have to live up to some standard . . . .

EP: So awards haven't affected your feelings towards your writing.

LC: I don't think so. Maybe I'd be a mewling, self-pitying creature if I hadn't won any awards!

EP: But you wouldn't be a post office worker or a banker or . . . .

LC: I'd still be a poet. You know in your heart that awards have nothing to do with your work. It's nice to get accolades. Who would say otherwise? And it's nice to get the money that goes along with it. But you're a fool if you let it go to your head.

And you asked about reviews . . . If the quality of reviewing in Canada had kept pace with the quality of the poetry, then maybe reviews would make a difference to one's writing and enrich the work to be written next. A few do that, but unfortunately, good critics are rarer than good writers. And I've noticed a particular nastiness in the newspaper reviewers in the last couple of years or so. Solway and Starnino in the *Post*, Fitzgerald in the *Globe*. They don't write insightful criticism that informs and enlightens. Instead their "reviews" are personal attacks on writers, full of the vitriol that can only come from jealousy and bitterness. That kind of small-minded review is detrimental to sustaining a rich literary environment. It destroys rather than enhances.

Nothing good comes from it, including good poetry from the reviewers themselves.

EP: How have your feelings about poetry, the reading and writing of it, changed since you were in you twenties?

LC: I don't remember – it was so long ago. *[laughter]*

EP: Maybe it hasn't changed. That basic urge, it's the same thing. Fire is fire.

LC: Writers have one or two themes they keep going back to, trying to get the poem, the novel, the short story right. I wrote about my dog when I was a kid; I'm still doing it.

EP: And it was a prayer, remember. And now you're back to prayers.

LC: Yes, it was a prayer. Everything I learned about poetry in grade one is perhaps all there is to know. Everything else is just a complication of very simple issues. I'm more patient with myself and with my own silent periods of not writing. I think I am more particular about what I read. I'm more demanding than I used to be. There are fewer poets who really satisfy me. That's just maturity, perhaps.

EP: Well, you do a basic wide reading – you lay down a foundation – and then hone in on what you like, what feeds your work.

LC: And what feeds your soul, I guess. Which is what poetry should ultimately do; it's how it makes such a profound difference to your life. There are maybe twenty poems that have changed me, in that really deep sense.

EP: I've heard people describe your work as "accessible." Sometimes this is criticism, other times it's praise. What do you feel about that word?

LC: I don't apologize for having an audience outside the university classroom – so do Al Purdy, Don McKay, P.K. Page, poets I admire. I strive for clarity. That doesn't mean the poems aren't layered or complex or that I don't pay very close attention to form and craft. I work very, very hard to make my poems say what they need to say, without any pretentiousness and muddle. It's definitely a stance I've taken. I can rework a line twenty times, until it's as clear as I can possibly get it, using the stained language that's all we have to use. If someone wants to be critical about that, then fine. If someone wants to praise that, that's fine too. Only a silly person would confuse clarity with simple thinking. Look at the haiku masters or one of my models, Margaret Atwood – you don't need a secret code to understand their work though a knowledge of mythology would certainly help with hers.

EP: But there is a distinction, don't you think . . . people muddy the water by thinking that clarity and accessibility are the same things.

LC: Yes, I think they do. Some also think that being clear is somehow less profound than being obscure, as Eliot was, for example, in *The Waste Land* – where you have to read the footnotes to understand exactly what's going on. I try to use the idioms of the place where I grew up, and the kind of family I come from. That's part of allowing myself the freedom of using my own voice.

EP: You didn't grow up in an English department or a cathedral.

LC: You can hide in language. I don't want to; I want to come out in language. I don't even know if there is a choice in the matter: you write the way you write because of who you are and that's shaped by all kinds of things, including what you've worked hard to learn about your craft.

EP: Right, it's not as if there are ten choices on the menu, and you can "click on" whichever you choose.

LC: It's part of my blood and bones to write the way I write, for better or for worse. That doesn't mean I haven't studied the craft of poetry and applied skills that I wasn't born with to my writing. Sometimes I read other people and I think, god, I'd like to write like that. But Patrick will remind me. He'll say, "You write like you write, and that's the way it is. And they can't do what you do either."

EP: Whose poetry at this point in your career do you go to for sustenance? Not past influences, but who are you reading now?

LC: Coleman Bark's translation of Rumi, *The Essential Rumi*. Rumi says the most gnomic things, simply and clearly. He wants his listeners to understand. Of course, he dictated his poems while he was twirling in ecstasy – he was a whirling dervish. I'll never approach his greatness or write like him, but I want to aim for his hallmark: profundity in simplicity. He exemplifies the height of what poetry is – succinct and surprising images that resonate with a meaning that can't be captured in mere words. And his metaphors are so fresh – he says, "this is that" without losing track of "this is this."

EP: They are like stones, something that is new – you see them shining beneath a stream of water, and they're new again. Yet they are so old.

LC: I'm liking Jim Harrison right now: *The Shape of the Human Journey*. And what I'm liking about him is – by the way, he wrote ghazals at the same time

John Thompson did, they were students together – is the unity within the disunity in forms that aren't ghazals. In his lyric poems he makes radical shifts between the stanzas; there aren't even the poetic transitions that we expect, and I haven't quite figured out how he does it. He brings disunity into a form known for its unity. His poems have structural integrity, and yet reading him is like watching a piece of crystal shatter; the poem occurs at the point of its shattering. Also he's a poet of place. He writes about Montana, about finding a cougar track in the sand, and from images like that you get a Zen sense of knowing what is present through knowing what isn't there.

EP: That's similar to my attraction to James Galvin, who writes out of Wyoming. Our allegiances cross borders – they are part of a region, of similar territories. What Galvin does, which I don't quite understand either, is he segues from the plain-speaking Wyoming voice into an abstraction, or a platitude that he uses ironically, or into an intellectual insight. The pieces of the poems are fitted together like tractor parts.

LC: I like the idea of poetry being composed of tractor parts. His Wyoming is also made up of neighbours, of people like Ray who he says is going to quit haying and concentrate on dying instead. That kind of understatement and conjunction of actions like haying and dying is typical of him. He gives you the sense of a small town, which you and I know well from having grown up in one, yet he makes of the people in them and the place itself a larger philosophic statement. And he does it smoothly. Also there's a bit of surrealism in his work.

EP: Yes, there is.

LC: It's a salty surrealism. There's the plain-speaking of the local folks like Ray, and then there are angels made out of pollen. Galvin helps me understand my dissatisfaction with Charles Simic in his later books. I used to read him all the time but I don't anymore. His surrealism is more ethereal than Galvin's. The latter connects the dreamlike and fantastic with the ordinary world he sees around him, so the resulting images seem deeper and richer. It's not merely what's in the head, but what's in the dust on the ground.

EP: Yes. It's what you're thinking when you walk outside and it's "cold as two sticks," as he says at the beginning of one of his poems.

LC: And what does that mean? Remember Wallace Stevens said that poems must resist, almost successfully, the intelligence. I think we always love the poems we don't quite get.

EP: What we aspire to.

LC: In the best poems, there's something that we're not quite understanding. And by reading them and thinking about them, we keep growing. We don't allow ourselves to stay in a comfortable place.

EP: And when the poems are really good, we never get everything, there's almost something new when we read them again.

LC: It's what you learn as a teacher: the good poems are the ones you can teach for ten years and never tire of. They're generous – they keep renewing themselves if you're willing to stay fresh too.

The Quiet Centre Inside

MARGARET AVISON

Interviewed by Sally Ito

Margaret Avison was born in Ontario in 1918. She has won two Governor General's Awards for Poetry – in 1960 for *A Winter Sun* (Routledge) and in 1989 for *No Time* (Lancelot). She holds three honorary doctorates and is an Officer of the Order of Canada.

Sally Ito is the author of two poetry collections, *Frogs in the Rain Barrel* (Nightwood, 1995) and *Season of Mercy* (Nightwood, 1999) and a collection of short stories entitled *Floating Shore* (Mercury, 1998). She lives in Winnipeg.

SI: In his poem "The Dead Poet," Al Purdy, speculating on the origins of his poetry, asks "how else explain myself to myself/ where does the song come from?" Do you have any explanation of where your voice came from, of why you became a poet?

MA: My mother valued, yes, overvalued, my earliest verse, even sent one piece to the local paper's children's page when I was seven. Nobody I played with knew or cared, so her pleasure pleased me. My mother's early encouragement did prompt me to go on writing, and to read whatever came my way later. Prose. Poetry was inaccessible at first. I started with Palgrave's *Golden Treasury*, and it palled! But I still can see the brown linen boards of D.H. Lawrence's *Poems* – accessible and explosively exciting. Soon I was writing echoes of T.S. Eliot too, and then of Elizabeth Bishop. Widening acquaintance with poetry, and life experience, gradually freed me to write as I liked. There was nobody to stop me.

SI: How have your feelings about poetry, the reading and writing of it, changed since you were in your twenties?

MA: Youth: lyric flow. Late teens: English courses and more verse music in my ear – too much Melville and T.S. Eliot for a while. In 1938 (at twenty) the poems in English from colonial Canada, though beautiful, seemed more relevant to field and forest than to the Depression and its looming solution, war. After 1945, American poetry came in from many contacts here and in the US. Experimenting energy peaked when our daily rounds brought bp Nichol and me together. By then new surges of vitality came with new Christian faith, and poetry lost its status as my first priority. Finally, life experience and aging led to delight in words' derivations and histories, a more deliberate style and some awareness of the need for exacting revision.

SI: Have you felt your vocation as a poet to be a solitary affair? How important do you think "community" is for the poet? (By "community" I mean a community of other poets and writers.) Do you find talking and consulting with other poets to be helpful? For example, you mention "experimenting energy" coming from your contact with bp Nichol.

MA: It has been solitary for me. In 1940 I graduated with a debt and needed a job. Depressed at first, I began to let the everyman quality of workdays whet me. The stress between nine to five and evening (books and notebook) proved stimulating – a pattern that was to persist. Family and family health concerns increased. Every experience feeds the reservoir that poetry taps. Of course, each of us makes choices. Only after twenty years' writing did I venture much. For example, Professor Warren Tallman organized an event at UBC which I attended. The stimulus of meeting with many writers was welcome, especially after meeting George Bowering and Marilyn Bowering over coffee. Moreover, down the years in Toronto I attended the readings organized by Raymond Souster, Toronto's eminent poet. A young, rosy-cheeked Leonard Cohen, with abundant black hair, came with work that evoked the huge dimensions A.M. Klein had opened to us all. There were fine American poets in the series, too. I enjoyed other writers as other opportunity offered, like that wonderful chance encounter with bp Nichol. However the fight for private time continued to be a primary concern.

SI: How did you meet bp? And what effect did he have on your work?

MA: We met in the University of Toronto library stacks in the early 1960s. He was then employed putting away books on a lower level and I had a carrel, a desk where my work materials could be left, during M.A. studies. As I walked towards that desk one morning, bp, an unknown stack boy, was waving a fist with a rolled up manuscript in it, saying softly but intensely to a co-worker "It's good. It's really good. They send it back after a half-glance, if that. Won't anybody READ my poetry?" Without breaking pace as I approached, I said "I will," and without a beat missed, bp slammed it into my hand. Instead of doing dutiful work at my desk, I read it with growing delight and when time came to go, I left a small note promising the precious manuscript back the next morning – although I made it clear that my enjoyment did not mean I could move bp any closer to publishers (no doubt he knew the same addresses). Of course I enthusiastically offered any words he wanted to use as a blurb. Over the months our correspondence flourished on scraps of paper – just fun to light the lower level where we were immured. I can't remember whether I attended some of bp's readings that year or later, or when I heard his group perform, or over what years received his delightful periodicals and mailings. (My set of such materials is now in York University Archives where a friend placed them when I had to clear my shelves in a sudden move.)

One morning, during library days, I vividly remember. Spring, a frantic season on campus, and bp elatedly cried, "Come out! A friend from Vancouver is outside! You've got to meet!" He and I and bill bissett sat in the sunny triangle of grass (northeast of the old building, now the medical library) and again, all the essentials were in place. bill's *th influenza uv logik* (Talonbooks, 1995) later showed the mutuality in that buoyant friendship-language. bill had a capacity for suffering, and bp for compassionate wholeness. Together they were discovering their own freedom of word and gesture. Influence? Little in writing. Concrete poetry, though, and the comic book (e.g. *Captain Poetry*) were now within my ken as a reader. I would play in now and then for the fun of those exchanged notes. One of my notes appeared in one of his papers once ("Eporphorial Harness"). Dear bp! The *person* he was nourished me over the years, humanly speaking.

SI: I know of some poets who have had their work used in liturgy and worship. Do you see your poetry as primarily something to be read in books? Or to be read aloud to an audience? Who do you see as your reader?

MA: I write to be read – I answer for myself only. I have enjoyed formal readings by other poets; oral rhetoric lifts the poetry off the page, sometimes. Tim Lilburn's is such, whether read or heard. My readers are the completers of what the text began. I address them as co-creators, unknown but for sure out there, and exacting.

SI: What *is* a poem, in your definition?

MA: We discussed this topic in a university English class I taught in the 1960s. My small senior "A" class set the topic they wanted to discuss from September to May as: "What Is a Poem?" That was their topic, up to me to devise a method. In each class someone was named to lead the next class's discussion, illustrating and explaining his definition based on one poem of his choosing, photocopied the week ahead so that everybody had a copy. When he presented *his* "A poem is . . . (such and such), the others were to challenge his definition from that poem and from any others they were planning to choose in turn or simply others that we all could look up in a common anthology. One by one, definitions were knocked down or edited down until in May we were all satisfied. Their conclusion: *A poem is that form of art in words that requires from the reader the same creative energy as from the writer.* To me, this was an exercise done in fun but at some level I concur with the conclusion they came to.

SI: I grew up as a writer in an environment of creative writing programs, of federal and provincial arts grants for writers and of early publication opportunities in literary magazines across the country. I know this is a much different environment than the one you experienced as a young writer in Canada in the forties and fifties.

MA: Yes. Before there were any grants, some younger poets fostered a politely anti-establishment stance. For example, F.R. Scott published a satirical poem on the Canadian Authors' Association's tea parties. In Montreal, Irving Layton and Louis Dudek led a more rambunctious break with the past, circulating mimeographed magazines, some in Toronto, too. While they were in Toronto, Miriam Waddington and Earle and Esther Birney encouraged writerly company. Time limits curtailed my participation. The Canada Council was born. I had a vision that it would set up kiosks everywhere, opening our books to everybody, to the publishers' delight. Repeatedly I urged this upon the Council. Government grants to individuals still evoked unhappy associations: McCarthyism in the US, propagandist art in the Soviet Union and censorship of writers in Nazi Germany. I had stated the alternative (to grants) so forcefully that, to be consistent, I never applied to the Canada Council for a grant. Yet I have gratefully accepted the Governor General's Award, twice. And I did apply for the Guggenheim Award when the opportunity was opened to me.

SI: How important have reviews, awards, other honours been to your feelings about your work? Is competition healthy or unhealthy for a poet?

MA: Any "recognition" – even a bad review – does help me. I write to (from and for) readers, and am therefore heartened to know somebody out there has read what I wrote. Awards? Cash helps, temporarily. Awards help publishers sell books, we hope. "Honours" can be an encouragement but can end up distracting from a writer's privacy and working time. "Competition?" The word's metallic taste is already there in "awards." Open competitions can launch new writers, true. Surely, though, no writer wants to "win" when that means another writer "loses" – and may for a time even believe the judges' assessment, not his own convictions.

SI: In your early years, did you have anything in the way of classes or an inspiring teacher that might have influenced you as a poet?

MA: I had contact for one term in the fall of grade nine, with one teacher, Gladys Storey, who influenced many, me among them. She was never my teacher, but she asked to see my notebook from home and made a few marginal comments in fine red ink. One of them counselled me not to "use the first person singular in any of your poems for ten years." After her death I learned more of writing just as reading and life enabled.

SI: Sage advice! Was there anything else in the early years of your career that encouraged you to become a poet?

MA: "Career?" I was a wage-earner. Any job I did well meant dangerous promotion towards a "career," i.e. a time-eating job. So I had to move on whenever "career" threatened. Daytime with everyman did make free time light up. I never thought of myself as "a poet," never wanted "to be a poet," and I wince if someone introduces me with reference to my poetry. The choice life made for me – is one with which I heartily concur: to "be" a human being, no more, no less. I *did* take the writing of poetry seriously as far back as I can remember – but never, God help me, did I or do I want to take myself as a poet seriously.

    Now back to Gladys Storey. In the fall of my grade nine year, she announced a "club" after school, 4 P.M., and people up to grade thirteen came. She read poems – ballads, English poets from several centuries and some recent writing, too. World War I permeated her thinking, and gave poignancy to her reading of Sassoon. We were spellbound. That first meeting, to help her assess who was interested in such a club, perhaps, she asked each person to bring some of their writing. Former pupils came back from university to sit in and absorb the selections of poetry – all from England – that enriched our understanding. She died after Christmas. I was in on only one term with the club, but the reading and her notes on my poems were a profound influence. In high school years my plan was to study math and physics in university. A burst appendix in the middle of grade thirteen meant I could not make up the labs in time. To avoid repeating a whole year, I switched to arts.

SI: How did your poetry writing develop in your university years?

MA: My undergraduate years were 1936-1940. All periods of English literature, especially the freshman course on Renaissance poetry, enriched my response to words and delighted my ears with new cadences, rhyme patterns, rhythms. In those days English began at the beginning, Old English and Chaucer, and ended with Thomas Hardy. Any contemporary poetry we read on our own, off-campus, like we did our own poem writing.

SI: And what of your years of post-graduate study? I know from reading your biography that you took an M.A. in English and that you also went to Chicago on a Guggenheim scholarship.

MA: There was a gap of twenty-three years between my B.A. and graduate school, which I entered in the mistaken hope of becoming a teacher. Teaching I enjoyed, but after two years of it other things came. Graduate school was made feasible by Ontario's subsidies, in order to staff colleges for a bulge of incoming students. Two good years of classes and writing the Byron thesis, and then three drearier years towards the doctoral written and oral exams gave me qualifications, "all but thesis." There has been no thesis. All cut into time to muse or write. The stack-time exchanges in verse with bp Nichol kept fresh air blowing in, as did the quiet centre inside from a brand new faith (conversion in January '63 of the year I enrolled). Some of *The Dumbfounding*'s poems came even then.

SI: What was your Chicago experience like?

MA: I received the Guggenheim in 1959. On the application I asked for "eight months in Chicago to live as a poet" – such I designated then for that purpose. Chicago was the place I chose because my ailing parents were accessible from there. My request was in general terms because I did not want to commit myself in advance to producing something at the end. In fact, most of my work was organizing, revising and typing old manuscripts. The outcome was a clean copy of the *Winter Sun* poems, a long accumulation with new poems of the

Chicago days interspersed. The experience was glorious. Wonderful libraries. The Art Institute near the Chicago Public Library. *Poetry* magazine on the same campus as the Chicago University Library. I visited *Poetry*: they had published a group of my poems earlier. There I met Frederick Bock, then the assistant editor, a fine poet who became a good friend until his untimely death from cancer. Everywhere the friendly Americans included me, if I could find time to socialize. I took time from working mainly to go where good jazz was playing, evenings.

SI: What was the critical climate like during your period of study in Chicago?

MA: The Chicago period blurs with other times. Dominant in the late fifties were critics who made the poem's text the primary object. They approved a closely textured style, significant in all its parts. I read and relished Blackmur, I.A. Richards . . . the "new critics." They had influence on us, but no poet writes from prescription. Frederick had been part of a creative writing class at Iowa University – the first time I had ever heard of such a class.

SI: Did you ever have a sense of yourself as a Canadian poet, in particular?

MA: Never "as a Canadian poet." My schooling had included British and ancient history, but little Canadian history. Knowing at least the southern part of Canada, BC to PEI firsthand, intrigued by Quebec, blank about US history, I did have a sense of belonging. The lack of patriotism here I judged a Canadian virtue. Books in English, poetry included, were without boundaries for a reader.

SI: What was your view of Canadian poetry?

MA: "Canadian poetry" struck my generation as echoing English verse *as* rural, remote from our experience of ardent pacifism, the Great Depression, then World War II with its sudden industrialization. Leo Kennedy's *The Shrouding* first woke me up to somebody in Canada who reacted as I did, and wrote poems.

SI: By "Canadian poetry," do you mean the work of earlier Canadian poets such as Bliss Carman, Archibald Lampman and Charles G.D. Roberts, for example?

MA: Yes. Carman, Lampman, Campbell, F.G. Scott (F.R.'s father), etc.

SI: I've not heard of Leo Kennedy. Who was he? How and where did you encounter his work?

MA: My generation read the first experimental periodicals and found him in the

McGill Fortnightly Review (we also found F.R. Scott, A.J.M. Smith and A.M. Klein there). Although he was born in England, Kennedy was educated in Quebec in Catholic schools and McGill. Here was someone with elegant form and a modern voice; we took notice when his book came out – *The Shrouding.* I do not know what happened to him later.

SI: Did your experience of pacifism, the Depression and the war create any conflict for you between poetry and politics? It sounds like you wanted poetry to be about something different than what you were currently reading at the time.

MA: Looking back, I think it was the "poetic language" that we all wanted to change. We learned music from the Georgians but we craved common spoken words in poems – *and* reference to contemporary experiences. It was natural for political identity to grow alongside wage-earner identity, around the edges, perhaps. Certainly I was involved with a political party and canvassed in pre-election weeks. I saw no conflict with poetry in this communal concern.

SI: I want to ask you now a question about writing in forms. You have written sonnets, especially in your earlier books, but did your desire to use "common spoken words in poems" eventually steer you more towards free verse?

MA: What felt passé were poetic subjects as much as elegant language, which demonstrated unawareness of a whole new social context to be spoken from, and to. Diction can declare the inclusiveness of communal concerns. Perhaps good writing is *always* non-elitist? As to your question, no. Everyday diction appears in various kinds of verse from the sixteenth century on. And the term "free" verse is purely negative – free from requirements. *All* verse must observe some constraints, rhythms, consonant patterns, echoes, stresses that fall as the meaning dictates, etc. These are unobtrusive requirements, but still not "free verse."

SI: Did you and your peers think of moving more towards narrative-style poems to bring that "story and novel" readership experience to contemporary poetry readers?

MA: Pondering what others in my time might have purposed reminded me of someone's quip that in those days *status quo* had become *fluxus quo.* Poetry readers will always be fewer than novel readers in our day, since journals and newspapers and work reports condition our reading habits. To be jerked about by shorter lines that yield meaning only after rereading and quiet consideration calls for unfamiliar habits. It was not so in Victorian England, when poetry had a wide and demanding audience. Poets tended to run to excess then. In our day we all found Earle Birney's "David" inimitably beautiful, of course. It was a narrative poem that every reader in Canada knew!

SI: I asked the previous question because a number of poets today are also prose writers. I myself write short stories and am currently working on a novel. I see working in the different genres as quite different experiences. Did you always only write poetry? Or did you ever want to write fiction?

MA: By my own choice, poetry was what I did. My prose writing has come through assignments: for example, a ghost-written biography paid for by the subject's children; a grade seven history text paid for by an educational publisher; pieces I was hired to do during my years of freelance work; occasional articles, invited usually, or book reviews, long ago. Novels require a capacity for plot structuring which has been left out of my makeup. Even narratives amongst my poems are, in the main, among the discards – they usually don't work.

SI: I think there is a distinct difference between the "kind of mind" required for writing the different genres. Tim Bowling has spoken of the art of writing poetry as a "discipline of consciousness." When you write poetry, do you have to be in a certain "state of mind" to do it? Is it a consciously cultivated state of mind or one that arises from the unconscious depths spontaneously?

MA: A "certain state of mind" concurs with the writing, yes. I think it comes of intensity of focus, i.e. not from "cultivating it," although I can remember doing so at thirteen or fourteen. When I wanted to write, I would play the melody of Schubert's "Am Meer," dreamily, at our piano – nobody else at home. Then I would go upstairs as carefully as if I were carrying a brimming cup, to the desk and the special pen and notebook for poems. I smile at the memory.

SI: Your playing of the piano reminds me of what other poets I know do – they get in the mood, so to speak, by reading poetry or listening to music. I do find reading other poets to be inspiring although I don't necessarily read them specifically to write poems. You speak of "intensity of focus" – do you find that to be a spontaneous thing or deliberate (in that you will concentrate on some-thing specific in order to produce a poem)?

MA: The question you have here is not clear to me. Fact, now: I resist having to write. Do so only when something nags me, preoccupies me, has to be cleared away. Analyzing my procedures is beyond *me* – though others write poems *and* write about process. We're each unique as human beings! E.g. Rilke, John Clare, Pope, Coleridge, my own family members!

SI: I understand your resistance to analysis of procedure. However, when I was taking creative writing in my undergraduate years, we were asked to "analyze" a poem we had written ourselves. For me, it turned out to be a rather illumi-nating exercise in terms of making something "unconscious" more conscious. P.K. Page wrote of "hearing a phrase" that came to one like a boomerang; one had to catch the thing before it curved away into the nether parts of the mind. From that phrase, she would then "build" the rest of the poem. I found that metaphor of the boomerang quite apt.

As the spiritual is often the topic of your poems, I wonder how you craft the metaphor for those "moments least accessible to lisping human terms" that you have described in your essay "Muse of Danger." Certainly you caution writers not to derive all their inspiration from such moments, but on those occasions when they do, how should they go about it? Or to be more specific, how do you go about it?

MA: The "how-to" will likely be unique for everyone in Christ writing poems. I was early struck by C.S. Lewis's warning not to use scriptural insight for poetry if it was meant for action. If it is an insight for poetry, my "method" is like trying to identify a hopping little bird before it flies – to discover something barely glimpsed, for my own sake.

SI: Yes, I do identify with that "method." I've often used poetry to "tease" out meaning from scripture – in particular, meaning from narrative passages where it is not always clear what motivates certain biblical characters As for other passages in scripture that are more "theological," I tend to want to work with them more in prose than in poetry although certain "notions" do occasionally hop about like the bird you speak of.

MA: Thanks to a friend, I'm learning not to use other people's words (the *jargon*, as the outsider hears it). She also warned me against moral-tag endings. Our faith is not fable.

SI: I agree; avoiding the "jargon" is of paramount concern. And moralizing is also a distinct temptation. It often parades itself as "closure" but may not be at all aesthetically pleasing or satisfying. The main problem I have discovered is finding a more deliberate and meditative sensibility that comes from a refining of spiritual consciousness. I was mildly surprised to see how precisely "mysticism" can be defined in the Catholic encyclopedia, for example. It kind of takes the lyrical "wind out of one's sails," if you know what I mean.

MA: "Mysticism" is a word I'm nervous about. Fruitful meditation is all I know. By that I mean a balance *I* need, to avoid inwardness.

SI: You spoke of "lyric flow" as part of your poetry in youth. And then in your later years, you thought of poetry in terms of a "delight in words' derivations and histories, a more deliberating style and some awareness of the need for exacting revision." I sense a shift here between the lyric to the more meditative – a shift that I am currently negotiating myself. I wonder how you made such a transition or shift.

MA: In my own experience lyric flow was a gift to youth, an overflowing ease
      like an athlete's ease, confident, full of energy and drive. One rides with
      it as far as possible. But to push on when it isn't a given is to risk writing
      parodies of one's own earlier poems. At that point, word, music, word-
      sounds, images no longer simply cluster and come almost of themselves.
      Contriving them is useless. Head-knowledge, life experience etc., gradu-
      ally change the process. Impulses of feeling become less important than
      quickened interest in some visual object, or a vividly imagined situation.
      This reads like a law for all poets! I speak only of what seemed true for
      me.

SI: In *Not Yet But Still*, how did you come to write about Job, in poetry? Since
      yours is such a long poem, I imagine that it wasn't spontaneous but a very
      deliberate and contemplative act.

MA: "*Job*?" At issue were two questions that had nagged at me over years, and had
      to be explored and cleared. (1) I had to face God's "permissive will," in suf-
      fering and hang on to that *and yet* Satan as instigator; and (2) in the light of
      Job's emotional struggle (through trying to figure it out), I needed to ponder
      the emotional component of the Godhead in the whole drama. That called for
      a solid, step-by-step restraint in form and language – hence, the style that put
      off any readers bringing in their own expectations of "a poem." One's natural
      reaction to the scriptural text would be overwhelming awe – hence wordless
      ness: this was the struggle behind putting down the words. Nobody has yet
      accepted my "Job" as a poem, so maybe it isn't. It can be discarded or forgot-
      ten: that's not my business.

SI: Did you see your writing of "Job" as a "practical application" of scripture in
      that the book of Job is one that demands meditation/contemplation rather
      than "service" in the form of action? I see your poem as a form of "hearing the
      Word and doing it."

MA: No – no "oughtiness" pushed me into it. Every believer reads the Book of Job
      over the years, finding shifting emphases, different questions etc. every time.
      I worried at one time about the validity of the teaching by Job's friends: should
      I heed it? Was it sound theology? If it was, then why did they need Job's
      prayers so sorely at the end? None of my earlier readings led to a poem. For
      this poem, my search was for God, as THE Friend. Underlying it was a recur-
      ring incredulity about the Father's love for me, I think. Certainly I wanted to
      know Him better as Person. And a person has emotions. What were His feel-
      ings – veiled by the scriptural text? That incentive made the poem a
      preoccupation until I took it on.

SI: Earlier you spoke of poetry "losing its status as [your] first priority." Was this a result of your "new Christian faith"? If so, how did poetry recover its place in your life afterwards?

MA: I was forty-three when I encountered the living Jesus. Up to then I had been "good," obeying Exodus 20:3-10 but unaware of a fallen nature. I was familiar with the stories of the Bible. The idea of the Fall had conveyed dark Miltonic imaginings. But suddenly, that day in 1963, the first two Commandments bowled me over – "Thou shalt have no other gods before Me" and "Thou shalt not make unto thee any graven image" – but I was steadied by Exodus 20:10-11 ("But the seventh day is the Sabbath of the Lord thy God.") We are to share the Creator's rest and joy – every week! What looked like a sacrifice (that "priority") turns out to be a good investment. On the brink of yielding, and accepting the Lord, I cried: "But don't touch the poetry!" As the "Person," in my *The Dumbfounding* says, at that point solid walls closed in. There was no deal till I threw in the poetry along with myself.

SI: I can certainly identify with that! I know you eschew the identity of the "poet" in order to avoid the vanity of the title, and yet as poetry writing is one of the things that humans do, it's not easy to depart from the identity it gives one if one does it well. In other words, it can still be seen as a kind of gift . . . certainly we can write our poetry for the eyes of God only, but is it not still meant for the eyes of humans as well? To nourish them in faith and worship? Otherwise we would all be satisfied in writing our poetry in the sand. What we do with the responses of humans, however, has more to do with ego than perhaps the actual writing of the poetry does. I don't know . . . I think the topic of selfhood in Christ and selfhood through writing is a constant source of conflict for some believers. It is for me.

       Going back to your earlier work, I was struck by your mastery of the sonnet. I'm curious as to how you developed such deftness at that form. I find that writing in forms requires a kind of diligence and concentration that that "lyric flow of youth" isn't always amenable to (I think here of Frost's old line about writing free verse like playing tennis with the net down . . .) I've sometimes experimented with biblical poetic forms – trying to write a psalm, for example – but I find it very, very difficult.

MA: I write with my ear. Some poetic forms originated in music. There is no parallel in prose creative writing. Sounds in poetry are musical, words are primarily tactile: to paraphrase some French writer, a writer's words are primarily not the ones in the dictionary, but the ones he knows from the reverse side where he can feel their surfaces, texture, knobbiness, curves . . . Playing with sound and texture becomes instinctive. No proper poet ever *planned* alliteration (that one was accidental!). Reading oceans of English poetry schools the ear to rhythm and rhyme. Doing it seldom just comes. There are patterns to learn. Rhythm is no problem if English verse is inside the ear. (Fighting off iambic pentameter where it is inappropriate, or dull, is the bigger problem.) Rhyme schemes have to be learned. This whole area is the place for analysis – not how a poem originates or how to make it come.

Tricks:

1) Write the rhyme scheme on the right margin of your page, every draft, so you don't have to keep checking line endings. As your lines establish the *a*-sound, the *b*-sound, etc., add the sound opposite *a* and *b* on the margin, etc.

2) If you are stuck with a weak word just for the sake of rhyme, and *cannot* do better, switch it to be the *earlier* line, so that the good rhyme will please the ear and (we hope) all will be forgiven.

3) If it's not getting in your ear fluently, quit the poem and do a *da dá da dá da dá* awhile to yourself. Too much sweating will show. It ought to begin to flow. I wrote one triolet (a poem of eight-syllabled lines where line one recurs as fourth and seventh, and line two as the eighth). It never had much life – too much carpentering and it never did become easy in the ear as I wrote. *Deftness*? Practice, and reading with your ear.

SI: Do you still write poems in forms? (I noticed a few rhyming poems in *Not Yet But Still*.)

MA: Sometimes. The themes and the way I feel about them guide the tone of voice, diction, level of style, formal or open lines.

SI: Another particular aspect of your poetry I find compelling and that I see throughout all your books is your use of weather and landscape imagery. I'm struck at how skillful you are in your descriptions of the seasons and the landscape at different times of the year. Your work seems to explore "terrains" – a word whose deeper meaning I've found in your work. I notice that many of your poems begin with a natural image – a gaze that leads into a deeper seeing. Is that often how your poems start – with that intensity of focus on some natural phenomenon? Does that first line (so many of which are stunning in their poetic impact) just come to you? And is it from there that you develop the rest of the poem?

MA: It is true that skies, weather, surroundings, do move me – but not *to* anything, not purposively. Just a form of rejoicing in natural being in general.

But first line "coming?" An image from gazing at something? No. Not in my experience. I'm sorry, I can't analyze how I work, though I know some poets can.

SI: With your poems, how much do you revise?

MA: Second day after writing, often extensively. Fussing with details, ongoingly. I wish I had done more of this early on!

SI: This brings me to ask how your books were put together. The typical thing today for a poet starting out is to "study" creative writing in a workshop or class, then publish a few poems in literary magazines and then eventually assemble the poems in some cohesive sequence and send out the manuscript to small presses. Somewhere along this process – and I would think this would vary from person to person – the "poet" identity is formed in the mind of the individual enough to provide him/her with the impetus to submit and/or often resubmit their work to publishers. Did your attitude about writing poetry change with the publication of a book? I don't intend this question to be about poetic identity per se but also about artistry in terms of getting a book 'out there to be read' and how deliberately shaping a book for readers is different than say, 'writing for oneself.'

MA: You ask about four things here: (1)Preparing manuscripts – selecting and discarding, reassessing and revising. (2)Submitting poems to periodicals: for me this began with high school and college student papers. Because I knew two people from other contexts on *The Canadian Forum* board, I submitted poems to that paper. And so on. (3)Arranging poems for a book: for it is usually scattering individual poems so that the reader will find an easy transition from page to page. I once tried a topical arrangement (*Not Yet But Still*) – a mistake, I now think. It forced a reader from too much entrée to too much pudding, all at once. (4)Finding a book publisher: it is indeed a matter of "submit and resubmit," as I found with *Winter Sun*, which was many times rejected, like most first books. My second book, *The Dumbfounding*, Denise Levertov *requested* when Norton New York requested *her* to assemble six poetry books pronto, to open out their catalogue which they considered too heavily academic. Then through his periodical I learned about William Pope and his Lancelot Press in Nova Scotia. He was friendly towards my manuscripts and published them until he retired from publishing.

SI: I know you have a new book coming out. What is it called?

MA: The new book, *Concrete and Wild Carrot*, should appear later this year. It will be published by Brick Books.

SI: As you look back on the many poems you've written, is there one in particular, or one book perhaps (excluding the most recent one), where you feel you came closest to an accurate rendering of your impression of life?

MA: No one poem, no. Over a lifetime of writing, "impression of life" undergoes many changes. I do notice recurrent responses to events and climates of opinion, punctuated by impulses of playfulness, and periods of withdrawal – time to digest all I've read and to refuse to keep up with all I haven't read. The one piece that says it all may lie up ahead somewhere, and seems to move on as I move on. This is not a negative statement!

The Provisional Shack of the Ear

TIM LILBURN

Interviewed by Shawna Lemay

Tim Lilburn has published several books including the poetry collections *To the River* (McClelland & Stewart, 1999) and *Moosewood Sandhills* (M&S, 1994) and the book of essays *Living in the World As If It Were Home* (Cormorant, 1999). He lives in Saskatoon.

Shawna Lemay is the author of *Against Paradise* (M&S, 2001) and *All the God-Sized Fruit* (McGill-Queen's, 1999), for which she won the Gerald Lampert Memorial Award and the Stephan G. Stephansson Alberta Book Award. She lives in Edmonton.

SL: Let's jump into the deep end, Tim, and talk about "the loneliness of human life outside Paradise." You used that phrase in an essay called "Contemplation and Cosmology" to describe an icon you had gazed at in New York. You described the male figure's "large sadness." Is this a touchstone image for you?

TL: I don't know if such loneliness is a touchstone for me, but I think it points to a sense many have that they are separated from some larger, natural community, a community that has the scent of a larger self. The story Plato puts into the mouth of Aristophanes of a split, circular self is another way of pointing at this: perhaps pointing to this absence is the only way we have to account for desire. And it's possible to imagine someone for whom the wanting arising out of such an experience of being bereft is primary. If I am not completely such a person, at least I have no difficulty understanding someone who is.

SL: In a *Moosewood Sandhills* poem called "In Paradiso," you end by saying "Things sprout a called-back collar of gold,/ the decay of something brighter." Reading this is something like running towards the gates and having them slammed in your face. The beautiful Almost. The question, then, is about decay, attention to decay – how important to your stance is the attention to the foul, the unsavory, the darkness?

TL: I like how you put that: the beautiful – almost. I think one must be very careful around beauty. It, after all, some form of it, will heal the ache mentioned above. It is the one thing, I suspect, that can do this and the imagination, as a result, is indefatigably and disastrously solicitous in this matter, always rushing forward winning simulacra of coming home. But if we console ourselves in this business of returning to the larger thing that we are – us as world, indistinguishable – it is no consolation at all. The sweet things the imagination places in our mouths – the sentimentalities, plans, philosophical claims – simply deepen our isolation, groove the habit of being plushly apart further in. So wait, I tell myself, don't be taken in: we can come only so close, it seems to me, to the things we mostly elementally desire. We can, however, be visited.

SL: Your poems are wonderfully secondary, if that's the word. Which is to say they are runoff from the slender, muscular school of the river. I think it's because of their secondariness that the poems have such integrity, such wholeness under their skin. A favourite couple of lines from *To the River*: "I don't amount to much./ This is a song, you sing it, then become it, the work of God." Can you tell me about your motivation to write poetry, the purity of that? Can we be vaguely mathematical? How many parts the song, to how many parts the singing, to how many parts becoming?

TL: I love your idea of "secondariness." I , too, am always most interested in the

interiority of poems, the life under the surface – never more than partly artic-
ulated, a place of hints and nudges. I like the sort of poem where the surface
– story, music, imagistic flow – is broken up (lake ice, mid-winter, after a
windy late November) yet beguiling. It pulls you in but doesn't provide a
home. Where the poem really lives is far inside itself. That's where it coheres,
but there it hardly knows what it's saying. It coheres far in but can't fully say
what its final shape is. As for singing and becoming, I don't split them.

SL: Thomas Merton, in his journals, in speaking about wanting "to write about
        everything," describes a sort of book "with a little of everything that creates
        itself out of everything. That has its own life. A faithful book. I no longer look
        at it as a 'book.'" Do you look at your poems as poems, your books as books?

TL: I am rather suspicious of writing (as Merton himself came to be) or writerly
        intent of calculating effect, preferring to trust, instead, plain attention. What I
        do is look, is listen as long as I can, as carefully, engage in a kind of auricular
        seeing: the poem seems to step forward into this. Forgive the Heideggarian
        sound of this – I don't want it. Let me rub it out a little by insisting that the
        attention doesn't *woo* the poem, doesn't liberate it from speechlessness and so
        on. The writer has little control over the poem (maybe none), nor does she or
        he do the poem any big favour by writing it down. I do (badly) the one thing
        I believe I can do which is turn toward things. Poems incidentally come out of
        this, but there is no guarantee they will.
             I think of both *Moosewood Sandhills* and *To the River* as book-length
        poems or better, long, segmented "speakings." I like the idea of such intent,
        almost endless utterance. I think of both books as, in part, long public per-
        formances stageable in the mind. What Merton says about faithful books,
        books with a life of their own, that do not strain for a particular pose, is good
        – books that have a surprising autonomy even from the author.

SL: You often refer to hollowed places – underground rooms, pits, saucers, inden-
        tations, holes. Is this a way of knowing, carving or inscribing yourself into the
        world? It seems a very lonely, sorrowful act. But then also one of wildness. Is
        this somehow a reaction to our exile from the garden? I read the image vari-
        ously as a sort of throwing oneself into the earth's big howl, a gentle lying
        down in the abyss, a drunken reaction to the unutterable. Could you talk about
        this recurring image?

TL: You need a place to stand. I think of pre-Patrick Irish monks living in trees –
        dendrites they were called. You can hear the confused, lonely love for the wor-
        shipped grove in the form of their lives. Or the very early Syrian
        contemplatives Ephrem the Singer (fourth century) talks about, "the mourn-
        ers, the dwellers on the mountains, in the hollows, in the rocks, in the clefts
        of the ground, the roaming ones." I don't quite know what I'm doing so I need

a place to wait and look, that provisional shack of the ear that Rilke describes in *Sonnets to Orpheus*. Also, I suppose such places are points where one might be found: an address in unmapability, your name in the telephone book of unlikeness. Eros appears to require some form of impoverishment. So, these places are mental and actual preparations, deer stands, availabilities.

SL: The result of this impoverished waiting can be exhaustion, and in your writing exhaustion is a gift, or a state that relinquishes gifts. You begin a poem called "You Sleep Your Way There" with the line: "You are so tired now." Which is an amazing first line, by the way – it plunges the reader directly into the deep well. In the same poem, the lines "You will never read all there is/ in the library of this dark." It's impossible to drink in the world wholly, to perceive the worlds in the world. But would you say exhaustion, giving up, even failure, is as close to perfection as we can come?

TL: It seems to me that failure runs through the project of intent – stirred seeing, necessary failure. The failure, for instance, of reason; of imagination; the failure of the project of satisfaction. Desire just rushes you into these losses and this, of course, feels uncomfortable, counterintuitive. You seem to be plucked out of yourself, set aside from yourself. If this is true (I think it might be) then what one might want to call grace or the daemonic wouldn't look at all graceful. It looks like deprival, itch, toppling, has the texture of a lit stupidity. Yes, giving up, but not as an elected state, not as concession. Instead, it's a matter of nothing working – the car doesn't start anymore – but the press of desire throughout this, desire increasingly unencrusted with visualization, anticipation, continues. The acceleration is sometimes sickening because the hurtling makes so little sense. So, exhaustion within the momentum of eros, giving up within that momentum. Let the telos, somehow, always be there for the hidden things, and then the failure will be good. It will add to the deposit of loneliness that drives the desire, the fuel of negation. Could one lose the feel of desire? Sure, I suppose so – and still be in the erotic drift – but I suspect this would be quite the labour. Just how deep does ascesis go? Just how negative can negative theology – where desire goes when pulled by some large thing it cannot name – be?

SL: Speaking of perfection . . . there is a line in a Charles Wright poem where he's looking out at his back yard, contemplating dead scattered leaves and the like, that goes: "Only perfection is sufficient, Simone Weil says./ Whew.../ Not even mercy or consolation can qualify." I've taken your books and Wright's books outside to read in the backyard at various times, and find the poems complementary. Do you read/admire Wright? Who are the poets to which you return and return?

TL: I read quite a bit and fairly widely. Where to begin in giving you a list of the writers I admire? Charles Wright, of course, Weil, Gary Snyder. This summer,

I'm reading again (and trying to write about) *The Cloud of Unknowing*. I also have been reading Richard of St. Victor's *The Twelve Patriarchs* and *The Mystical Ark*, the two books that drive *The Cloud*. Robert Bringhurst's Haida translations, his Ghandl book; some eastern European poets like Aleksander Wat and Vladimir Holan; Isaac of Stella; Yehuda Amichai; Leo Strauss on Plato; Pierre Hadot on Plotinus; a scholarly work on early Syrian monasticism; Jan Zwicky, Don McKay; Merton's later journals. I don't read a great deal of fiction, but I do like essays, books on mystical theology (treatises on eros). These last books are not the same as poetry but they feed in roughly the same way. Eugenio Montale entrances, Ikkyu, Osip Mandelstam, shimmering psychagogic books like Exodus, Isaiah, the Gospels, the middle dialogues of Plato, the *Odyssey*, twelfth century Cistercian writers, big talkers like Ginsberg and Li Bai: this is what my reading has been more or less in the last few years.

SL: What I love about Wright is his ability to casually shift registers and I also love his sauntering lines. In *Tourist to Ecstasy* you seemed more interested in a sort of full-tilt galloping intensity, and also with hitting multiple registers. Your poems in the next two books are still intense, they still shift, but more subtly. What happened to cause this change, or did it just happen? Put another way, how have your feelings about poetry, both the reading and writing of it, changed since you were in your twenties?

TL: The shift in style between *Tourist to Ecstasy* and *Moosewood Sandhills* just seemed to happen, as you say. I always go through a period of silence and confusion after a book – this depressed, shapeless time after *Tourist to Ecstasy* lasted a little better than a year. I was living north of Sault Ste. Marie during much of that year, on the shore of Batchawana Bay, and was experimenting with some new forms of address in poetry, and I felt they were getting nowhere (much later, however, I looked at them and liked them). I returned to Saskatchewan in the summer of 1990 (after having been away fifteen years), had a house on some land outside of Saskatoon and a new sort of work was coming to me. It made me quite nervous at first – too pared down, too slow, too tired – and I resisted it. I feel roughly the same way incidentally about the work I'm now doing, after a two-year trough following *To the River*: nervous, resistant, uncomprehending, fatalistic (this is all that's on offer) – both glum and excited.

      About the last part of your question: in my twenties I was more interested as a reader in the use of narrative poetry, anecdote. Much of the poetry published in Canada at that time – all of it, maybe – was built around a story, straightforwardly presented – decorated, deepened with small lyrical flourishes. I'm much less interested in the compositional power of the story now and very interested in – what? – penetration, prayer states, hearing into things. Obviously I'm not sure what to call it, but I'm amazed now by how self-evident it seemed to me twenty or so years ago that narrative was the only possible armature for poetry. It's not clear to me, though, what you get if you place intense listening, say, at the centre of the poem, or if you make the speed, the headlongness of language, the cohering force in a poem. Also, before, I saw poetry as chiefly individual poems and believed the function of these was essentially decorative – poems that caught your attention and seemed beautiful or clever.

Now I tend to see poetry as a probe, an instrument for homemaking, like philosophy, but more efficient at this than most of the philosophy that has been done over the last four hundred years. Poetry, when it's saturated with listening, is a residue, I now think, of the true way of doing philosophy, but if it ever "outed" itself as this, contemporary professional philosophy would attack it with its institutional white blood cells. Our culture is anti-erotic, anti-philosophical (even when doing philosophy), anti-metaphoric: it loves it when poetry is modest in its ambition. During my thirties, I read a great deal of Robert Lowell and his generation – John Berryman, Delmore Schwartz, Theodore Roethke, Elizabeth Bishop – and learned much from them.

SL: I'm a little reluctant to pose the next mandatory question which has to do with voice, and where you think yours came from, and why in heavens did you become a poet. I have a feeling that people become too preoccupied with this idea of voice. And whoever does think of becoming a poet? Maybe that's just my own particular frustration.

TL: I'm not really sure about voice – you sound as if you aren't either. I like the work of poets who seem swallowed by a particular obsession, who seem helpless before this, who seem not even to have much control over the speech the obsession orchestrates, and are drawn and drawn, and seem to lose the sense that they could be watched in this, that they should worry about how this transfixity might appear to others. There's a sort of innocence and intensity in their being lost in a preoccupation. I didn't plan to be a poet, though I've been trying to write since my early teens. Poetry is not the sort of vocation that would occur to a male growing up in working-class Regina in the late fifties and sixties, where hockey, fighting, general thuggery and eventually finding a decent job made up the usual range of possibilities. But I always liked the way words could hang together, floating, could find an incantatory stride and say something you knew was true but had never said. I'm not saying I have had a particular love for language. I'm not sure how such an affection would feel. I just kept wanting to say things that had a quick, intuitive aptness about them. Later, I had a desire to replicate musically some charge, some electrical leaping, I thought was in the world. So writing not as virtuousity or self-expression but as fidelity.

SL: Do you ever think of your poems as letters, love letters? In his introduction to your book of essays, *Living in the World as if It Were Home*, Dennis Lee called the essays love letters, and it seems that could go for the poems as well. Maybe all poems. The way that letters speak into a silence, and then the way you are both intimately connected to the writer at the same time as being violently separate. You've already likened your poems to long "speakings," which is a satisfying thought, but because they're also pollen-drenched, desire-filled ecstasies, I can't help thinking of them as love letters.

TL: Poems as love letters? Well, maybe. As fidelities, probes, adulatory mimeses, keenings, rages, headlongnesses: these names seem better. If poems in fact grow from a practice of listening, they are acts of self-overriding obedience. And it seems to me that if this is true, poems as obedience, a certain sort of poetry, core stuff, elemental, will vanish if what makes for fidelity (devotion, deference, sublation of self) isn't there. So you can't separate poetry from the contemplative life, which just makes the poverty of writing poetry all the greater. You never amass a bank account, and if you are foolish enough to believe you have, you are in danger of losing everything.

SL: Your poems, which are so much about looking, seeing, also inspire a silence in the reader. They're as full of listening as they are of looking. What does silence mean to the poem?

TL: Well, silence – and within the silence an alert craning – is what I think poems grow out of. Not-having is a form of silence, too, not feeling your hands encircle the language, sensing you are in the wrong place in what you are writing, not feeling pulled. Writing, for me, often starts back in these states of deprival. Then there's the silence that is deference to the otherness of one's experience, the otherness of things. I'm not much interested in observing the clumsy self-absorption of my naming: you can invite the other things to say what they are. Writing – thinking – as erotic passivity. What do you think of that? I have a question for you: why your occupation of others' voices? I like it. Why, though?

SL: Well . . . erotic passivity. I think that's an excellent way of looking at writing. Since my last book I've more and more thought of writing as being about wait-ing, and I've thought a lot about keeping the writing muscle working – a balance between these two. I'm always saying these words of Samuel Beckett in my head: "Try again. Fail again. Fail better." I admit I'm trying to write the perfect poem, and I don't know what it is. And what would happen if the per-fect poem were to occur? I guess the paper would spontaneously combust. I'm obviously reaching for the unreachable. And why not? I loved it when you said earlier that you were in a state both glum and excited which is pretty much where writing always deposits me, into this state – of devastation and ravish-ment. There's an impatience too in me though and some strange always-thought that I just might be dead tomorrow that leaves me unable to completely embrace passivity. Writing, I want to be in the deep well, but don't always manage to get there. That could have something to do with having a three-year-old running around the house.

The last couple of years I've spent looking at things – baubles, bric-a-brac, fruit, flowers – and writing about them. It's a way of taking a small amount of time (because this is what I have at the moment) to fall in love and become wildly delighted with a sliver or detail of the world. Anyway, after doing this I can't imagine writing poems again where I take on a voice. But then it seemed a natural thing to do. Because I'm intensely shy. Because it was a way of moving about, observing, looking outside of oneself and travelling without actually leaving the room. It was also a way of figuring out how to live as an artist, a female artist. I've worried a lot about *being* fraudulent, but then I'm still also intrigued by surfaces, by fakery, how we see, and by how things ring true, or not. I might some day return to the art forger somehow as a way of examining the worlds inside worlds. Maybe all the rest of my writing will be about the removal of masks . . . It's interesting to me to think of how writers come to their subject matter. Maybe it's accident, or whatever is there in front of you. I mean, if I hadn't married a still-life artist would I be so entranced by art and everyday objects? Would you be saying the same sorts of things some-how if you lived by the ocean and not a river? If you lived in a desert, say, or next to the San Diego Zoo?

TL: I've often thought how hard it would be to move and have to try to take up another landscape. It would involve learning another language, an extreme and maybe undoable apprenticeship. But "writing as being about waiting" – yes, yes – and I'm struck by how little one has if this is true. Sure, potentially the whole world, but nothing, absolutely nothing, to jiggle that potency into act (except maybe further poverty, but if you use deprival as an instrument, you're really screwed). So you stand there, nearly weightless (complaint has no substance), ontologically hybristic (you want everything), trying to keep the apparatus of the ear up and running.

I also like what you say about spending time being "wildly delighted with a sliver or a detail of the world." I imagine the weight of you going into a pear. The heft, the solidity of seeing – paper mâché pear or real – and the weight of the pear going into you. Everything seems to get more dense when this sort of minute, thick looking goes on. The act also strikes me as generous and politi-cal, coming down on the side of the reality of things – a pastime inevitably acknowledging, and unlike almost all other activities in late capitalism, where a sort of flect solipsism drains substance from the world, drains distance, there-ness, the discrete nature of things. Sure, where you're placed, in a marriage, by a river, lays down the lines for writing, or at least the latter has for me. The hard part is finding out where further to go when the river is finished with you.

SL: Your writing is obviously informed by Christian scholarship, steeped with it. I guess I'm tempted (or feel oddly compelled) to ask you a sort of biographical question related to your relationship to faith – how you moved from a United Church background to a Roman Catholic one and then to where you are now. But maybe a better question is how do you feel about the biographical intruding into the reading of poetry? For myself I'd rather skip it, but also admit to being semi-ashamedly interested in other poets' biographies. When I hear of a writer who has (or had) young kids I want to know, how are they negotiating that? Is there some part of the writer's life that you're in any way fixated on?

TL: About religious affiliation – I grew up in the United Church, but stopped attending in my teens. My late teens were convulsive, borderline hellish (though all this had a kind of benign inevitability about it) – drinking, drugs, psychiatric problems. I became a Catholic in my early twenties after a summer of reading John of the Cross, Walter Hilton, *The Cloud of Unknowing*, Thomas à Kempis and Merton – though it wouldn't be correct to say I read my way into the church – and I discovered that I loved the liturgy. In my late twenties, I became a Jesuit – I'm very glad for that. Right now, as practice goes, I'm undetermined. My reading is solidly in the Christian contemplative tradition, with buttresses touching Plato, the Pythagoreans and Weil, but I'm also interested in Lao Tzu and Chuang Tzu and Buddhist thought from the Tang period, and much else. I like biography, too – I sometimes read the contributors' notes in magazines before the poems and the stories, but I do rather struggle around talking about personal details.

SL: How important have reviews, awards been to your feelings about your work? Is competition healthy or unhealthy for a poet? I guess that there is no such thing as competition for you. In a poem in *To the River* called "Pitch" you say, "You must be this without knowing you are." You have to lose the self-consciousness. In another poem, "Slow World," talking about willows, "you walk into the thicket/ of the book and are poor." It seems to me that you couldn't see your way into this kind of poverty if you were preoccupied with competition. You've got to be pretty stripped down to write this kind of fall-on-your-knees stuff. Could you talk about the importance of friendships with other poets perhaps?

TL: Well, I do try to keep that volume – awards, reviews – turned as low as possible in my life, though a perceptive review can make a great difference – you feel heard. Friendships are far more important; what a handful of close readers make of my work, over the long run, is more significant for me than larger, public recognition. I believe the books, in the end, find whom they need to find.

SL: Do you ever look back at what you've written?

TL: I am always looking back on what I've written. I keep playing with the things, seeing if they'll walk further, declare more of themselves, step more out of where they're recessed. I'll sit with a poem for a year or more, not trying to rewrite really, but to hear it better. Where does it want to go? Letting the thing be feral and uncurl.

SL: Because I'm really obsessed by "things," and inspired to ask by a line in "There Is No Presence" ("What glitters in things is a mountain, it can't be held in the mouth."), is there any object you need, or rather like, shall we say, nearby while you write? Any rituals? And then the actual writing, pen to paper, which I think is always interesting. You once mentioned to me that your writing is "accretions." I've loved the thought of that – that your poems are built up like that. When I reread your poems, especially the last two books, I come across some knock-your-socks-off line and I think, "How could I have missed that?" Which is just the line resonating in a different way, I bet. And maybe that comes from the density and depths of the poems. Do you have an architecture in mind?

TL: I usually don't know where the poem is going when I start out, but I do often have a scent of the end – something pulls. I suppose this is what draws me to poems: the air can twitch with exigence. But the practice in which the poem or essay appears is bigger than any artifact that may rise in it, and more important. The product, however, almost inevitably claims the attention and the work sometimes can be retrieving this attention and placing it in the service of the ear, the waiting.

SL: "So nothing will ever be enough." (from "You Sleep Your Way There"). There's such tremendous fullness and consolation in such a line. Where will you go next? What obsesses? Where does your gaze fall? This is an obvious way to end the interview, talking about future work, but there's something to be said for getting to work. Annie Dillard quotes Chinese Chan Buddhist master Hongren: "Work, work! . . . Work! Don't waste a moment . . . Calm yourself, quiet yourself, master your senses. Work, work! Just dress in old clothes, eat simple food . . . feign ignorance, appear inarticulate. This is most economical with energy, yet effective." Have you ever noticed that your favorite writers have never written enough? If I wish I'd asked so many more questions, I console myself by sending you back to work!

TL: Thank you for the Hongren quotation. What am I up to these days? I'm working on another poetry collection that I'm thinking of calling "Kill-site" (these new pieces make me rather nervous) and a collection of essays on desire – half of these will be tight readings of Plato, The Cloud, perhaps Bernard of Clairvaux and others like John Scotus Eriugena: the rest of it will be more personal writing, more autobiographical in a way than anything I've done before. And I've just finished editing a book of essays by Dennis Lee, Don McKay, Robert Bringhurst and Jan Zwicky (I've contributed a couple of pieces, as well). It's called Thinking and Singing: Poetry and the Practice of Philosophy. It tracks for some way poetry's migration into what philosophy really is.

Following the Breath into Form

MIRIAM WADDINGTON

Interviewed by Barbara Nickel

Miriam Waddington was born in Winnipeg, grew up on the prairies, and has been writing and publishing poetry and criticism for fifty-seven years. Her books include *Apartment Seven: Essays Selected and New* (Oxford, 1989), *Collected Poems* (Oxford, 1987), and *The Last Landscape* (Oxford, 1992). She now lives in Vancouver.

Barbara Nickel's book of poetry, *The Gladys Elegies* (Coteau, 1997), won the 1998 Pat Lowther Award. She has poems forthcoming in *London Magazine* (UK) and the *Notre Dame Review* (US). She currently teaches in the Creative Writing Program at the University of British Columbia.

BN: In your essay "Mrs. Maza's Salon" in *Apartment Seven*, you write at length about your friendship, as a girl, with the poet Ida Maza and the influence of other poets prominent in the Yiddish literary world who frequented her salon in Montreal. As someone who didn't come to poetry until I was in my mid-twenties, I'm curious about your very early start. When did you actually write your first poem?

MW: I was in grade six at Machray School in Winnipeg, a public school. My teacher, Miss Jones, said to the class, "Write a poem about spring." So I wrote my poem – it rhymed *abab*. It was a ballad, I now realize looking back, about transformation. It was a story of a knight and his lady – there was a dragon. They came to a river, the knight and dragon had a battle, the knight was killed. The lady was wearing a mauve dress and she lay down and died of grief. Her dress became the violets. There was a girl in my class – there's always a girl like this in every class – who was the monitor, you know the type. She wore a navy tunic with pleats and a white blouse. She got to clean the blackboard and wash and hull the strawberries for the teachers' room, but Miss Jones read *my* poem out in class. She said, "That was a very good poem. You should keep writing." That was all I needed. I was off to the races.

BN: What kind of poems influenced you at that time?

MW: I remember liking ballads. My favourite was "Sir Patrick Spens." There's a wonderful image at the end – a ship with an entire court went out to sea and sank to the bottom. So there's a whole court at the bottom of the ocean seen through clear water: "Half owre, half owre to Aberdour/ 'Tis fifty fathoms deep./ And there sleeps good Sir Patrick Spens/ With the Scots lords at his feet." There were others – "Where have you been Edward, my son . . ." I love all ballads. They all tell a story and rhyme, and are always of human interest. What more do you want?

BN: What other poems influenced you?

MW: We always had poems in our reader at school, but when I really started to read poetry, I read Edna St. Vincent Millay and all the women poets.

BN: What was it about Millay that you admired?

MW: I read her when I was fourteen years old, perhaps twelve. I still think she's a good lyric poet. She's a good poet to start with, especially for romantic pre-teens. I admired her lyricism, her rhythm, and she was accessible. She didn't make herself obscure. I find women poets tend not to be obscure whereas male poets obfuscate meaning. Also men often have a deaf ear. Seldom do women. Although some women imitate male poets and so they have a deaf ear, too.

BN: When I read lines of yours like "Lady in the blue/ dress with the/ sideward
      smile,/ I see you at your/ easel in the field/ beside your house/ painting the
      blur/ of long ago summer . . ." ("Lady in Blue: Homage to Montreal"), I feel
      I'm connecting to a voice that is about a woman's particular understanding of
      the world. Do you prefer reading women to men?

MW: I always preferred reading women writers. I don't know why but I still do. For
      me they are easier to understand. Genders give people different interests.
      There's a bias in gender that you have to make allowances for.

BN: And perhaps learn from as well? The work of Coles and Heaney and Rilke and
      Lowell are by my side along with the women poets I always carry with me. Do
      you read male poets?

MW: Sure. I read Shakespeare often. He's the best of them. But at the moment, I
      can't think of any others. In terms of gender, I don't ask myself if it's a woman
      or a man but I just seem to gravitate to women poets. At readings, male poets
      are usually arrogant and proud of themselves and busy being peacocks and
      show-offs. Take a male poet on tour across the country. He's very proud of his
      achievement and he certainly shows it. Women are not like that. They may be
      proud of their achievements but they don't show it in the same way. I don't
      worry about it. I know I'm a good poet – I don't have to prove it to anybody.
      If you're insecure you feel you have to prove yourself, but that's a big waste
      of time.

BN: You've written extensively about the poet A.M. Klein. In your essay "Alone:
      Klein's Rocking Chair," you call his poem "The Portrait of the Poet as
      Landscape" capable of becoming "the autobiography for all Canadians."
      Would what you're saying about male poets apply to him?

MW: I suppose it's not fair to generalize. Klein was rather unusual. I never heard
      him read his poetry. But I heard him give many, many speeches.

BN: Klein brings me back to Jewish Montreal, Mrs. Maza's salon, and your youth
      in that poetic milieu. Did you have a sense early on of yourself as a poet?

MW: When I got to high school, my short stories and poems were published in the
      high school magazine. I didn't think of myself as a writer, but just someone
      who wrote stories and poems.

BN: I'm thinking of your poem "The Returner," with its regular but subtle rhyme
      scheme and rhythm, its secure sense of place: "There is the house of the sum-
      mer days/ With the last year's nest among the eaves/ And a skeleton heap of
      old dead leaves." Didn't you win a prize for that in high school?

MW: It was an arts and letters competition for the whole city. One of my teachers was writing poetry and entered the competition but I won. I felt really great about that. It didn't make a big difference to my poetry writing, but it felt great that the judge was Duncan Campbell Scott. I was only in the third form in high school – about grade ten.

BN: Were you ever taught to write poetry?

MW: I was never taught writing. But we had a very good music teacher. She taught us a lot of sea shanties, like "Way haul away, we'll haul away Joe." She made you love music. She was a great influence.

BN: As I mentioned earlier, I came to poetry quite late. I might never have pursued it had I not taken the M.F.A. Program in Creative Writing at UBC. It was a life-changing course of study for me. Do you think writing can be taught?

MW: It should never be taught. I think it's a terrible thing to have all these people around with degrees in creative writing from universities. It's just foisting a lot of wannabe writers on the world. And most of it is really bad writing. I don't believe in creative writing classes, although good things can happen in some classes – usually the good things have nothing to do with writing.

BN: In the many years you spent teaching English literature at York University, did you ever teach writing?

MW: I tried to avoid it. Once I had to teach it when another professor was away. In one class there was a boy who when I first met him had buckteeth . . . he was a mess . . . he couldn't write. But he told a story one day and got recognition from the class. He became a transformed person because of it – I've never seen such a transformation in a student. He really cleaned himself up. He was never a good writer but his teeth retreated and his storytelling was good. So something except writing came out of it. But I always hated teaching creative writing.

BN: Many of my questions are leading to a question I'll ask later about the origin of a poet's voice. Along these lines, I'm wondering if your parents encouraged you in your poetic pursuits?

MW: I didn't bother them with it. I didn't talk about it and my brothers teased me about it. At home we always had interesting visitors – Russians. They'd sit down at the table and there would be conversation and singing and lots of food – a typical Russian party. It was very jolly. My father had a good tenor and someone played the piano. I also belonged to a singing group. There was a teacher who ran that every Friday night. There was a lot of singing in my childhood and I think this encouraged my writing of poetry. We also had a lot of books in our house. My first language was Yiddish and we had to speak Yiddish at home. I went to a [Jewish] parochial school until grade four. I had wonderful teachers. We had classes in English in the morning and classes in Yiddish in the afternoon. And then there was Hebrew as a second language, which was always difficult.

BN: Did you write poems in Yiddish?

MW: No. I always thought in English and wrote in English. I had twin brothers. When they were four and I was six they couldn't speak English and I had to speak to them on the street in Yiddish. I remember being ashamed.

BN: That reminds me of my Mennonite family. My mother as a girl was instructed by her father not to speak German, her first language, on the streets of her Saskatchewan village during World War II. A common place in both of our experience is that we each come from distinct ethnic/religious groups. As a Jew, have you felt like an outsider in Canada?

MW: Always. Listen – I grew up hearing "Dirty Jew, dirty Jew" yelled at me by the Ukrainian kids in the alley. There was a hierarchy [in the schools] that most teachers observed. They didn't make any allowances for ethnicity as they do now. But I never noticed discrimination from teachers. Our teachers were good – most were Scottish immigrants.

BN: I've written poems about my experience as a Mennonite, mostly about the par-adoxical sense of entrapment and release I feel in that web of family and history and religious beliefs. In your work, I'm thinking of a poem like "Disguises" – "On Dizengoff Street in/ Tel Aviv you were the/ bearded Jew in sandals/ the profile of Abraham/ making history come/ true . . ." How do you write about your Jewish identity?

MW: I can't tell you. It's a big mystery. It should remain a mystery.

BN: Back to origins of voice. I gather that John Sutherland was a big influence. You even wrote an elegy for him in *The Season's Lovers*. Under what circumstances did you first meet him? How did he affect your life as a poet?

MW: He was the editor of a little stapled-together magazine called *First Statement*. He was a natural born critic at a time when there wasn't much criticism in Canada. There were two magazines – *First Statement*, which the Brits called "native" and *Preview*, which they called "cosmopolitan," mostly run by the British – P.K. Page was one of them. So *First Statement* was in Montreal, I was in Toronto. *First Statement* published some of my poems, and that's how I met

John Sutherland. We became good friends. We wrote to each other every day for a time, all about Canadian literature. I destroyed all those letters – I thought they were too impersonal. He had a sister, Betty Sutherland, who was married to Irving Layton. John and Betty ran *First Statement* together. They handset and published my first poetry book – 200 copies of *Green World*.

BN: What was publishing like in those days?

MW: It was very hard to get published. There were two publishers – Macmillan, who wasn't interested in poetry, and Ryerson. I was very lucky that Ryerson published my next book, *The Second Silence*.

There was a little magazine in Vancouver called *Contemporary Verse* edited by Alan Crawley. He was a wonderful editor and did a lot for Canadian poetry. He always wrote letters back about your poems. The magazine was mimeographed with printed covers. I don't think they paid poets back then. Maybe Alan Crawley did, and if he did, it was out of his own pocket. He wasn't a mentor, but he was very important to my poetry. He was a very good critic, in a general way . . . Dorothy Livesay and a group in Winnipeg later started *Contemporary Verse 2* when she was writer-in-residence there.

BN: That magazine, committed to a woman's experience, published my first poem. Did you have any significant female mentors?

MW: Dorothy Livesay wasn't a mentor to me in any way, shape or form. But we became good friends in 1941 when she first visited Toronto. Then in 1942 I took a trip by train with my bicycle across Canada and saw her again. We corresponded all our lives. We wrote about what we were writing, and about our lives.

BN: Did you send each other poems?

MW: Oh yes.

BN: Did you critique each other's poems?

MW: Not very specifically. I don't think we tore them apart – just commented generally. I have some of those letters and would like to publish them. Dorothy and I remained lifelong friends. We corresponded until she died.

BN: How did the war affect literary life in Canada in the 1940s?

MW: I don't think it touched us much. Raymond Souster joined the air force. He wrote me letters almost every day. But the war didn't affect funding because there wasn't any funding.

BN: I'm interested in your dual career as a social worker and a writer. As a musi-
cian and a writer, I've struggled with trying to find a balance between the two.
On the one hand, I write about music and so it feeds my writing, but on the
other hand, time spent involved in the musical life takes away from time I
could spend on my writing. Did you feel that your career in social work con-
flicted with or fed your writing life?

MW: Everything I did fed my writing life. A poem like "Journey to the Clinic" is an
example. I have written many poems that stem from my social work. I think I
always wrote about everything that was going on in my life – poems about
alcoholics, drug takers, people on the street.

BN: But how did you find a balance between social work, family and then teach-
ing full-time? How did you find the time to write?

MW: You always find the time. I don't know how or when. But I always wrote. I had
a lot of energy in those days.

BN: I'd like to move now to some of the technical aspects of your poetry. When I
first discovered the sonnet form, I felt somehow that I'd come home. Maybe it
was because I'm a violinist. The regular rhythm and rhyme felt like the rhythm
of music and reflected those themes of entrapment and release I talked about
earlier. So I wonder about your use of regular metre and rhyme in poems of
the first two collections. Say, a poem like "My Lessons in the Jail" – "Walk into
the prison, that domed citadel,/ That yellow skull of stone and sutured steel,/
Walk under their mottoes, show your pass,/ Salute their Christ to whom you
cannot kneel." What was it about the traditional stanzaic form that attracted
you?

MW: I never thought about imposing a form. It just happened. The poem has to find
its own form and I think that's the way it has to be. I think it's terrible to come
at something with a bunch of notes and then impose a form. Someone I knew
at Banff did that. And I remember someone else once writing a long letter to
me asking, "What form should I use?" This is really ridiculous. Form is not
separate from content, so you can't even discuss it. I never tried to write to
form. If I found that I wanted a certain form for a poem, it just came to me. I
realized then and still realize now that form is a whole big issue. But for me,
meaning was the most important thing, more important than anything.

BN: I feel that I have a different project than many of my peers because I write in
form. Was what you were writing, specifically the verse forms, a departure
from what your contemporaries were writing in the 1950s?

MW: I didn't pay much attention to what other people were doing. I read them all. But I just concentrated on writing from my own life experiences.

BN: Many have commented on the way your use of form changed in 1966 with *The Glass Trumpet*. L.R. Ricou, in the essay "Into My Green World: The Poetry of Miriam Waddington" in *Essays on Canadian Writing*, calls this your "most noticeable technical development." How would you describe this change?

MW: I started to break up the line.

BN: Why?

MW: No reason except that the poem demanded it. It was demanding its own form.

BN: What about the use of spaces instead of commas?

MW: Later I looked at those poems and thought that it was affected, but I can't change it now. I never gave a thought to form. If a poem doesn't find its own form, it isn't a good poem.

BN: Even when writing formal poems where the end of the line is determined by a rhyme pattern, I often will use that last word to turn the corner and drive me onto the next line. And I rely heavily on enjambment to try and keep a rhythmical flow through the sonnets. In a poem like "Provincial," which came after the big change in 1966, all of your lines are enjambed, with end-stops at the end of each stanza. Do you have a certain method of breaking the line and the stanza?

MW: It has to satisfy my eye and ear.

BN: How does rewriting work for you?

MW: I revised and revised and revised and I worked and worked and worked while I was writing. But once I was finished I left it alone. Sartre said, "Revision is the essence of writing" and I think that's true.

BN: Do you use a computer?

MW: I've never used a computer and I wouldn't compose on a typewriter either. I have to do it in longhand. I rework and rework and rework while I'm writing. Once I'm finished, I never go back. That really attacks the integrity of a poem. A poem has to find its own life and you shouldn't destroy that. You know when a poem is finished. A poem is a kind of act. It's an organic thing.

BN: In your essay "Poetry as Communication" in *Apartment Seven*, you mention, "the writing and reading of poetry is physical or physiological . . ." What do you mean by this?

MW: A poem is physiological. Of course, there are many complex factors involved. But the physiology of a poem involves rhyme and rhythm, your own voice, your breath, without you thinking about it. I didn't write a sonnet until later on in my life and then it just came naturally. I came to the end of the poem and realized that it was a sonnet. Form is not separable from content.

BN: I guess one obvious physical characteristic of a poem would be its voice. How would you describe the voice in your poems?

MW: I wouldn't even try. With some poets you can recognize the voice. Dorothy Livesay for instance had a soprano voice – a high-pitched voice. But I don't know any other poet as well as her. Voice is made up of a lot of elements. It's very hard to tell what goes into it. It's complicated. But it *is* physiological – it has to do with rhythm and breath. I don't have more than one voice. A voice must be characteristic – so that you can distinguish one poet from another. I never write in anyone's voice but my own. Browning tried to adopt different voices.

BN: That's a technique I've tried. Adopting another voice allows me to say things I wouldn't, perhaps, when writing in my own voice, while still exploring themes relevant to me. When involved in this, I've come back to reading "My Last Duchess" many times. Do you think Browning was successful?

MW: Yes, I think it worked for him. It's a good strategy for contemporary poets as well.

BN: Do you see a difference between your public and your private voice, say, the difference between a poem like "Green World," which feels more inwardly focused, and "My Lessons in Jail," which grew from your experience in social work?

MW: It's all part of experience. I never wrote about anything I didn't experience. Never.

BN: Another physical aspect of poetry would be its rhyme. How do you feel about it?

MW: I don't ever look for it. It happens by itself. I don't think you should struggle for it or artificially impose it.

BN: I think my process is the opposite. Struggling to get a rhyme scheme pushes me into a corner and I'm forced to search and search for a word that never would have surfaced had I not had the restriction of coming up with the rhyme. And then when the right word comes it's like a gift, and it can really direct the meaning of the poem. In those cases the physical, the musical aspect of the poem is actually leading the way. It reminds me of Rilke when he called rhyme "a goddess of secret and ancient coincidences" and said, "she is very capricious: she comes as happiness comes, hands filled with an achievement that is already in flower." But I feel that I have to struggle first to find that already-flowering achievement. Did you *ever* consciously write using rhyme?

MW: Maybe, when I first started. But not for a long time.

BN: I'm impressed at the number of composers who have chosen to set your poems to music, from Chester Duncan's setting for mezzo soprano and piano of "Sea Bells," to Ruth Watson Henderson's "Crazy Times," a work commissioned by the Toronto Mendelssohn Youth Choir that set five of your poems including "When the shoe is on the other foot for a change." How did this come about?

MW: I knew several composers. I went to Yaddo, an artist's retreat, and met composers. One or two read my poetry and decided to set it to music.

BN: In good songs, text and music work together to achieve a balance where neither medium dominates. There are song lyrics that could never stand without music, and there are poems that need to stand alone and could never fuse with music. What is it about your poetry that works with music?

MW: A lot of poets have a deaf ear. It just has to be musical, rhythmic – it has to follow your breath.

BN: I'd love to have my poems set to music but imagine I'd also be a little on edge at the performance – worrying that the balance I was just talking about wouldn't be achieved, that the music would overpower the words or vice versa. What is the experience of listening to performances of the fusion of music with your words?

MW: It's exciting. It's a translation into another medium altogether ... I'm fascinated by what composers do. Stephen Chatman at UBC has set a number of my poems into wonderful songs and I just love them.

BN: It must be very satisfying to have such interest in your work from composers. I was wondering how important reviews, awards, and other honours have been to your feelings about your work? Do you think competition healthy or unhealthy for a poet?

MW: Competition isn't healthy for anyone but recognition is very important. It means that someone is responding to your work. No experience is complete without a response. A response means you aren't writing into nothingness. It's very discouraging to write and never get a response. I'm sure I would have written more if I'd received more recognition. But I never courted recognition. I didn't want disciples and I didn't want to be a disciple. In the words of an old union song – "I want no bosses over me."

BN: I know what you mean about "writing into nothingness," especially in terms of the physical aspects of poetry we talked about earlier. For me, like music, a poem isn't complete until it's heard out loud. How do you feel about giving readings?

MW: I enjoy giving them. Back east I gave many readings to schools, at least twice a week. I really loved to read in schools. The students were always very responsive – I especially liked to read to grades nine and up. I would hate to read to an unresponsive audience.

BN: Did you ever experience this?

MW: Not that I can remember. A completely unresponsive audience would be hard to find.

BN: I want to move now to the question I was leading to before about the origins of voice. In his poem "The Dead Poet," Al Purdy, speculating on the origins of his poetry, asks "how else explain myself to myself/ where does the song come from?" Do you have any explanation of where your voice came from, of why you became a poet?

MW: No. It's a mystery and should remain a mystery. I'm not that interested in the creative process – that's for the professors to work out. Who knows where a voice comes from? You're born with it. It's a gift. You're very lucky if you have it. I've had a few gifts in my life. I was lucky to be born on the prairies. I was lucky to be a poet. I had some wonderful teachers. A good teacher responds to a certain quality in a student and encourages it. Like Miss Jones. And in Philadelphia at the School of Social Work I had two wonderful teachers who encouraged me as a person and as a writer. Teachers are very important in people's lives.

BN: I was also born and raised on the prairies, and so I'm particularly drawn to your poems about that landscape. In your first book, *Green World*, there's a poem, "Gimli," about the place in Manitoba where you spent time as a child: "I travel over you a swift railway track/ Spinning to Gimli's summer sudden beach." How do you remember Gimli?

MW: We always rented a cottage there, on Lake Winnipeg. To me, it was like an ocean. I remember bathing in the water, and found myself floating without ever being taught to swim.

BN: That reminds me of what you said earlier about a poem finding its own form, like the time you wrote a sonnet without trying. Was your poetic process something like learning to swim?

MW: Yes, I think so.

BN: Do you miss the prairies?

MW: Yes. When I die, my ashes will be scattered on the prairie outside of Winnipeg. It [the prairie] teaches a good lesson – honesty. There are no barriers to seeing what's there. The lesson of the prairies is honesty, openness, clear vision.

BN: How have your feelings about poetry, the reading and writing of it, changed since you were in your twenties?

MW: I don't think much has changed. They've only deepened, only intensified.

BN: Perhaps one thing for poets that doesn't change is the way poetry seems to always permeate all aspects of life. As you said earlier, everything you did fed your writing life. How does this affect life as one gets older? Doctors retire, bankers retire – do poets?

MW: I'm sure not. I'm always writing.

BN: What are you working on now?

MW: I'm writing some very good poems called "Songs of Old Age." But I haven't sent anything out since 1992.

BN: Why not?

MW: No time, no energy. There's a lot involved in sending out. I have enough to worry about keeping track of my pills.

Going Down to Where the Roots Begin

ERIC ORMSBY

Interviewed by Carmine Starnino

Eric Ormsby was born in Atlanta, Georgia, grew up in Florida, and resides in Montreal, where he is a professor at the Institute of Islamic Studies at McGill. His poetry has been published in four collections, including *Araby* (Signal/Véhicule, 2001) and *For a Modest God* (Grove, 1997), and in journals such as *The New Yorker, The New Republic, Paris Review, Descant* and *Parnassus*.

Carmine Starnino is a Montreal poet and critic who has published two collections: *The New World* (Signal/Véhicule, 1997) which won the 1998 Gerald Lampert Memorial Award, and *Credo* (McGill-Queen's, 2000), which won the CAA Prize for Poetry. *A Lover's Quarrel*, a book of criticism on Canadian poetry, is forthcoming from Porcupine's Quill.

CS: Why the long wait in publishing your poems?

EO: I might say, "Why the rush to publish?" It's better to wait and let time sift your work. The fact is I've always written for purely personal reasons. I never thought of writing as a "career." I was even rather embarrassed by it; it was like a secret vice I was ashamed to disclose but which I couldn't stop indulging. Then too I'd always kept my writing separate from my professional life, in the beginning as a librarian and administrator and then as professor. When my poems first came out and attracted a little notice, I was deeply uncomfortable. My fellow administrators greeted the news with about as much elation as if they'd learned I had herpes. On a deeper level though, it was, had always been, a precondition of my writing that it be a strictly private endeavour.

CS: Circumstances weren't so different for me. Many older Italians I knew regarded my literary ambitions with great suspicion. To the immigrant sensibility, writing – indeed, all art – is seen as a leisure activity. My parents, God bless them, have been supremely supportive, but I must say that there are other family members, mostly men, who continue to dismiss what I do as an effeminate whimsy. But I'm curious: what finally drove you to make your writing public?

EO: A very good friend of mine – the friend, in fact, who first got me writing poetry seriously, back in 1958 – died quite suddenly and unexpectedly in 1982 and left behind his own unpublished poetry. He hadn't tried to publish anything either. It wasn't until I began sending his work out to magazines that I realized how difficult the whole process really was. Eventually I did succeed in getting a number of his poems into print, but I began thinking that I had better send out my own work. I started submitting poems to various magazines: of course, most of them were rejected. But one day, after a year or so of trying, two finally were accepted by *Chelsea* magazine in New York. For about five or six years after that, I sent work out week after week, partly in order to understand what the situation actually was in the "world of poetry," as I now heard it called, as distinct from "poetry" itself – another often quite incompatible realm. Editors returned poems for the strangest reasons or they accepted them for even stranger reasons – poems I hadn't expected anyone to like! The first poem I had published in *The New Yorker*, in 1989, was one of these seeming anomalies. I wrote "My Mother in Old Age" as a poem for my mother and only stuck it into the submission to fill out the envelope. But not long before that I had written a sequence of poems that I recognized immediately as good: these are the Lazarus poems in my first book and they represented a turning point for me. I sent them to *Shenandoah* which took four of the five. The fifth I placed in *The Quarterly*.

CS: Funny, I wouldn't have thought of the Lazarus poems as a turning point.

EO: I was dealing with a notion that was close to me: the sense that though I had written for so long – almost 25 years by then! – I had not really emerged, and that these poems signified a coming back to life. A resurrection, even if a reluctant one. In those poems I also began for the first time to find a voice all my own.

CS: Let's talk a bit about that voice. In "Origins," for example, you declare that you want "to go down to where the roots begin,/ to find words nested in their almond skin,/ the seed-curls of their birth, their sprigs of origin." I've always found those lines to be a terrifically rich declaration of intent – that of retrieving the raw, original potency of words.

EO: Well, yes, the idea in "Origins" is that words have a pristine origin to which I'm trying to return. But the poem also crystallized attitudes I had held for a long time about the past. In the poem, for example, there's the line: "At night the dead set words upon my tongue." I had always believed that poetry comes out of one's connection with the dead and that words are a gift to you from them, like heirlooms handed lovingly down and yet, unlike heirlooms, vividly alive. Perhaps this reflects the fact, too, that I grew up in a house that was steeped in the shadows not of forgotten, but of disappointed, ancestors.

CS: Disappointed?

EO: As a child I was made aware of grandparents, of aunts and of uncles, of cousins, who had had vast aspirations which were always somehow defeated in the end. Remember, my own grandfather grew up during Reconstruction in the South and though he was an unusually genial man, always felt that he had been denied opportunities to succeed and better himself. I grew up amid anecdotes of his impoverished childhood, as well as of the schemes and failures of others, such as my grandmother's own father, an Englishman transplanted to Tennessee who failed at practically everything he touched. One of his plans, for instance, involved growing hops, of all things, on the Cumberland Plateau where all the inhabitants were notorious teetotallers. Hops! An utterly useless crop in that place and at that time, and of course he went bankrupt, much to the amusement of his neighbours. His folly is still a source of comic legend in that region of Tennessee. As a child I picked up a strong sense of my forebears' disappointment. Perhaps I hoped to accomplish something as a way of vindicating them. Still later, when I became a Catholic, the Church's doctrine of the Communion of the Saints – the teaching that every soul is still living though in an unseen dimension – worked a strong influence on me.

CS: That's really interesting. As you know, I've conceived of much of my poetry as a salute to my Old World legacy. Fundamentally what I'm trying to do is find ways to surprise the reader, to take what is culturally so familiar to me and give it back – as Seamus Heaney writes – "with a clean new music in it." But I can't say that my decision to have a go at the immigrant subject involved such a powerful sense of responsibility. It was really done out of a kind of opportunism. As poets, we always want to write the sort of poems that flatter our sense of what a poem should be. Being a big fan of Heaney, I wanted, like him, to write earth-reeking poems and was lucky enough to come from a race of earth-reekers. Do you still trust in that doctrine?

EO: I don't know if I still believe that, but it did help keep my motives in perspective. That's why, in my view, poetry ultimately has nothing to do with publication or prizes or acclaim. Because I'm writing not merely for the immediate reader but also for those with whom I can no longer communicate directly, those whose own aspirations once affected me deeply.

CS: And as for your voice?

EO: As for "voice," I've always understood this quite literally. When I wrote my first poems way back in the summer of 1958, I could hear, if I listened with the utmost attention, a strange sort of talking in my head that had nothing to do with my speaking voice and which demanded an almost trance-like attention on my part. I can even remember the July day and the room where I was standing when I first became aware of it. I recognized then that this was my "daemon," in the Socratic sense. So from the beginning writing entailed the utmost attention followed by a struggle to transcribe that innermost voice. By "transcribe" I mean finding a style in which to reproduce that interior summons literally. It took me years. Nowadays the voice is becoming harder to hear, or perhaps I am growing deafer to it.

CS: Would you say, then, that there's a spiritual premise to your poems?

EO: Yes, not perhaps in any doctrinal way although I was a practicing Catholic for a long time. I began writing on a daily basis over twenty years ago initially as a "spiritual exercise" for Lent. This entailed writing and finishing a new poem every day for forty days. I wanted to realize what Kafka meant when he spoke about "writing as a form of prayer." It was a wonderful discipline, and my first two collections have several poems which were written in this way.

CS: I was once a practicing Catholic as well – in fact I was headed straight for the seminary! – and while I don't believe in the sufficiency of a religious life anymore, I do recognize great creative opportunities in its myths and rituals. Much of the challenge in writing Credo, for example, was finding ways to appropriately translate the experience and vocabulary of those religious convictions.

Most importantly, I wanted to write poems that could credit the instinctive religiosity of working with words, the notion of writing as worship.

EO: I too believe that there's a sacramental sense in my poetry, and I hope my language exhibits that quality: that of words vibrating over many octaves and possessing transformative power. I believe quite strongly in what Baudelaire called "correspondences," the conviction that things are not only what they appear to be in themselves but that they correspond to something else, either from within the mind or within another realm. This has always governed my poems about plants or animals.

CS: You've shown more sympathetic fascination for animals and plants – they appear in your poems with greater distinctiveness, eccentricity and poise – than people. Why is that?

EO: People are difficult to write about well in verse – especially in verse that aspires to be densely textured and musical. Chaucer and Browning and of course Shakespeare are the great exemplars. But in my own smaller way, that's what *Araby* represented: an effort to write poems about people, poems that are both authentic and memorable. I've always been drawn to nature and taken inspiration from it. I grew up in Florida, a paradise for a child. All year round you have flowering plants, sunshine, swamps, forests, jungles, the Everglades, the ocean! But while writing about natural things isn't easy, it's easier than creating a credible character. When I started writing seriously about nature, however, I suddenly realized that I was also writing about myself, only obliquely. The poems which worked best were those in which I had left myself out, but in which, using some outside object, I was writing about human life, my life. A colleague who read my first collection said to me that I really should stop writing about "weeds and grasses" and tackle something important like "the failure of my marriage." What he didn't realize was that I had tackled that very topic but had expressed it at a remove through a series of intense verse meditations on the lives and forms of various plants or animals. Now, with *Araby*, I have begun to work my laborious way upward along the evolutionary chain from lichens and wood fungus to camels, vultures, baboons, and finally, humans! *[laughter]*

CS: What was the intention behind the representational zest of your nature poems?

EO: My original and governing impulse was to look at a thing, to look at it absolutely, and then to try to say something about its essential nature, whether a pickerel weed or a sea shell or a grackle or my mother's face. For a long time and certainly during the writing of my first two books, and even perhaps my third, I believed that description alone, if done accurately, could stand by itself. After all, things in life, in nature, don't come to us freighted with commentary or directions, at least in the first pristine instant of encounter. For me everything you needed to know about the subject, not only factually but also *emotionally*, would be implicit in the description, if the description were unswervingly faithful. Isn't this what Flaubert tried to do in prose? To present a scene or a character or an object – remember Emma's parasol or Charles's grotesque school cap? – with such fidelity that it not only hovers before the reader's eyes but carries an irresistible emotional charge that comes with the revelation of its innermost nature? Such writing requires a terrific intensity of concentration and this is hard to sustain. There were some poems of this type on which I spent two or more years, my mullein poem, for example. I put it through incessant revision; the drafts and notes dominate my notebooks of that period, during which I constantly looked at and studied the plant in different seasons, photographed and sketched it, tried stubbornly to inhabit it. Though I was in part inspired by Rilke and his *Dinggedichte*, "thing-poems," I went far beyond this, in the end, to an obsessive intensity that I now find a bit frightening.

CS: So what's the project now?

EO: I have almost completed a fifth collection of poems, many of them quite wacky; these are the poems on various household utensils, like the one about the whisk that appeared in *The New Yorker* earlier this year. This book also contains a tragic poem on the potato and a wildly erotic one on the vacuum cleaner – a first in poetry, I believe – as well as a bizarre folkloric sequence drawn from the fairy tale of Rumpelstiltskin. This last project I began around 1984 and it has been simmering ever since. But my main project is what I call my "Big Book," the book in which I want to do everything of which I am capable in poetry and attempt some things I may not be capable of. The book is called *Time's Covenant* – the phrase is from Eliot's *Four Quartets* – and is centred on a mythical utopian settlement named Covenant. It is a town, and a book, teeming with characters who appear in numerous guises, in daguerreotypes and snapshots, in letters and journals and albums, in glimpses from kitchen windows, and who reappear over time in all the disguises which time drapes us in as we grow and age. I have the ambition to do something which is quite common in the novel but rare in poetry. I've always loved the device, which occurs throughout Balzac or Proust or Faulkner or Anthony Powell, by which a particular personage pops up, disappears and then resurfaces over some interval of time in the course of the narrative. Such recurrences not only give a sculpted and three-dimensional portrait of a person but also create the felt sense of the passage of time. This is among the aspects of the novel which I most admire but which poetry almost never attempts.

CS: Maybe in the epics?

EO: Yes, you have it in the epics. In Dante or Virgil, neither Aeneas nor Dante is
      the same personage at the end of his journey that he was at the outset. Homer,
      of course, does this. As for giving a sense of time passing, think of the famous
      scene in which Odysseus's dog Argos, grown old and frail, recognizes him
      after twenty years. The full impact of his long absence is felt at that instant.
      But it is hard if not impossible to express the actual passage of time in a poem,
      especially in a lyric poem, though it has been done brilliantly by a few poets
      – Eliot, in particular, but also Yeats. Express it, that is, so that the reader leaves
      the work with the sense of having himself *experienced* time. Then too a novel
      depends upon the novelist's skill in handling all the pedestrian transitions of
      the characters from one place, or time, to the next. Paul Valéry wrote that he
      could never be a novelist because he couldn't bring himself to write such a
      sentence as "The marquise went out at five o'clock." In a narrative poem too
      this can easily degenerate into padding. But the real question is whether a
      poem can recreate the sense of lived time, and this is what I am attempting to
      do in the "big" book. It's already well over a hundred pages, and there are
      swarms of characters but I still have to devise credible ways of uniting and
      linking the sequences.

CS: You mentioned Flaubert, Proust, Balzac and Valéry. I know of your admiration
      for Ponge – whom I adore – and Baudelaire. What is it about French literature
      that attracts you?

EO: French has always been important to me. My great-grandmother was French
      and my grandmother still spoke French a bit at home and said her prayers at
      night in French. Our bookshelves were full of French novels which always
      intrigued me as a child because of their brittle pages that broke off in my fin-
      gers and their indecipherable titles. Later, when I learned French well as a
      teenager I began reading the literature with an explorer's passion. My first
      great "discovery" was Baudelaire and I memorized almost all of *Les Fleurs du
      Mal* in the original. He had a huge influence on me. I loved the way he was
      able to condense immense experience – whole lifetimes, as Flaubert said of
      him – into a single line. The density of his lines intrigued me. It was the same
      with Virgil a bit later, that sense of language made molten and slowly cooling
      as you encounter it. Then there were Villon, Hugo, Mallarmé, Rimbaud,
      Apollinaire, and later, for a long time, Claudel and Valéry, both of whom I still
      consider the greatest French poets of the past century. But also Ponge and
      Michaux and Supervielle and many others. At times I became so steeped in
      this tradition that I fancied myself a French poet condemned to write in
      English.
            But other languages, and other traditions, have always been important
      too. I studied several languages in order to read the poetry: Arabic and Persian,
      of course, but also Italian, Spanish and German and more recently, thanks to
      my wife Irena, Czech. In college I majored in Greek and Latin, and I still know

much of Sappho by heart in Greek. These studies gave me the odd sensation at times that English was rather an impoverished language and, quite definitely, that too much contemporary poetry in English was paltry and anorexic.

CS: You've spoken often about English poetry's feeble state, often attributing the cause to certain "limits" that we've pre-programmed, as it were, into our verbal ingenuity, thereby hobbling it. But are there things that *can't* be expressed in poetry?

EO: Dante thought so – he struggles with that problem in the *Paradiso*. Certain things seem to be inexpressible, but maybe that is because we are still incapable of expressing them. Like everyone else I have intuitions and premonitions and what Henry James called "glimmerings" every day, which I doubt that I could formulate in poetry. But I wonder, is this the drawback of poetry or of myself? I am sure that it is the latter; I have the strong presumption that anything which we can feel we can also express, if only because language and feeling are inextricably bound up with each other.

CS: How have your feelings about poetry, the reading and writing of it, changed since you were in your twenties?

EO: In my twenties I read and wrote poetry with greater single-mindedness and perhaps with a more passionate intensity but I lacked the discipline and the restraint necessary for creating a fully finished poem. I wrote wildly and often well, I think, but in a more fragmentary, sporadic and scattered manner. I have a fat trunk full of my earlier effusions which I peek into occasionally and it both startles and oppresses me. I keep in mind what the Persian poet Hafiz wrote, "Love at first seemed easy, and then the problems began." It is the same with writing poetry. As the problems begin you must respond in a more complex and subtle way than you did at first but what you lose in intensity you gain in depth.

CS: How about the issue of recognition? Has that been a concern since you've started publishing? I myself have begun wondering about this idea of "fame," not in the sense of reputation, mind you, but in the sense that Keats talked about it: the Parnassian idea of eternity, of being remembered as long as the language exists. That's not a sensible thing to admit to nowadays, I know, but tell me: reviews, awards, have these been important to your feelings about your work? Is competition healthy or unhealthy for a poet?

EO: I've received very few reviews and even fewer awards. Happily the reviews have almost all been intelligent. These have taught me much about my own work, about aspects of it, for example, of which I was unaware, not to mention the faults, the excesses, in which I've indulged. The usual criticism, often all too accurate, is that I push the language too far; you yourself have pointed this out, though I seem to remember that you liked this tendency.

CS: I did – and do. I certainly see the risks, but I also recognize that those risks, in their full flourish, have helped you to secure some persuasive effects.

EO: In the end I've been awfully lucky in my reviewers, both Canadian and American; their enthusiasm for my work has made up for their scarcity. Awards I consider largely destructive, particularly for the recipients but also for those who don't win. Of course, we all want to be recognized and prizes appear to confer recognition. But unfortunately, the winner of an award invariably feels that he or she has been justified. Not only may this be wrong – in fact, it all too often is – but awards persuade poets to repeat themselves, to cease to grow, since they are always hoping to regain the plaudits they received earlier. And even though losing is not as bad as winning, the losers often feel absurdly devastated.

CS: Yes, as poets we can be a pretty doleful bunch. This is the sort of thing no one warns you about, how so much of one's life as poet may likely be bound up in bitterness: bitterness at the rejections, at the bad reviews, at the "insult" of being passed over and ignored. Archibald MacLeish said something once I've never forgotten: "Believe in your own work. No poem was ever suppressed – if it *was* a poem. Belayed, yes. Muffled. Ignored for a generation or a century. But not suppressed." I console myself with that. But how do you accommodate that kind of thinking with the competitive impatience to have your career happen *right away*? You don't, obviously. You just hope that it happens sooner rather than later.

EO: Except that more and more young poets (and some old ones too) write now with their eyes on this or that prize. This is poisonous. As for competition, I think it was Bartók who remarked that competition is for racehorses, not for artists. I share his view.

CS: Do you feel part of the scene in this country?

EO: No, not at all. I came to Canada when I was forty-five. Though I became a Canadian citizen and genuinely love Canada, I recognize that I'll never feel "Canadian," even if I'm not always sure what that means! You have to grow up with this or imbibe it early on – it can't be force-fed later.

CS: Yet your poetry, in its robust verbal alertness, has much in common with Canadian poets like E.J. Pratt, P.K. Page, Tim Lilburn, A.M. Klein, Peter Van Toorn, David Solway and Michael Harris. Do you feel more comfortable being considered an American poet?

EO: No, although I do think that I respond as a poet more in what I understand to be an American way. Many of my themes are explicitly "American" – for example, in my sequence in *Coastlines* on my Florida childhood. And yet, that book also contains a suite of poems on Nova Scotia. My dual identity, or dual self-confusion, is something I have in common with Clark Blaise, another writer I admire who seems caught between two identities – who has a superfluity of identities, or none. But in America I no longer seem to fit in either.

CS: Why do you say that?

EO: America has begun to seem unfamiliar to me, at times nearly alien. The America with which I still identify passionately is the America of a different time. I grew up with a decided hankering for the nineteenth century, maybe because of my grandmother who was still strongly rooted in that time. I inhabit a mythical or remembered America in my imagination and inevitably, that doesn't coincide with present-day reality. I feel a bit as if I were Rip Van Winkle having a long dream about America. Of course, not surprisingly, given this perspective, I don't write in a currently fashionable manner. Possibly too because I began publishing later in life I'm now categorized in a different way than I might have been had I published at twenty-five. Still, I don't say this to complain. I've always very deliberately kept myself apart from those considerations which struck me as dangerous. And it was only after coming to Canada that I became involved in any literary scene, if you can call what I do being "involved."

CS: Why dangerous?

EO: For me the main obstacle to writing well has always been self-consciousness. I have always had to devise tricks to fool myself into forgetting what I was doing. The critic inside you must be distracted momentarily if you are to write anything original or distinctive and I have invented dozens of ways to distract that intimate enemy at the crucial moment. If I were conscious when writing that X or Y or Z would eventually read it, or that the poem might appear in this journal or that, it would be hard, if not impossible, to face the blank sheet of paper with the necessary spirit of adventure.

CS: Speaking of consciousness, something struck me when I was going over some your work, and I'd like to read some lines out to you. "Gazing at Waves": "the horizon glitters like an eye/ peeping through a sleepy eyelid." "Mutanabbi Remembers his Father": "Sometimes, half in sleep, when the dreaming mind/ confuses past and present smokily." "December": "[a]t night,/ our dreams infringe and pool,/ our common terrors shake us in sleep." "Wood Fungus": "if you pry them from their chosen oak,/ they seem shut fast, like the eyes of sleepers." Your essay "Questions for Stones": "the infinite delineations of the sand dunes, which move their slopes and crests incessantly like a troubled sleeper twitching his covers all night long . . ." Why the obsession with sleep?

EO: What magnificent lines! Did I write those? *[laughter]* Frankly, I hadn't noticed all the multiple allusions you've brought together so perceptively. When I started writing poetry every day, I discovered that if I wrote when just out of sleep, I was able to come up with interesting, sometimes highly bizarre, images that I would not have discovered otherwise. Sleep and dream became my muses. But more prosaically, I have always had trouble sleeping, even in childhood, and so sleep appears to me as a charmed and privileged state. Like the ancients or like the early Arabs, I regard dreams, even the horrendous ones, as gifts from somewhere else. Of course, intelligence inhibits the half-waking dream-state. Sometimes you have to trust in the magical nonsense your drowsy brain produces. You can assess and refine it later.

CS: Here's another: "If only recollection could cohere! If only/ memory were cogent once again!" You've always had this acute sense of the vaporousness of memory – so much so that I often wonder if the verbal density of your poetry isn't a compensatory act.

EO: I like the words in my poems to have the texture and the density that things possess. In this I admire Celan, however uneven his late poetry is. His words are like shards you pick up from the ground, like nuggets or chunks of ore. They're thick and veiled and impenetrable. They possess a material character; they aren't mere instruments of "communication," as his interpreters like to think. As for the compensatory act, that's interesting. In my second book, which I wrote in the house in Florida where I grew up, I found myself over-whelmed by the past. I understood then that nostalgia was not that mildly agreeable state of reverie we sometimes allow ourselves, but that it could be toxic. Nostalgia can paralyze. You begin to think of the past as fixed but, as I realized, it is not. The past is continually changing and revising itself even as – perhaps because – you are trying to recover it. I came to realize that not even the past was set forever, and this realization was at once painful and liberating.

CS: So, as poet, what do you trust in that situation?

EO: You cling to form. Form isn't merely an adornment. Form is not extrinsic. Form has to arise out of the necessity of the subject. The subject can dictate a sonnet or it can demand free verse but whatever form is chosen must be true to its origin in the subject. I have no sympathy for the "New Formalists" who write villanelles to show that they can do so. The poem has to assume the shape proper to it, and its form, like its language, has to be newly minted, even if it's been done thousands of times before. Form is all that we have. Form is the only means by which I can give you a sense of what my experience has been, or you can give me yours. Mere description isn't enough. Form is what allows an experience to be so objectified that another can enter it as you yourself did. A poem must not be shapeless but rather, possess a unique shape acting, as Coleridge said, under laws of its own devising. The laws can be self-generated but they must be palpable. If you pick up a poem by Geoffrey Hill, you know that this poem, whether you like the poem or not, has been cast into its form out of necessity; an aura of inevitability hovers over it.

CS: Yes. Very few experiences are, in themselves, interesting. Many poets think that if the subject is significant, the poem is significant. I often wonder, though, why poets treat this idea – the idea of form as the corroborating force in conveying experience in a poem – so disdainfully.

EO: Perhaps because it involves renunciation. You have to forgo immediate feedback. You have to resist displaying the poem until it has taken on its proper shape. You must be willing to renounce gratification, often for a long time, for the sake of making a work of art. I think of form as the ultimate way in which civilized people convey something to one another. It's a courtesy, an aesthetic courtesy. If someone presents me with the inchoate blob of his own experience, why should I care? There needs to be artisanal pride and respect for your reader. If poets were carpenters and made chairs the way many of them today write poems we'd all be sitting in a heap of splinters on the floor.

CS: What are some of the things you look for when you read a poem?

EO: First, if the language has texture. Which is why I responded so immediately to your own "Cornage" sequence. It was instantly apparent that here was a verbal density and a texture that were gratifying and intriguing. Then, a tension must be present in the poem that is quite separate from the dynamic congruence between sound and meaning; there has to be some provocative interplay within and among the words themselves. As if there were a magnetic current of repulsion and attraction in the words, in the sounds. In the poetry of Yeats, where this current flows constantly, the lines have a coiled and tensile energy. If that complex charge isn't there, and it usually isn't, there may of course be something else of interest; the poet may have some wit or humour or insight and present it with skill. That's of value too. But generally, if the language doesn't catch me, I don't read on.

CS: I agree. For me, a poem's first duty is language, and to the joy that gives language its ardor and abundance. Interestingly, however, I've found – and I don't know if it's the same for you – that I read poetry differently when I'm asked to write about it. Not that I look for different things, but that my attention to a poem's ideas, my sensitivity to its sounds, is more concentrated. The effort of writing critically frees me to think – and react – with greater clarity.

EO: Yes, when you write about poetry you can't remain content with your own subjective pleasure. You have to find a way in which to communicate that pleasure to another reader. I don't believe that there aren't objective criteria for judging poetry. Quite the opposite: while it's sometimes true that you cannot explain the secret of certain great poems or lines, you can always explain why one poem works well and another does not. Also, when I read as a critic I try to rid myself of my preconceptions as best I can. I'd always loved the poetry of Eugenio Montale, for example, but when I was recently asked to write about him I ended up spending over a year on the project. I had to read in a more concentrated way. As a result I began to understand aspects of his work that I had not even noticed before. While I like his verse as much as ever, I now see it quite differently. This is a valuable process and quite different from the kind of reading you do as a poet.

CS: What do you respond to first as a critic?

EO: Whether the work is honest. I believe in the correspondence theory of truth as Aquinas defined it: *Veritas est adaequatio rei et intellectus.* Truth requires some actual correspondence between intellect and thing, between word and thing, an "adequation" – to mangle the Latin! – of the mind and the object it apprehends. For me dishonest poetry, or prose, is untrue to the phenomenon it addresses. Writers who have garnered too much attention tend to fall easily into dishonesty; they pander to the taste that rewarded them by repeating *ad nauseam* whatever style or tone or mannerism first made them celebrated. Having been rewarded for a certain kind of work they keep repeating it rather than going further into new or uncertain or venturesome topics or styles. These are the poets whom their sycophants keep terming "avant garde" and "daring" and "cutting edge," but they deserve none of these epithets. They write the way a pasta machine extrudes noodles.

CS: Has the critical writing helped you as a poet?

EO: Not really. I was always quite critical of myself, too much so. But critical writing has taught me the value of deletion. I've become very fond of cutting out things. Amazing how much it can improve a poem! I find that hard, though, because my ultimate model in English is Shakespeare who is incredibly abundant. But to tell you the truth, Carmine, I do not honestly feel that the two, poetry and criticism, are compatible. I am sure that if I stopped writing prose I would write more poetry.

CS: Ah, well, that's where I'll have to part ways with you. I definitely feel that all my critical writing has accelerated my apprenticeship as poet. I don't think it's necessarily made me a better poet, but after spending so much time trying to depict the success or failure of other poets, I find that my instincts are sharper, my intuitions more alert, when I return to my own work. But why do you do it, Eric? If there's an artisanal pride in writing poetry, is there an artisanal duty in writing criticism?

EO: Yes. There's a duty. Writing criticism is important because the standards by which works of art are judged today are appallingly low. Good poetry can't flourish where bad standards prevail. Look at what garners acclaim, the squalor of the work, the pretension and sham! If we had good criticism we might have better poetry. Yet most reviews in North America are too easy: they tend to praise when they should criticize. Worse, Canada doesn't have a large enough number of good venues for publishing essays and reviews. Still the chief problem here is the lack of a good critical sense, or the fear of exercising it. If anybody comes along and is critical of a work – as you yourself have often done – it causes consternation, because people are not used to it. But there should be consternation; unthinking praise is not only meaningless, it is harmful. The situation is not much better in the US. I was told, for example, that reviewers for *The New York Times Book Review* are instructed not to write negative reviews. And it's true that you rarely do see a negative review there. I don't think that negative reviews are automatically good but the reader of a review should have the confidence that the reviewer is employing at least some critical acumen. In any case, to get back to your question, many poets I admire wrote fine criticism – Coleridge, or Eliot, for example.

CS: Eliot's point, though, was that as a critic one also argues for the kind of poetry one wants to write. Do you believe that?

EO: Yes. I do have an aesthetic and criticism is one medium by which I can promote it. In verse too, I try to exemplify the writing I admire, but people don't appear to notice that aspect of the poetry. That's good: I don't wish to be a programmatic or tendentious writer; nothing could interest me less. Of course, most people would rather read a book review than a poem – who can blame them given what's touted as good? Through criticism then I may be able to reach a wider audience.

CS.   And you still feel that you're open to other kinds of writing?

EO: I try to be open but I don't always succeed. There are poets and whole "schools" of poetry which are admired by many but in which I see little of value. Olson, bp Nichol, the Black Mountain poets, for example. In the sixties I endured so many readings of that amazingly forgettable verse. I kept thinking that I must be wrong to find it unappealing. Now I think otherwise. If one of their admirers could explain to me what beauty or wit or relevance he finds in their work, I would be prepared to change my mind. But I find that, strange to say, none of the admirers can account for their fondness for, say, *The Maximus Poems.*

CS: I don't have much sympathy for those poets either. But how would you account for your aversion to them?

EO: Ultimately, I don't feel as though such poets are uniquely possessed by their language. Their words do not emerge from them as if they were originating with them. And I recognize this flatness instantly when I pick up their books. If you hear a good cellist play you know that he or she is good from the first note; the attack they make with the bow tells you this in your nerve endings. With a poem you feel that, too – there are good notes and there are false notes. You hear them at once.

CS: I noticed a copy of *The Contemporary Canadian Poem Anthology* on your desk. When did you get it?

EO: I purchased it in 1986 just before moving to Montreal. I already knew of certain popular Canadian writers – Robertson Davies and Marian Engle, for example – but I wanted to find out more about the poetry, which is not well known in the US.

CS: What did you think of the work?

EO: I am sorry to say that I didn't find anything terribly distinctive. Once here I began regularly visiting bookstores like The Double Hook and I read up on the people whose work was being talked about at that moment, poets like Patrick Lane and Lorna Crozier. Their work didn't impress me. The constant muting of the voice, the smug understatements, the obsessive use of the plain unadorned phrase, was unappealing. It seemed as though most Canadian poets were refugees from some American poetic movement of fifties. Of course, I did find a few good poets. I was aware of Irving Layton though I had never read his poetry before, and I was very impressed with his work. Layton seemed to me part of a great tradition, not merely of some narrow local trend. Pratt I had read years before and found tremendous. At that time I became interested in Quebecois poets such as Emile Nelligan.

CS: What are your thoughts on Quebecois poetry?

EO: Often it appears to be stronger and more confident than its Anglo counterpart. Robert Melançon, for example, is a superb poet, a true master. I admire Gaston Miron, St-Denys Garneau, and Robert Marteau, too, though Marteau is really

French. These poets haven't severed their connection with the mother country; they see the language and the poetry as a continuum. Perhaps this is one happy side effect of the otherwise daffy emphasis on "La Francophonie." I've always been puzzled as to why more English Canadian poets don't take advantage of the fact that, like the Quebecois, they have access to the larger poetic tradition in a way that American poets do not.

CS: Americans don't have this access?

EO: Not in the same way. You'd be considered an oddity if you wrote as an English poet in America. Take the case of the late Hyam Plutzik, a marvelous poet whom Ted Hughes and others championed. He tried to recreate a credible Shakespearean voice in American verse but his success doomed his verse to obscurity. Only a few other poets read and admire him, to the majority he appears impossibly archaic or affected. But it's not simply that American poets are rejecting British models (if anything they ape things British) but that they have a strong notion of what an American "voice" should be. The notion of "voice" has imposed itself in fact to the point of eccentricity. In the best American poets the search for a voice is inseparable from a rather lavish pleasure in their own identities. We can thank Whitman for this, thank him for the excesses as well as the successes.

CS: Do you think there's a Canadian identity to our poetry?

EO: Not yet. To me it seems that the writers who are usually held up as typical of Canadian poetry fail to do justice to what that poetry might be, both in manner and in content.

CS: What do you think is missing?

EO: For one thing, a true sense of the land itself. Of course, Pratt did try to get at the geography in a special way, and succeeded, I think. But in general I find little in Canadian poetry that is infused with that innate sense of an immense landscape you find in poets like Whitman or Robinson Jeffers. You do find it some: Bruce Taylor and Tim Lilburn, to name two. Still, in general, that instinctive identification with the native earth out of which a genuine national literature can arise strikes me as missing here, though it is very much present in Quebecois verse. The German poet Hölderlin wrote "Remain true to the earth," but I don't find very many English Canadian poets doing, or even attempting, this – to grasp the immensity of the Canadian earth in a visionary way.

CS: What about the Prairie poets? What about Al Purdy?

EO: They don't strike me as unmistakably Canadian. There's a generic quality to their work. They could be writing anywhere. Don't get me wrong: there are marvelous poets writing in English here, especially in Montreal – Norm Sibum comes to mind – but elsewhere in Canada as well. But too much Canadian verse focuses on matters inimical to poetry and which diminish it as art. Inserting irrelevant political messages, for example, as Lowther did in some of her weak later poems, or self-censorship in conformity with political correctness. That, I'm afraid, is what appears too frequently in the average Canadian literary journal: carefully monitored verse with no element of surprise or of audacity.

CS: You once said in an interview with P. Scott Lawrence that the language doesn't fail us, we fail the language.

EO: I believe that. English poetry is not *intrinsically* lacking; it's impoverished because of current practices. Poets have grown up with the dogma that all must be stripped bare, the adjective is your enemy, there can be no adverb. Happily, the language is too big, and it outwits us all in the end. When you write you're like a momentary passenger on a high-speed train. The language has been gathering strength behind you for centuries before you were born, and it will roar on after you are gone; you're ticketed to ride it for a tiny station-hop. I don't mean here the Heideggerian notion that "language speaks us," but that we have to be aware, if only subliminally, when we write, that we form – if I may switch metaphor – only a few small but perhaps indispensable droplets in a great wave, and that this obliges us to write with humility but also with as much daring as we can muster.

The Messenger Never Arrives

MARGARET ATWOOD

Interviewed by Norm Sacuta

Margaret Atwood is the author of more than twenty-five books of poetry, fiction and non-fiction, and her work has been translated into more than thirty languages. Her novel *The Blind Assassin* (McClelland & Stewart) won the 2000 Booker Prize. Her poetry collections include *The Journals of Susanna Moodie* (Oxford, 1970) and *Morning in the Burned House* (M&S, 1995). She lives in Toronto.

Norm Sacuta's first poetry collection, *Garments of the Known*, was published in 2001 by Nightwood Editions. He lives in Edmonton where he works full time as a writer and editor. He is currently completing a novel.

NS: When I asked Tim Bowling about what the audience would be for this book, he suggested a general audience – that is, a general poetry-reading audience. This would be in contrast with an academic readership, so I've tried to gear my questions to cover general topics rather than specific poems.

MA: So, a general poetry readership? But do we even know what general poetry readers are? Actually, they're probably other poets.

NS: Exactly. So I decided to ask questions that I thought other poets might be interested in. I did look at previous interviews with you and that was a bit frustrating since, basically, you've been asked everything. So if these repeat what came before I apologize.

MA: Well, you know, you might get a different answer.

NS: One of those previous interviews was with Graeme Gibson from a collection of compiled interviews called *Conversations*. You said to him – and this interview was over thirty years ago – that you learned to write poetry, unlike the way you learned to write novels, through a Canadian tradition. There was a strong Canadian tradition in poetry that went back in time, unlike novels, which you learned to write from non-Canadians. I wanted to ask you about that. How, for you, has that poetry tradition changed? Were the poets that were important to you then as important for you now? Has the poetry tradition changed for you, as it obviously has within Canada over the past thirty years?

MA: I think we're talking forty years ago. That interview may have been 1972, but obviously what I'm talking about is the material that I was reading in the fifties and the beginning of the sixties. The poets I was reading up to '61, well, a lot of people hadn't appeared yet. Michael Ondaatje, obviously, wasn't around. He's younger than me and was probably nineteen then. Purdy was only available in a rather peculiar pamphlet called *Emu Remember!* Alden Nowlan had only appeared at that time in pamphlet form as well, although I knew about those pamphlets because I knew the person who published them. And lots of other people who have come along since just weren't there yet – George Bowering didn't publish until a couple of years after that, and I knew Gwendolyn MacEwen but she didn't come out with a book until *The Rising Fire*. The people who had already published and who would already have been appearing in anthologies included P.K. Page and Margaret Avison, whom I reviewed as an undergraduate. I don't think I understood the poetry, but I reviewed it anyway. James Reaney, who had not yet done any of those plays. Irving Layton and Leonard Cohen, up to a point. A.M. Klein was very important to me – so, people who were very active in the thirties, forties and fifties. But among that group there were a number of very accomplished women poets.

NS: Was Anne Wilkinson well known in that period?

MA   Yes, and I knew her work. I got *The Hangman Ties the Holly*, in first edition, early on – around 1960.

NS: My first introduction to her work was about ten years ago with a new volume of the collected poems [*The Poetry of Anne Wilkinson*, Exile, 1990]. She's been a huge influence on my own work. The poems and images are amazing.

MA: Yes they are, and she died early, as you know. But it was possible, then, to just pick up those sorts of editions in second-hand bookstores. For instance, I have an edition of Klein's *Hitlariad*, probably the only complete one that's ever appeared.

NS: What about some of the earlier writers even before then? We've all read Pratt –

MA: We hadn't then! But I'd read a lot of Pratt and Earle Birney. I would say that Earle Birney and E.J. Pratt are the backbones of *Survival*, but that was ten years later. In the early sixties, A.J.M. Smith's anthology had more or less just come out. Also, the first *Oxford Book of Canadian Verse in English* and it wasn't just in English then – it was bilingual. There was a Penguin book as well and *The Blasted Pine*. Do you know it? It was an anthology put together by Smith and F.R. Scott – "disrespectful verse," satire and yelling at people and bawling them out with political poems and ripping a few skins off. Some of the poems in that collection are very funny and interesting.

NS: I suspected that many of the influences I've had – and this was part of the reason I wanted to do this interview – have been influences on you. Poets like Wilkinson and Gwendolyn MacEwen.

MA: Yes, up to a point. But early to appear in the sixties was John Newlove, who I think is a very, very good poet and much overlooked.

NS: Yes, I admire his work as well. And it's interesting, because much of the poetry that I did end up being taught in my university years at the University of Alberta and UBC ended up not being the poetry that I was particularly interested in.

MA: What were you taught?

NS: Well, a lot of what came out of the *Tish* movement – Fred Wah or Daphne Marlatt, for example, although I do quite admire Marlatt's novels. And sound poetry to some extent because I was at U of A when Stephen Scobie was there doing his work with Doug Barbour. I'm wondering – and I'm not trying to get you into the arguments that still divide poetry in Canada between narrative and anti-narrative verse – but what are your views on narrative in poetry? Because it seems to me, even with your more recent work in *Morning in the Burned House*, you haven't strayed from it.

MA: Well, there's a long tradition *[laughs]*, and it's called Homer. It's a most post-modern old poem, but actually there are two older poems that are even more postmodern than Homer's. That would be the "Song of Songs," which was indeed stuck together from a group of different poems, and ancient Sumerian poetry. I mean, in the postmodern, as in these two poetries, you can't often figure out what's going on. Who's talking? And different styles bounce off one another, thereby giving you the fragmentary effects which, in ancient Sumerian poems, is really a fragmentary effect in a physical sense, because what you're doing is sticking together old clay tablets, and who knows whether you have them in the right order?

NS: And even with the traditions of fiction from the past, from the eighteenth and nineteenth centuries, you have examples of more interesting postmodern sensibilities, I think, than have come out in contemporary culture.

MA: Sterne, yes, it's all there. It's like fashion, I think. If you follow fashion at all. If you do fashion speeded up – you remember those time-lapse films of flowers opening that you used to get in school? If you do it with fashion you can see the skirt shrink, the sleeves become important, the shoulders balloon, and they become bigger and bigger and bigger and then they disappear; and then the bustle becomes important, it gets bigger and then it shrinks; and then the skirts raise, and then the ankle becomes important. You can go through all of these combinations, but essentially what you have is the human body. That's what you're stuck with. This or that can be bigger or smaller, and this or that can be emphasized, or this or that colour can become important, but really you've only got so many colours. You can call them different things – taupe or mauve or whatever – but essentially it's a limited palette. It's what we can *see*. You can't do infrared or ultraviolet unless you use certain kinds of lighting. You can't put those colours into clothing because nobody can see them.

So what do we have with poetry, or literature in general? We have the human psyche, lord love it, and we have language. And you can arrange those elements as you may, but you're still going to have the human psyche and language, in different combinations, with this or that emphasized. There was a period when we went in for fear and literature was gothicized, and then we had fleeing maidens. Then fleeing maidens got overdone and Jane Austen did maidens not fleeing. Instead they stirred their tea and thought, "All those fleeing maidens are really silly." So things develop to their utmost, and then somebody else does something else. There's no *progress* in art.

NS: There's reflection and reaction.

MA: There's change. There's reflection and exploration, reaction, change. Movement here and there, but you can't say that a Picasso is necessarily better than a Neolithic cave painting. We can say this is a good Picasso or a bad Picasso, but we can't say Picasso-ness – this thing that he does – is in essence better art than the cave painting. It isn't. So a certain amount of snobbery gets into these things. People saying that this or that is *cutting edge*. Well it usually means they are using a razor that was in use 150 years ago and people have forgotten about it. "Sound poetry" was very cutting edge when it began, this wave of it, but what was it really? Chanting. And chanting is very old.

NS: And the best of what was happening in Canada with sound poets like the Four Horsemen, they often acknowledged that what they were doing went back to that tradition of chanting.

MA: Yes, they were drawing attention to an area that had been neglected. And that's what art often does – it draws attention to an area that has been neglected. For instance, once upon a time art was not about people changing diapers, and then the border got pushed and that element of life, which had been in the wings, got included. But then if the new thing becomes old – changing diapers – you want something different. A trend gets pushed to its extreme, it's forced to do as much as it can do, and then something else comes along. If not, you're just stuck as a culture and can't make anything new.

NS: Speaking of trends in Canadian poetry, I've noticed that *Grain* magazine has been running a prose poem competition for a number of years now – or short, short stories – and certainly you've been interested in that genre with *Good Bones* and *Murder in the Dark*. Do you consider those two collections to be prose poems?

MA: Absolutely – early in that trend, in Canada anyway.

NS: What about that form holds interest for you?

MA: Well, the prose poem as such was originally French and it was much more closely aligned to symbolism and the suggestiveness of language than a lot of those little things in my books, which draw upon, really, a ton of different areas. What they essentially have in common is that they're short. Some of them are shaggy dog jokes, and some of them are sci-fi pieces. Some of them are prose poems proper, whereas others are mini-narratives. Little adventure stories. They're miniatures of all sorts of things. Some are little detective stories and some are miniature furniture descriptions.

NS: They're self-contained.

MA: They're self-contained, and one of my influences from way back, since we were talking influences earlier, would be Kafka's parables, which are NOT prose poems. They're little parables. And some of the earliest forms of narrative we have are, in fact, parables. Things like Aesop's fables – little mini-narratives. The fox is interested in some grapes, but can't reach them, etc. Very short. Very peculiar and to the point. Anyone delving into the folk tradition will know that there are these small narratives that are suggestive and peculiar, and you don't really know where they came from. There they sit.

NS: Those sorts of things – the parables – tend to have a moral message or a moral code to them, whereas yours don't.

MA: The older fables do, yes, but the whole point about Kafka's fables is that they don't. Not as such. Not in relation to right behaviour.

NS: Moving into the modern dilemma.

MA: No, moving into the unresolvable. In fact, they are already in the unresolvable. We know the messenger will never arrive, but nevertheless . . . .

NS: What about the other direction – the long poem? Many critics have suggested that *Susanna Moodie* or *Power Politics* are long poems in themselves, but I'm not so sure. I don't want to ask "Why have you never tried an epic poem like bp Nichol's 'The Martyrology'?" but I guess that's exactly what I am asking.

MA: It didn't interest me – it's not my area of a) talent and b) energy. If I want to write a long narrative I write a novel. It's not that I don't like long poems – I'm Tennyson folk myself. *Idylls of the King*. But you have to be in the mood for it.

NS: And *In Memoriam*, too.

MA: Yes, but that's not a long poem. And I would contend that there's a difference between a long poem and a cycle or sequence. For instance, Shakespeare's sonnets, although nobody knows what order they should be in, they are essentially a sequence. *In Memoriam* is a sequence arranged in three cycles. People were doing that when I was a young poet – various people were doing these arrangements of shorter poems that were strung together into a narrative. *The Waste Land,* of course, is such a thing. A number of poems stuck together, and within each section different kinds of poetry are bounced off against one another. And I've always liked that – bouncing one form of representation off another. But I am by no means the only writer to be interested in that. If you take a look at *Mrs. Dalloway*, for instance, one of the first things that happens in it is that she sees a sky-writer – an airplane writing something across the sky. And no one can quite make out what it is. The messenger never arrives. But what it turns out to be – or what she thinks it says – is KREMO. Advertising had become a thing by then, so lots of people took that form or representation of reality and stuck it into another form, namely literature.

NS: In his poem, "The Dead Poet," Al Purdy, speculating on the origins of his poetry, asks "how else explain myself to myself/ where does the song come from?" Do you have an explanation of where your voice comes from, and perhaps, why you became a poet?

MA: Zero. Zero explanation. I have no idea.

NS: In an earlier interview I think you were asked a very similar question and you said that you really didn't want to know where your voice comes from.

MA: I don't know where it comes from, I've never known where it comes from and I don't want to know where it comes from. It was a sudden development. People say, well, when did you decide you wanted to be a writer, but I didn't decide. It was an occurrence.

NS: You've said that you started to write when you were very, very young and took a long break until you were sixteen, then started again. Was it something in that period that led to you wanting to write again. I know you were young, but –

MA: I didn't want to write. I didn't want to write even when I started writing. It wasn't a desire that preceded an act. It was an act that preceded a desire. There's this interesting book called *God, a Biography* by Jack Miles, which I highly recommend – it's lots of fun. But one of the things he does is take the Bible as if it were a book-book. Forget all the theology and stuff that you learned in the church, and everything that's accumulated around it. You take it as a book. You pick up this book and open it and you have a character called God. So, what do we know about God, this character in the book, through what he says, what he does and through what others say about him? And how does he develop – because he does develop just like any other major character in a book. One of the things that becomes obvious is that God doesn't know "Thou shalt not kill" until he sees somebody kill someone. There's no prohibition against murder until Cain kills Abel. It's after that event that God decides he doesn't like murder. It's like Tigger – he doesn't know what he likes to eat. So I started writing without having decided first that I was going to start writing.

NS: And are you still reading Canadian poetry regularly?

MA: I don't read anything regularly. I read things in bursts. And I've been reading poetry in bursts because of the Griffin prize and the fact that I'm a trustee, so it behooves me to read the short list.

NS: Are there any contemporary poets, new ones, that you've discovered?

MA: I don't discover things, really. People who discover things are other poets who are very close to the place where the river meets the road; that is, they are editing anthologies and magazines, and are in touch with other people of their own generation. So a new person will come along, and they might discover that person through a magazine submission and then they'll phone up their friends or be having a beer somewhere and they'll say, "Have you read so-and-so?" That's how it goes. If you trust your friend's judgment then you'll get the book and read it. But usually – and it's why I support the idea of them – it's through little magazines that people enter that arena, where they can be discovered by someone. By the time they're in book form, believe me, I ain't the discoverer! Other people have done the discovery. I was at the discovery end when I was doing the poetry list for the House of Anansi, which I did for several years. I was not only reading new manuscripts, but putting together collections for people who had been around for a while. For instance, bill bissett. I took a stack of his mimeo things that was this tall [indicates about twelve inches] and whittled it down, and believe me, it was a labour of love!

NS: Have your feelings about poetry, the reading and writing of it, changed since you were in your twenties?

MA: Well, in my twenties I was very active as a poet, partly because I had day jobs, or I was studying, and I couldn't write novels. The only thing I could write was poetry and I wrote the poetry in the space left over from all the other things I was supposed to be doing. I was a night writer, and had the big bags under my eyes and the dark circles and the stumbling-around-in-the-daytime behaviour. So that changed when I didn't have to have a day job anymore. Shortly after that time, I also had a baby. But I was more prolific in poetry in the sixties and seventies than I have been since, partly for those reasons and also because I've been writing novels.

NS: You said at one point you liked poetry because you could write a poem in an evening. You could get that sense of completion by writing and finishing a poem, unlike a novel, which is continuous and ongoing.

MA: A novel is work. You can have a flash of inspiration in about the same amount of time it takes to have it with a poem, but then you have to sit down and work it all out. That can be a long, hard, drudgy process, with a lot of revision. Not that you don't revise a poem as well, but –

NS: So is it still a source of invigoration for you when you sit down and do a poem?

MA: Well, again, I don't *do* a poem. It's an occurrence. I sit and write down a poem. It's in your head first, you know that, and it's not something you can anticipate. You can't work at it apart from revising and typing out.

NS: Is what you're saying – and I agree, usually my poem is in my head and I simply get it out – but do you then create meaning as you write? Is there sometimes simply an image there and then?

MA: What is meaning? Meaning is when you've got two things. You can't have meaning when you have just one thing. So meaning is a system of relationships, amongst all kinds of things, but in the poem the relationship is between certain letters, certain sounds, certain rhythms, and then the meaning – if we want to say there is such a thing as *a* meaning, which there isn't. There are different meanings. You can find that out very easily just by substituting a word of the same "meaning" for the word that's already there in a poem and you can see how deeply altered that poem becomes, even though it may "mean" the same thing. In the high school précis sense of the word "meaning," which I've always been against, a poem becomes a box of crackerjacks, within which is embedded a cheap little prize –

NS: – that we have to get at, somehow. Push all the words aside and there it is!

MA: To quote Quentin Crisp when he was a film critic, what do Shakespeare's sonnets boil down to, viewed in this way? To the fact that Shakespeare loved Mr. H. more than Mr. H. loved Shakespeare. Which "if that were all, would indeed be banal." In some ways you can't deal without such meanings, but if that's all the poem is, you might as well just be writing ads in the personals section.

NS: I want to turn to the idea of identity politics – because being in Edmonton the whole notion of identity politics becomes appealing as a strategy for, well . . . .

MA: For pestering the government.

NS: Yes, exactly. I'm gay, so a lot of the politics in Alberta places me in a category that sometimes I'm comfortable with, and other times I'm very uncomfortable occupying.

MA: So you have to be a spokesperson for "gaiety."

NS: Yes. I'm bringing this up because in many, many interviews you are referred to as a feminist writer.

MA: Well, obviously, I can't speak for all women just as you can't speak for all gay people. There's such diversity. One person in that category says *tomato* and the other says *tomah-toe*. People in these categories may have certain problems in common, but they don't necessarily have certain interests or personality traits or tastes in clothing in common. All the things about being a human being may be different, except for that one thing. And having a set of problems in common shoves people together because they may sometimes wish to over-come those problems. But if you're a writer then it becomes another sort of problem because those people want you to represent them in every respect. And it's a bit easier, being a poet, in that way, but if you are a novelist you might find yourself face to face with the fact that the gay people in your books should be loveable and wonderful and talented and handsome and without a flaw. And all the other people should be boring. And it's that form of identity politics that is inimical to art. It's the opposite of what art does, and it cuts off exploration and substitutes dogma. So, whenever that becomes an issue, just say, "Take a hike. If you're not willing to accept the fact that I'm a poet, then get yourself someone else to head up the committee."

NS: But what is it, then, that leads to a successful infusion of the political into poetry, because Adrienne Rich is very good at that – especially in a collection like *Diving into the Wreck*. The politics is there, but –

MA: Adrienne Rich is a genius! In that particular book, especially. Again you can't determine where the intersection may take place. I would say that when things become deeply felt, that is when they can enter art. Things are not deeply felt when they're being dictated to you by someone else, who may indeed deeply feel them but may not be an artist. Usually these stances and politics are worked out by groups of people, hammering away to get something they want. It's very instigated. The main thing is not to take dictation. Don't take dicta-tion from anyone who thinks he knows better what you should be saying than you do. As for women as a category – forget it! Half the population of the globe have certain problems in common, but everything else is different. People say women want this, or women want that, and I usually think *bullshit*. *Which* women, and under what circumstances?

NS: What social or political situation . . . .

MA: Which country, how rich are they, what colour? It's all difference.

NS: How important are reviews, awards and other honours to your feelings about your work?

MA: *[an old woman's voice]* At my age? *[laughs]* I think, how shall we put it, if people get such things too young it ruins them. If people get them too old, it doesn't make any difference. They're already bitter.

NS: That's what Jean Rhys said when she won a major award for *Wide Sargasso Sea*. "It has come too late . . ."

MA: This process started quite early for me. I won second prize in a doll's dress-sewing contest when I was in grade five. Not first prize! And I didn't win the Consumer Gas Miss Homemaker's Contest either.

NS: How long ago was that?

MA: High school. Me and my friend Sally were the entrants from our high school. You had to make a meatloaf, iron a shirt and make something else with gas.

NS: Did you even place?

MA: I think there was only a First, but we all got little bracelets with golden bells and fake pearls on them. What else have I won that's odd? I've won a number of peculiar things. I won the Swedish Humour Award, which my publishers almost killed me over. They had to go collect it, and it was an open amphitheatre in the pouring rain. The prize was a huge crystal ball, or bowl, possibly, and they took it back to the office and someone stole it.

NS: So you never saw it?

MA: Nope. So somebody has got it somewhere. I suppose it has my name engraved on it. Anyway, yes, people get very caught up in it all. The people who love these things are the publishers and people in the book trade. And awards can be very helpful to young writers entering the field. An award can get them noticed in ways they might not otherwise have been noticed. But they can also be a horribly disappointing process for people. We think it doesn't matter, and we make fun of it, and say it's only a jury, or it's just people's taste, or a do-dad that you get at the end of the road, but there is something about human beings and symbolism that makes it probably more important than it should be. And what I say to young writers – well, I've never said it to young writers, but I'll say it to you – go to the stationery store and get a bunch of those gold legal stickers. Get them embossed – put something in the middle, plants or animals. Trees are better than dandelions, lions are better than mice – then stick them on your books and people will think you've won something. Even you may think you've won something. It's a very tangled area, and the other horrifying thing is that awards attract awards. People think that if you got this gizmo over here you should probably be considered for that one over there. Anyway, who am I be to say anything negative? I, who have somewhat benefited from these sorts of items. I say somewhat because I think when I won the Governor General's in 1967 it created a batch of instant enemies.

NS: I can imagine, in poetry especially.

MA: Envy is not a motive to be ruled out. Or people think, "Oh, big shot, let's take a few acres of air out of her balloon." So you become a target as well as an icon.

NS: Is competition healthy or unhealthy between poets?

MA: I think male poets feel competitive with one another, and female poets, at least until recently – no! I bite my tongue and take it back. Because I can think of a couple of female poets that were competitive in a very unpleasant way. But women poets tended to feel isolated – poetry, in my youth, was a group activity for men and a solitary activity for women. I may now be completely out to lunch and it may have all changed – for instance women gay poets may feel they can band together and represent a group in some way. But in the sixties, when people were editing magazines, it was pretty much men doing it. I never felt competitive with fellow poets. I didn't think that my job was somehow to squash them into the ground. It's not that I'm lacking in competitiveness – give me a good doll's dress contest and I'll be as competitive as the next person. But poets in those days were such a small beleaguered group, as with Canadian writers in general, that the point was not to be competitive but to increase the opportunities, which meant increasing them for everybody and to increase the audience to open poetry up to all comers. And I'm not a saint here; it was a sign of the times. I'm sure if I were just appearing now I would feel competitive. Now there are grants and people you have to impress and lots of publishing houses and way more people writing. The only other female person I knew who was my own age and writing poetry when I was beginning was Gwen, and who could feel competitive with her? She was from outer space! You can't compete with a Martian.

NS: bp Nichol, in "The Martyrology," didn't really want to ever bring closure to his poem. So this is a good place to end our discussion: how do you know when a poem's finished?

MA: When nothing more can be done. It's the same with a novel. You come to the point where it's either good or bad or mediocre, but it's finished. You can't do anything more. When nothing more can be done.

Peek-a-Boo

PHYLLIS WEBB

Interviewed by Jay Ruzesky

Phyllis Webb lives and paints on Salt Spring Island, BC. She is an Officer of the Order of Canada and has won the Governor General's Award for *The Vision Tree: Selected Poems* (Talonbooks, 1982) and the BC Gas Lifetime Achievement Award (1999). Her selected prose is collected in *Nothing But Brush Strokes* (NeWest, 1995).

Jay Ruzesky's most recent book is *Blue Himalayan Poppies* (Nightwood, 2001). Other books include *Painting the Yellow House Blue* (Anansi, 1994) and *Writing on the Wall* (Outlaw, 1996). He lives in Victoria, BC, and teaches at Malaspina University-College in Duncan, BC.

PW: I don't want to say anything. I have no message for the world!

JR: I loved your essay on "Poetry and Psychobiography" [*Nothing But Brush Strokes*]. The idea of it fascinates me. You talk about the invasion of Anne Sexton's privacy in biographical approaches to her work and yet the only way you can do that is by providing some of the details of her life – brief sketches I admit – but details that are what that voyeuristic way of looking at a life involves. Was that a difficult piece to write?

PW: Yes it was. I've spent many hours with psychiatrists in my life. I remember hearing something on the radio about disclosure and I almost passed out. It's that sense of the loss of control over your private space and your private mind that upset me about the Anne Sexton incident when the psychiatrist released the tapes. It seems amazing to me that a doctor would do that, and it's all very fascinating and we're all interested. It's that ambivalence of being either the subject or the object. This causes me a lot of confusion. I recently turned down an invitation to a conference at which they'll be discussing some of my work and I realize that is the problem again. Will I be a subject or an object? That dichotomy is existentially very frightening.

JR: Can you explain what you mean by that dichotomy? Why is it frightening?

PW: It's a woman's problem of being an object – a scx object and that frightening loss of personhood. Being the thing discussed . . . The person and the work get confused – the impression that "my work is me." If my work is being discussed perhaps I feel that I am being objectified and analyzed and dissected. I don't want to be identified or confused with the work and I don't want to be there while I'm being discussed. The body of work is not me. There is a kind of sexual anxiety there of being on display. I'm such a private person and I've gone to extremes to remain private, apart from my public performances.

JR: Which isn't necessarily you.

PW: No, that's the mask. I'm curious about the subject of that essay, which is psychobiography and the use of titillating private life details and the whole mystery of why that is almost more interesting to people than the work.

JR: Do you have a sense of why?

PW: I offer a theory in the essay which is that it's a return to the source of creativity, of biological creation, of how we are made. It goes back to who screwed whom. It's the secret of life that we're all consumed with finding out about.

JR: Biography informs literature. Most people are interested in biography after they do some reading. You read about a writer because you know something about their work and that information informs your past and future reading of that work.

PW: In a way it probably shouldn't. It's unfortunate that we have lives. The work doesn't need that dimension.

JR: There is the idea of the purity of the poem; it ought to be able to speak for itself and often does. And yet we're interested in biography. Sylvia Plath is a good example. Many of her poems are marvelous and I read them before I knew much of anything about her, but I think "Lady Lazarus" is somehow more potent when you know something about her life. Maybe it's a sense of the poem seeming more authentic. Is that what draws us to biography? The desire for authenticity?

PW: You mean that this is the true story?

JR: It's not so much a factual truth. Readers want to know that they're being told something real.

PW: We don't want to be conned. But the work of the imagination can float free of that biographical data. It never really floats free of the self. I'm curious about that hunger for "this is based on a true story" as they say on television. It's supposed to make writing more real but if it's fiction or fantasy it's not real. A made thing is not real life. Poems are creations. I don't know what would be the true story except maybe a police report.

JR: Like reality TV. That must be what's so compelling about it. Real drunks being arrested by real cops. Somehow that's fascinating in a way that it wouldn't be if I made it up.

PW: Do you think that's because our experience is not satisfying for ourselves? That we have to have someone else's experience because there's a lack of depth in our experience? To fill "lives of quiet desperation." People are living quiet lives of emptiness and this provides a thrill.

JR: Real TV would do that but I don't know if that makes the world more thrilling.

PW: You can also watch them bungee jumping or being towed by a boat or other activities that adventure stories once fulfilled, and detective fiction would have also filled that need.

JR: My theory is connected with those lives of quiet desperation. Maybe many people don't feel their lives are very real. I read a book a few years ago called

Mr. Wilson's Cabinet of Wonder [by Lawrence Weschler], which was about strange things in the Museum of Jurassic Technology in Los Angeles. Some of the exhibits are true and some are not and what that does is it inspires a kind of wonder. There are things . . . ants with huge horns, that seem like they shouldn't be true but they are, and other things that are believable but aren't true and I think that we have a kind of engagement with the world that is like that. It's about wanting to be impressed by the world. We want to be open to being in awe of the things that are around us.

PW: Ants with huge horns sound marvelous and suggest to me that we're in the realm of magic realism. The magic and the real playing tag, a very serious game. Awe and wonder bring us close to the mystical, the hope of climbing out of the boxes we live in from day to day.

JR: I'm very interested in what happens when the magic and the real come together. There's a beautiful line somewhere between truth and lies that writers play with all the time. When I'm teaching I often talk about the idea of the well-made mask. Fiction (whether it's poetry or prose) reflects some of the features of the real face beneath the mask and the mask reflects the face but it's also shaped and crafted to take on a kind of expression of its own. The reason it has an effect though is that there's an essence of the face that comes through. Normally you would see the eyes for example.

PW: True, even if it's a wolf mask.

JR: Because perhaps there's an essence of the wolf in the face beneath. The mask draws us in but it's what's behind the mask that has the impact. The authentic stuff coming through.

PW: So are we trying to tear the mask off? Perhaps. In which case there is not enough appreciation for the mask maker and maybe for the beauty or the ugliness of the mask.
        On a confessional note, I do find it hard to read novels by friends. I know something about their lives and there is a terrible temptation all the time I'm reading to say, "Is this true?" I feel it's a sickness almost and I wonder why I am doing this. Is this an aspect of fiction that it sends off a message to say, come on and read me? Figure me out if you can?

JR: In another essay in *Nothing But Brush Strokes* ["The Muse Figure"] you say that "we do not have muses." Can you explain? Is the naked truth something that anyone can strive for in the age of information?

PW: I guess I said we, but *I* don't. It's a matter of personality now. It was formerly a tradition, a kind of manner of behaving as a poet. It's also a way of projecting another part of the self so that it's over your shoulder or advising or communing with you. It's more a male construct because usually the muse was female so I always felt I had to have a male muse if I had a muse. A lot of my mentors have been men but I wouldn't have called them muses and I wouldn't think of the beautiful male being a muse in the way that the female has been for male writers and artists. The white goddess was represented, according to Robert Graves, as a naked woman. I don't think she's always naked. I have trouble with the whole thing. Do you have a muse?

JR: No, I don't think so, but I like the idea as a representation of the naked truth. Back to authenticity again. In your poem "Two Pears: A Still Life" [*The Sea Is Also a Garden*], in the last line pears become "secret, original, a dream of candor." It's the word "candor" I react to. It's an act of faith and trust to tell the truth and to expose yourself even through the mask of poetry; to express something that is deeply one's own.

PW: Sir Philip Sidney said "look in thy heart, and write" and that has a kind of directness without too much embellishment and it seems to me a way of evading a lot of what I do which is to be intellectual and witty. I'm not sure how often I look in my heart and write. I did occasionally. I don't think that's the place to write from all the time and I don't know that the naked truth is what it's about all the time either. I don't think I have a heart anymore so maybe that's why I've stopped writing; it wore out.

JR: Do you mean that?

PW: I don't know. I'm sort of heartless I think.

JR: Some of your poems that strike me most are your love poems. "Propositions" [*The Sea Is Also a Garden*] is a beautiful poem.

PW: I must agree. That's one of the miracles that happened. It was written very quickly in Paris. It's mathematically balanced. Someone worked it out mathematically.

JR: I don't know that I felt drawn to add things up.

PW: It's very one, two, one, two.

JR: And very moving about what love is and wholeness. The last line about the half moon.

PW: I still think of that when I look out the window and see the half moon. I think of my own line.

JR: "a half moon, its hidden wholeness there." *Naked Poems* as well are wonderful love poems.

PW: Not all of them are love poems. The "Suite of Lies" is not love poems.

JR: There are several layers there. It's also about the love of language.

PW: It's about poetry too. Yes.

JR: Those poems have had a big influence on other writers. Do you think romantic love will always be a driving force in literature? Is it an endless subject or are all poems love poems of a kind?

PW: The kind of love poems that are written now are not like the old lyrics. The way people write about love now seems to be much more bristly. It's honest. It's more about the difficulties of relationships than about falling in love. The romantic love poem tends toward the lyrical. If you think of Anne Carson, for instance, always writing about love: but how acidic she is and how funny. This is a complicated approach to love. I think there's no such thing as a straightforward simple . . . I'm thinking about Leonard Cohen's early poem about Annie but he's a singer: he's still in the lyric, the singing lyric.

JR: It's probably harder to write that kind of love poem.

PW: I keep getting images of thorns and scratches. Maybe it all changed with Margaret Atwood's *Power Politics* – "you fit into me/ like a hook into an eye." In Canadian literature that was probably the turning point in the love poem with the entry of this female voice: the sharpness, the vitriolic tone. There's a real intelligence at work which cuts into the lyric outburst. *Power Politics* was a landmark in Canadian literature in the sixties. There's more about married love now, it seems to me. If you think of Sharon Olds, there's more daddy love, too. The poet is more willing to grapple with actual relationship and is less outside admiring the object. It's much more relational and that's why it's more complicated and bitter and edgy.

JR: It's a sign of the culture where relationships have changed so much in the last century. There's a lot of questioning of societally conditioned love.

PW: But the basic formula hasn't changed despite all the questioning for centuries. We're still doing the same old thing – getting married, getting divorced. That's what appalls me about gay marriages, the desire to fall into a worn-out mode. But it won't wear out, it still has a lot of life.

JR: You were politically active early on, running for the CCF, and you were later involved with Amnesty International.

PW: I started a group on the Island [Salt Spring] but I burned out after two or three years. That was in the eighties. We had a very good group going here but then I moved to Victoria.

JR: It seems that your poems became more political the more you wrote, more overtly political in poems like "Prison Report" and "Treblinka Gas Chamber" and much of *Hanging Fire*. Was that a conscious decision?

PW: No. I'm always preoccupied with these things. Some of it did come out of the Amnesty work. I met Jacobo Timmerman in Toronto at an Amnesty meeting and I was struck by his gentleness and his good humour after what he'd been through. I read part of his book that was reprinted in *The New Yorker* and then I wrote the poem. There was a direct Amnesty connection for "Prison Report," but I wrote "Treblinka Gas Chamber" in the seventies. When I look back at earlier titles from the fifties and sixties they do seem more personal. I probably wanted to become more overt. I wanted to expand. It was a movement away from the personal, private kind of poem. And also I was maturing.

JR: I wonder if it has anything to do simply with the world you found yourself in. You were brought up through the war. But my sense is that politics are even more desperate now.

PW: I've always felt desperate about social conditions.

JR: Why write poetry then? Did you have to wrestle with the idea that you were writing poems rather than being a social activist?

PW: I felt, and still do feel, that I ought to be doing something. But I wasn't made for that kind of public life. I was too private and too easily damaged and the use of the language is so offensive in its rhetoric and clichés . . . How do you live from day to day speaking that way? All that fed into my nausea at the thought of entering public life. But I still feel guilty. I feel I should be doing more. But that's puritanical and protestant. Social good has always been something I've cared about.

JR: Do the poems serve a social function?

PW: Yes. Poetry "makes nothing happen" as we know, but there's a slight consciousness-raising.

JR: And you were directly involved in politics. You can't always be the one chained to the tree.

PW: My time with *Ideas* at CBC, my work generally at CBC, was very important and that was certainly political. We were a radical bunch and a lot of our programs dealt with very, very important social issues. That's probably when I was most effective in a public way. Teaching, too. That's also socially useful.

JR: When did you stop writing? *Hanging Fire* was the last book of poetry.

PW: That was 1990. It came out in '91, but it's dated '90. There'll probably never be another book.

JR: You say probably.

PW: Well, you never know! I think it's very unlikely. I psychologically date it from my mother's death, which was in '92 I think. And in '93 I started painting. *Hanging Fire* has a lot of anger in it. I wonder if it scared me that I had revealed my anger so openly. John Hulcoop did a review in which he emphasized the anger in the book. There's a lot of feminist anger, social anger and other kinds.

JR: It's more subversive.

PW: But there wasn't much attention paid to it when it came out.

JR: I sent you a question about what Joseph Beuys said, rather famously, that the "Silence of Marcel Duchamp is Overrated." I think he was referring to the anti-art sentiment implied in Duchamp's reported decision to turn away from art and just to play chess, and also to the ego involved in that decision. As though Duchamp wanted to see whether the world could do without his art. But I don't think, when you're not writing, that it has anything to do with ego.

PW: That sort of hit me. Silence and seeing if the world can go on without your art. It's like, "Well, fuck you if you're not going to read my book and give me a prize or something." *[laughs]* I realize I don't want to be forgotten, and not just my work.

JR: That's understandable but Duchamp was quite ego-driven I think.

PW: What artist isn't? The Dada movement certainly tried to get an effect and be noticed.

JR: There's a story about Satie and his piece called "Entr'acte" It was performed at an intermission for some other event and everyone stopped to listen, so he had to run around and tell everyone to "Quit listening, quit listening." It was not at all about what happened inside the concert hall where everyone was supposed to listen politely. I don't know if Duchamp really intended just to stop and play chess.

PW: I realize what also fed my withdrawal. It was not so much about stopping writing as withdrawing from being a "poet." I made a trip to author festivals in Australia and New Zealand and I wondered "Why am I doing this to myself?" It was so difficult. I always had quite a bit of ham in me, I did like performing, but I thought "I'm too old for this, running around, getting up on stages and showing off." When I came home I decided "No more public appearances," and I've pretty much stuck to that except for memorial occasions or ecological ones. And that led to the examination of the problem of the ego and identity and the poetic identity. I wanted to see if I existed apart from my identity as a poet. That was an important part of who I thought I was. So, gone, gone, gone.

All those things combined: the non-reception of *Hanging Fire*, the death of my mother – which in some ways was a great relief because she was a hundred and one and our relationship was painful and there's been a hangover from that – those things and this decision to cease being a performer more or less, hiding away here. That's when the painting erupted. Then I had to go through the ego problem again with the painting because you want to show your work. You want to show that you've done something. Here I am again. Sign it. Peek-a-boo.

JR: Well, it's a process that involves reception at some point.

PW: Yes. At the moment I'm wondering if I'll exhibit in the summer show this year with the Alliance of Salt Spring Artists. I think my painting is getting worse. I got very excited about painting because I had to teach myself everything. There was a great excitement about learning. I seemed to be so hungry for knowledge about painting. I'd always been passionate about painting. I'd known a lot of painters and so on.

JR: Some of the prose pieces in *Nothing But Brush Strokes* were written since you started painting. But it's interesting that one of the first problems you were dealing with when you started painting was the problem of the ego.

PW: Yes, and I'm still struggling with it although I feel much freer now. I do feel I worked through something. I've just been reading a short essay in *Brick* by Jim Harrison on Zen practice which throws some light on my perhaps misguided struggle to escape myself. He says, "In our practice the self is not pushed away, it drifts away." Which shows I'm not much of a Buddhist.

JR: Maybe you had a sense that some of the work would become public and it would be easy to anticipate that someone would say "Here's Phyllis the poet and she's trying to paint."

PW: There's nothing false about that statement. She's trying to paint. I'm aware that there's a lot of bad painting in the world and I'm just adding to it.

JR: I don't know about that. Can I ask you about collage? It seems to be a disorderly medium. It naturally, I think, moves toward abstraction. You begin with what may be a recognizable image or a bunch of them and by putting them together in unique ways and altering perspectives you make the familiar unrecognizable or at least you force people to see those images in a way they wouldn't have otherwise. It sounds a little like what a good poem ought to do.

PW: I'm getting myself to see. Not necessarily with any sense of an audience.
       I'm not sure that collage necessarily tends toward abstraction. It disrupts habits of perception, as you say. There's an element of the puzzle about it – and in fact I've been working recently on some paintings with pieces of crossword puzzles, acrylic combined with collage on canvas.

JR: There's a kind of breaking down involved in collage – cutting up photos you've taken. And then a reconstruction. Do you find the process ameliorative, maybe transformative?

PW: Yes. There's a thrill in that double take, knowing what the original images were and seeing them deconstructed, or reconstructed, into something new. I think I'm only beginning to understand Pound's dictum: Make it new.

JR: The idea of deconstructing and reconstructing sums up the pleasure there is in making any kind of art.

PW: I had a conversation recently about literary theory which aesthetic appreciation has been torn from. Most theoretical dissertations are not concerned with beauty or an aesthetic sense of the work. They are much more subject-related or structure- or technique-related but not a lot to do with the pleasure that's part of our pleasure of writing, of production, of making things. There's all that pleasure. "The pleasure of the text" – Roland Barthes's phrase. For me, there's a lot of pleasure in writing and painting and collage, and you want to give pleasure as well by producing something splendid.
       I've been interested in the spatial problems I have to solve. I guess there is a sense of an audience because obviously in order to make a work coherent somehow, if I choose to show anybody, there's a slight sense, like writing a poem, that you have to engage or interest or involve and reveal. But it's not terribly deliberate. It is somehow just there at the back of the mind that someone might want to look at this or happen to look at it and then see something or just appreciate my aesthetic sensibility which is another aspect of the poetic production – that you are the maker of possibly beautiful things.

JR: In "Might Have Been: The Tedious Shores" [*Nothing But Brush Strokes*] you say that at first the creative activity of painting seemed meaningless, and yet it appears to have great meaning for you to the extent that it put off depression.

PW: I had a problem with the meaninglessness of it all. That was a feeling of being a novice and therefore insecure. And not being very good at it.

JR: You were excited to be learning.

PW: As you say in *your* essay ["Writing On The Wall," *Brick* 53], "the meaning of life is being here." The meaning of bad painting is it's fun to do.

JR: At some point you were beginning to write. Do you remember having the same feeling about that?

PW: No. I don't think so. That's the difference between feeling like an amateur in painting and deeply knowing that writing poetry had a profound meaning for me that is inexplicable, really. You ask where does it come from: I don't know but I've always had a great respect for my writing life and I don't have that as an attempting painter. I just enjoy doing it and it keeps me out of depression. It's my anti-depressant. I hate the idea of art as therapy but there is a therapeutic aspect to it.

JR: There always is.

PW: I don't think we'd go on doing it if it didn't cure us in some way, heal us, make us more whole. Then you smash up again, put it all together again.

JR: It's the process of sorting through, the self-questioning and trying to find answers. If that wasn't happening it wouldn't be worth doing.

PW: The major impulse that led me to write was depression and it also led me to the silence. Depression was a profound part of my life for most of my life and writing was a way of surviving in a sense. Not that all my books are depressive.

JR: In fact the opposite.

PW: Yes, joyful and funny sometimes. But my constant struggle with breakdown and depression through the years was a way of making sense of what was going on, fighting suicide and all that.

JR: You were saying in the car that you weren't sure that you wanted to talk about poetry.

PW: When you asked me about how I felt when I was writing in my twenties I thought "I'm seventy-four, I can't remember that far back." How did I feel? I don't know. It was very inspirational. I just got hit and zapped by poems.

JR: You say in "Might-have-been: The Tedious Shores" that you had something like an ecstatic experience that drove you to write. Something happened in Montreal that made you know that you should write.

PW: I went there *because* I was writing. I was walking through the grounds at McGill. It's in one of my early poems, "The Colour of the Light" [*The Vision Tree*]. These are the pigeons: "how clear were the colours of pigeons/ and how mysterious the animation of children/ playing in trees." It was one of those moments. I worked as a secretary and I was also a student. I would walk through the grounds a lot. That was a very memorable experience but it's hard to recall the process of writing. It was a cluster of images. It was a moment. You said ecstatic?

JR: I'll read it: "I moved to Montreal and had not a mystical experience but something like it which revealed to me that my destiny was to be a poet."

PW: How interesting. I was already writing, I'd been writing before I went to Montreal. But that's about "Earth Descending" [*The Vision Tree*]. That was the poem. Do you know it? It's about the planet Earth tumbling. This was a turning-point poem for me because of its cosmic dimensions.

JR: Which has been a continuing obsession.

PW: I was very existentialist at that time and it *was* the existentialist time so it has that impulse in it. I lived in a basement apartment and I remember writing "Earth Descending" in the bedroom. It was a turning point although I'd been serious about writing before. I was encouraged to write by Frank Scott and being taken seriously means you take yourself seriously, you feel some responsibility. Louis Dudek also helped me a lot and I began to move with other writers and people who belonged to that group in Montreal. When you have like-minded people who are committed it becomes a way of life.

JR: I suspect that these days it might be easier to find that community of like-minded people. There simply weren't that many people writing then.

PW: There are thousands now! I had a more organic literary life. It was attached to my life and it was immediate and was about getting together. You mentioned Toronto but I was too busy in Toronto.

JR: Was the atmosphere different in Toronto?

PW: Yes, and I didn't really have time. I worked very hard at the CBC in public affairs for five years. I was thinking that the difference was immense. I didn't produce a book in that time except *Naked Poems*. I resolved the technical problem of using the question form in the final section. That was published while I was there. I was frustrated as a poet.

JR: How do you mean you resolved the problem? What was the nature of it?

PW: The sentence structure was either/or, and/but – these dyadic structures which are part of our thinking unfortunately. I remember where I was sitting in my apartment and I thought "Ah! Questions!" It just broke through and I was able to finish it. Later I wrote an essay on the question as an instrument of torture.

JR: Which made me nervous about coming here to talk to you!

PW: I used to do a lot of interviews, too, so I know about that business of asking questions.

JR: Who was part of the community in Toronto?

PW: I occasionally saw Ray Souster, and Al Purdy, and Earle Birney. Victor Coleman, Michael Ondaatje, Eli Mandel – he was a dear friend. In my work I ran into a lot of writers

JR: Gwendolyn MacEwen?

PW: Yes, of course! There was a reading at the Bohemian Embassy, which was a coffee house. Al Purdy and I read each other's poems. We hated it. I hated the way he read my poems and he hated the way I read his. I suppose I did have literary connections. Joe Rosenblatt, too.

JR: Have you seen the NFB film about Gwendolyn MacEwen? It was based on Rosemary Sullivan's book [*Shadow Maker: The Life of Gwendolyn MacEwen*]. There's some good old footage from the Bohemian Embassy. A very young Margaret Atwood and so on.

PW: Gwendolyn was always there and her husband, Milton [Acorn]. I knew Margaret Atwood because I did a series of CBC television programs and I had up-and-coming poets on the final one. I must have been more connected than I thought but it felt very different from Montreal.

JR: When did you meet Leonard Cohen?

PW: That was in the fifties. I met him at Irving Layton's when Louis Dudek brought him. He was Louis's protégé. That's where we became friends. We aren't now. I didn't hear from him after I moved out here until I went to his concert in Victoria.

JR: I saw you at that concert. Did you go back and see him?

PW: Yes. I don't think he quite recognized me and I teased him about it but he said, "Of course I did darlin'."

JR: Did he become part of that circle?

PW: Yes. Then he went to New York, to Columbia. He came back and forth but I was moving around too. We were good friends and I saw a fair amount of him when we were both in town.

JR: The friendships you had with that group, did that involve a sharing of work?

PW: That's what it was all about actually. Mainly we met at Irving's house which was out in the suburbs and also at Frank's [Scott's] house. Occasionally I met Irving or Louis at a restaurant. They were quite large gatherings. Al, Irving, Frank, Louis, Eli, Leonard, Miriam Waddington, Betty Layton and kids. But we didn't workshop.

     Irving was a very strong personality. Even when you consider the others who were in the room. He was so expansive and so ideologically focused. He knew what he was doing. Contact Press was in formation so that was also a subject of interest. And *CIV/n*, which was a magazine that Louis and Aileen Collins published. There was a lot of small publishing. Louis believed in small presses and literary magazines and wrote his thesis on small presses. There was a lot of commitment to poetry. We sometimes attempted to meet with French writers, Quebecois writers, and we'd get together once and then nothing more would happen. I guess it was the language. There were these efforts. Frank was translating. He translated Anne Hébert. I've lost touch with Quebecois writing. I read Nicole Brossard in English now.

JR: Someone who is starting to write now probably reads contemporary Canadian writers. If they go to university there are classes in Canadian literature and creative writing. It's not very difficult to become part of a literary circle simply by showing up. It must have been very different for you.

PW: I was just lucky to land in this milieu.

JR: Another twenty years earlier it would have been even more difficult.

PW: Yes, but when you think about A.J.M. Smith, F.R. Scott and that McGill group, that was thirty years before . . . I think people do find each other. It's a kind of radar that writers and artists have. That reminds me of *Contemporary Verse*, which Dorothy Livesay was involved in. I published there and that was a kind of gathering place. Not physically, but once you'd published in that magazine or *Northern Review* you felt part of that community and you sort of knew people even though you didn't know them. All across the country. I knew all the poets in the country at one time I think. It wasn't very hard. You did meet them.

JR: Which is not possible now. There are thousands of people writing. Every now and then I come across a poet and realize that this person has seven books! I've never heard of them and I wonder why.

PW: I can't keep up. I do try in some kind of way. I get the *Malahat Review, Capilano Review* and *West Coast Line*. Visually things are getting very interesting with other languages coming in, Mandarin and so on, and I get excited about that. I never know where poetry is going. Where can it go?

JR: I notice in *Hanging Fire* and also in *Water and Light* that there are references to what I might call popular culture sneaking in: "the Home Hardware catalogue," "Toad of Toad Hall," "the aisles of Safeway," of "Pharmasave." Were you conscious of those references to such contemporary mundane things? They don't seem as present in the earlier poems.

PW: Maybe that's brand naming or something. Perhaps I was keeping up with the times. That kind of pop culture or mass culture reference is permissible. Maybe a bit trendy. The Pharmasave thing of course happened. The Safeway sign was just an emblem. They come out of my experience.

JR: But they root things in the present in a particular way.

PW: They will be passé very soon. That was probably a kind of loosening up, less high-seriousness. Letting those things in. I wonder if Sharon Thesen was of some influence there. It was around me. People write like that now and perhaps we didn't before. It was not high art to refer to movies and television programs.

JR: I couldn't imagine Rilke talking about the grocery store.

PW: He probably never went to one. I imagine he was always looked after.

JR: He talks about going to a farm to get a glass of whole milk every day and about going to a vegetarian restaurant in Paris, which wouldn't have been fashionable. Maybe it's more a reflection on the culture than on your writing; television, film and advertising are a bigger part of the experience of living now.

    I was supposed to talk to you about reviews and awards. You talked a little about the non-reception of *Hanging Fire*.

PW: Competition. Is it good, is it bad? I don't know. But winning prizes does help financially, that's the big thing, and it gives you a little stroke, several strokes. I like what Erin Mouré says about the artist's life, how artists finance the production of art with their lives. I think that's wonderful that we finance and subsidize with our lives.

JR: I love your idea that the correct response to a poem is another poem.

PW: The *proper* response to a poem is another poem. Actually, it was someone else who said that and I can't remember who it was. Maybe Oscar Wilde. People seem to think I made it up.

JR: Do you still think it's true?

PW: That is an ideal response and it would be lovely if it happened but I don't think it happens often. Very rarely.

JR: There is a dialogue that goes on. Mark Strand talks about the "secret life of poetry" where a poem refers to another poem. You might not have to know that but it adds another layer.

PW: In a way that's what I'm saying; that is the proper response to a poem.

JR: It's a dialogue, these poems talking to each other through the ages.

PW: It's true. Even with the anxiety of influence, or maybe out of the anxiety of influence, the influence of anxiety. The tradition in action in liveliness.

JR: Is it an anxiety? I get students to write an imitation. One doesn't want a student to become someone else but there's the response that some students have that they don't want to read anything because they don't want it to influence them.

PW: Yes I know. I laugh but you know I had to stop reading Dylan Thomas in the fifties because he had such an incredible influence on me. I loved him and I read him a lot, over and over again, and it kept coming into the poetry so I had to put him away, cast him out.

JR: Putting him away is different than . . . .

PW: Not having read him at all.

JR: I was thinking about Rilke. I'm asking about him because you refer to him enough times that you must think he's important.

PW: He was for me. I read him in the fifties. I was blown away and I didn't understand very much either. Knowing it's in translation you don't know what you're getting. That so much should come through in translation is amazing; they become English poems or at least they did for me. There's a kind of romantic sense to those poems and still a lyrical impulse there, very strong. They were so different from anything I'd ever read. The way he talked about relationships was so extraordinary, archetypal, the angels and all that. They had a huge influence on me. Huge. I did a radio program on his letters. This was for *CBC Wednesday Night*. I really got down to the nitty gritty of old Rainer. Karl Siegler has translated the *Sonnets to Orpheus*. It's a lovely translation. I love everything he did. I read *The Notebooks of Malte Laurids Brigge* when I was in Paris. I should read him again now.

JR: Have you done that a lot, reread people?

PW: I reread something of Henry James every summer. It's so odd that I keep going back to Henry James but I can reread him forever. My memory is so bad it's like reading something fresh.

JR: In another essay you mention that you were reading Canadian literature when you were a student at UBC.

PW: There was Ira Dilworth's anthology which we used. He was a Vancouver person, a local book. It had Birney, Pratt, Livesay, Page, Scott and all those people. It was my introduction, yes.

JR: Would you say they were as much of an influence on what you were writing early on as Thomas, say.

PW: Oh yes. I don't know how much they influenced my style but they allowed me to write. That was a world I could perhaps enter. Those poems influenced me enormously: Earle Birney's "Vancouver Lights," and P.K. Page. Dorothy Livesay was also very important. I was very political then. It aimed me in my direction. There was a Canadian literature there.

JR: Were there creative writing classes at UBC when you were there?

PW: Earle Birney had started his classes then but I didn't take them. I didn't think I was a real poet. I was writing poetry but I didn't take myself that seriously. So I never took a creative writing course.

JR: You've taught them.

PW: Yes. And you want to know if it can be taught.

JR: No. Of course it can be taught. It's a ridiculous question isn't it? If nothing else it teaches people to be better readers and there are tools and things you can learn about technique. I don't know if you can be taught to have an eye for recognizing what to write about but you can certainly teach people a thing or two about expression. I'm interested in what the process of teaching was like for you. Was it inspiring?

PW: It was inspiring and stimulating. It didn't stop me from writing as I thought it would. One year I did teach full time and that was a bit tough, but the way I taught – which was not every year – helped me because I liked to keep in touch with young people and with the university and see what's going on. So I enjoyed it for the most part except for the occasional horrific moment in teaching which we all have had. I just enjoyed teaching. Or maybe it's not teaching, leading a class, letting a class happen, whatever you would call it.

JR: In "A Long Line of Baby Caterpillars" you say, "Take away my wisdom and my categories!" which strikes me as a very Taoist or maybe Buddhist idea. What is real is inexpressible. I wonder if there is a connection there to silence.

PW: That is why I take a lot of pleasure in painting. It is a release from language and meaning. But also "take away my wisdom" points to my sense that there is no end to learning and understanding and experience. Wisdom sounds so final. "Categories" refers, of course, to that rationality and ordering with which we are imbued from a very early age. Our filing system minds – all very useful and efficiency-making but again tending towards finality, the false sense of security that goes out the window the moment our expectations and plans are upset, undone.

JR: In your essay "On the Line" [*Nothing But Brush Strokes*] you discuss the importance of sound in your poems. Have you always had a sense of language as music? Did you read aloud to yourself as you composed? Did you listen to music when you wrote? Do you do it now when you paint?

PW: I don't suppose I would have written poetry if I hadn't had a good ear. I've
      often said that when I write a poem "I play by ear" – which I did when I played
      the piano long ago. A way of composing poems, crooning along. I would work
      over a poem by reciting it over and over, if only in my head, until I thought I'd
      got it right, a sound-haunting for perhaps a week. And then it could go fly a
      kite and so could I. The poem was done. I don't think I listened to music while
      writing. I sometimes do when I paint. I love opera and chamber music, though
      I'm not very knowledgeable even after all these years. I always went to con-
      certs wherever I lived – Montreal, London, Paris, Vancouver – before I got
      phobic about public spaces. Now it's CDs and tapes and of course the radio,
      but I do live a lot in silence. I can't take too much speech coming from me.
      Silence is my natural mode.

The Wisdom of Falling

DON DOMANSKI

Interviewed by S.D. Johnson

Don Domanski was born and raised on Cape Breton Island, and presently lives in Halifax, Nova Scotia. He has published seven books of poetry, including *Parish of the Physic Moon* (McClelland & Stewart, 1998).

S. D. Johnson is the author of *Pale Grace* (Thistledown, 1995), and *Hymns to Phenomena* (Thistledown, 2000), which won the inaugural ReLit award for poetry. She lives in Saskatoon with a cat and a mannequin.

SDJ: How important have reviews, awards, other honours been to your feelings about your work? Is competition healthy or unhealthy for a poet?

DD: It's always nice to receive recognition, to hear that someone appreciates what you are doing, etc., but in the end the poem knows nothing of contests and awards. Al Purdy once compared the world of poetry to a race at a horse track. You never knew who would win in the end. From where the poem sits, there is no race, no horse or track, not a jockey to be found. To my mind competition is meaningless. It's background noise that sometimes gets turned up to a volume that's annoying, nothing more. On the one hand, it's good that a poet gets some attention, that his or her book is put under the spotlight for a while. It's also good to actually make some money from poetry. On the other hand, it has become somewhat of a blood sport and far too much attention is given to it, sometimes at the cost of the work itself.

It can be argued, of course, that everything can be interpreted as politics, even the arts. But one thing that a political agenda doesn't have is silence and at poetry's centre there's the silence of a world turning. This is also found at the centre of a stone or at the axis of a tree. To my way of thinking, that silence is the main importance. Out of it come the manifestations, all the beings we call words. It's not that honours and awards aren't important. They are in terms of income and the acknowledgement of work. It's just that the need to be competitive appears to be growing, taking on a whole reality of its own, with its own justifications and that worries me. At this point, competition seems so often to be overshadowing the poem itself, eclipsing what is written on that silence.

SDJ: In his poem "The Dead Poet," Al Purdy, speculating on the origins of his poetry, asks "how else explain myself to myself/ where does the song come from?" Do you have any explanation of where your voice came from, of why you became a poet?

DD: It's difficult to explain this. Possibly it defies rational explanation. Perhaps it's simply another random call from the noosphere? When I look at my background, I can see no direct link to poetry other than simply being a human being. No books in my house, no kindly parents trying to open up the world of art for me. The only glimmer of light that I can see by way of explanation is a need to communicate and this comes from early in my childhood. But having said that I should add that it felt like the world was communicating to me, explaining itself on some level. This, I think, is probably very common, both to children who will one day become poets and to children who will become mechanics or jockeys. The difference was that I took it very seriously and still do. At some point, I needed to also speak, to interconnect with this sense of the world. My need – without knowing it – was for some non-linear way to express myself, because that was how I experienced the world.

My first interest was in painting. The language of colour and form seemed far deeper than simply stating a fact or an idea. Once again, I should say that this wasn't happening on a conscious level, perhaps on a cellular level, possibly I had an over-imaginative lymphatic system, but it was happening nevertheless. The problem was that my parents couldn't afford more than a few art lessons, so somehow I turned to poetry at fifteen. I say "somehow" because I don't honestly know how it happened. I never liked poetry in school, avoided it if I could, but it became both tongue and grip, a way to speak and hold on to that sense of things, that connective tissue along which ran a dialogue that I could only faintly hear, but that bit of hearing was and is the joy of it. I think there's a lot of paint in my work, lots of brushstrokes, a very visual sense of things.

So the logical conclusion to come to is that I substituted one art form for another and perhaps that's true to a degree. But I see it not as a displacement or a real shift of focus; rather, it feels part of a whole. Possibly it's better put as an interlingual rendition, a translation of the same drive. Whether it's keyboard or brush or chisel, whatever you're using, it has as its source that same impulse, the same unknowing that comes from allowing the world to speak, and that little whisper to run up the spine.

SDJ: When you speak of unknowing, I'm automatically thinking of E.D. Blodgett and Tim Lilburn, two poets I would closely align you with because of a shared negative transcendence, an address to a "Thou" which is bound mostly to the shadows, of which you only occasionally get the slightest glimpse. Am I wrong to associate your work with these poets more closely than other Canadian poets?

DD: No, you're not wrong to associate me with Blodgett and Lilburn. I feel very close to what they're doing, but I also feel close to other Canadian poets as well. They are both poets I have the greatest admiration for, and yes, there is certainly a connection in terms of negative transcendence. I would define it, in part at least, as an acceptance of sorrow, what the Japanese refer to as "the slender sadness," that runs through every moment of existence. The Japanese are talking about nature, not just humanity, about the fleetingness of lives lived in a world where nothing can be saved, where each new second eliminates the last and nothing can really be accumulated or held onto, where there are no handrails to guide you, no structures to lean upon. Unknowing, by my definition, is entering that state of being with a joy and wonder that comes from that very impermanency, from the absolute dispossession of everything we love and cherish. The wonder is that anything at all exists. The joy is that it does, even if it is as momentary as a human life. We can live this as a partial mode of attention or we can live within its movements, its cycles and treasure the phases, the round of it. We cannot grasp the world nor put it into an order. We can only experience it. For me, the "Thou" you refer to is simply the deepest end of that experience, seen for an instant and then gone. It's another moment you cannot cling to. An ascetic disciplinarian might push through that and see God. I have no desire to push towards an explanation, to delineate beyond the experience itself. For me, the poem is enough by way of an accounting. Hopefully, it captures a human response to transcendence. The poem is one way of unknowing, of accepting "the slender sadness" of the world.

SDJ: The concept of "the slender sadness" is very beautiful. Do you remember when you first discovered Eastern religion and thought? How has it influenced your work?

DD: I began to read about Eastern religion and thought at the same time I started to write poetry, at the age of fifteen. I read about Hinduism, Buddhism, Taoism, etc. while reading poetry for the first time in any real sense. I found in those Eastern texts something that seemed very close to my own feelings about the world, about how one should *be* in the world. From Taoism and Buddhism especially I learnt so much that has been helpful to me in my approach to life. I learnt much about compassion and inwardness, about looking at reality not just from my small perspective, not just from a linear perspective and looking without desiring what I saw.

Then you see things as coming from a common rising out of nothingness. All life, all matter rising up at once in numberless forms and all of it intimately connected and dependent. There's a lovely quote from the Dalai Lama, "All sentient beings are our fathers and mothers," because all living things are joined. Without all the rest, you and I wouldn't be here. You didn't just get here via your mother, but also by way of the rest of humanity and by way of the wolf, the maggot, ears of corn, etc. All the birth through billions of years of incalculable plants and animals got you here. That's just one example of a way of thinking that seemed very natural to me. I've also read Christian mystics like Meister Eckhart, Sufi teachers like Mevlana, Hasan of Basrah, Rabi'a al-Adawiya, etc., the Gnostics, Jewish Mystics like Rabbi Israel ben Eliezer and Rabbi Dov Baer, Hindu Mystics like Sri Ramakrishna. Also *The Bhagavad Gita* and the *Upanisads* were of great importance. Anyway, the list is long and I won't bore you with all that. It's enough to say that this has had an effect on how I view things, has added immeasurably to how I see and interact with reality.

In the end, I'm a spiritual free-range chicken, pecking here and there, finding what suits the hunger of a moment. In turn, this has influenced my poetry in an immense way, leading me to explore things from a different viewpoint than I would have otherwise. Art and religion are extremely close on some levels. I'm sure that religion was begun by artists back in the Paleolithic or far earlier. So much of art is like religion, a belief in the wonder of the moment transfixed, without the dogma and nonsense. Artists should reclaim religion as their own. In many ways, it's going back to their roots, roots that run deep beneath the greensward, deeper than any church.

SDJ: How have your feelings about poetry, the reading and writing of it, changed since you were in your twenties?

DD: Well, I think I'm far more open now to the possibilities of poetry. In my twenties, I was hunched over the grindstone, trying to form a style and presence in my work which would carry me through. Not that I'm certain now of that "presence." It continues to change and, hopefully grow, but I've learned that it transcends, in many ways, personal intentions and that was a revelation of sorts. I've had to learn to be open to that, to let it sweep me along. I might for instance be writing about an experience during the night, but slowly it becomes day in the poem and the whole experience itself changes. I allow and encourage that to happen. A mountain in a poem might become a blade of grass, but perhaps it was a blade of grass all along and I didn't know. Perhaps there's no difference between the two.

     The desire for metamorphosis is a lot stronger now. When I was in my twenties, once I sunk my teeth into an idea or concept I wouldn't let go. Now I carry no idea or concept to the page. The Chinese have a saying: "A blank page contains the infinite." I try to allow for the infinite, while at the same time speaking out of the space of existence. I've learned over the years that the two are one, that they coexist, lean on one another and that the poem sees no difference between them. Much of what happens in a poem is a matter of chance. The poet must be ready to honour that, to pay heed to it and not hold too fervently to the concept or intention that started it. That intention, in the end, only got you to sit in front of the page or computer screen. It puts bums on seats, but doesn't write the poem. That comes from elsewhere. It's a matter of getting to elsewhere, which has nothing at all to do with goals or destinations. It has to do with letting go, with the free fall of images, which generate a descent into things. Since my twenties, I've learned to fall better, to trip over chance, to stumble over my own sense of what the poem should be and to see the wisdom of falling.

     In terms of reading poetry, I want to be influenced far more now than I did in my twenties. Back then, there was a real sense of being cloistered away from influence, being overly protective of my work. Since then, I've realized that each of us stands on the shoulders of thousands of men and women who have gone on before us. It isn't just one hand holding the pen or moving across the keyboard. This sense of connectiveness has gone a long way in appreciating the poetry of others, of realizing that the poem written has only a bit of myself in it and far more of the world, of other poets, both dead and alive. When you stop influence, you're imprisoning the language. You're killing what started you writing in the first place, the voice of others. I should mention that it isn't always a poet's voice or even a human voice. It can also be, and often is, the voice of the non-human, a deer for instance, or the presence of a cloud. That presence is also a voice to listen to, to be influenced by. That cloud can help you fall into language.

SDJ: "I cannot paint an angel because I have never seen one," said the painter and political radical Gustave Courbet. This emphasis on the everyday, which is predominant as well in Canadian poetry, has also been emphasized in Maoist China, in the Soviet Union during the Stalinist terror and in Nazi Germany. Angels and fantastic creatures inhabit all of your books, from *The Cape Breton Book of the Dead* to *Parish of the Physic Moon*. How would you justify yourself to Courbet, and to the majority of the Canadian literati? Do you think such encompassing realism exists in a freethinking society, or do you think it suggests there is something wrong with Canadian culture? Do you ever feel that your imagination is under attack?

DD: I think that's pinning reality down quite severely. I've seen Courbet's work at the Musée d'Orsay and his figures so often look like tired angels, somewhat bemused and exhausted from divinity. Myths in their myriad forms are a part of the human psyche, whether we accept them or not. I respond to them and, in doing so, I think I'm receiving a fuller view of what it means to be human. Some people believe devils and angels exist. While others would take the view that they're a creation of human imagination. Either way that makes them real from where I stand. The poem is an act of the imagination. I don't think that makes it any less real than the city of Toronto or Halifax, which are also acts of the imagination, as are a minotaur and manticore. The "everyday" is the grand act of the human imagination. Nothing that we have constructed comes near to it in terms of sheer inventiveness. There is no "everyday," no "normal" day.

There is no "everyday," no "normal" day.

Yet we all pretend there is. We all add to the myth. It's an act of pretense which helps us survive, to feel there's ground under our feet, when we know full well that beneath that ground there is an eternity of stars and galaxies, a great unknown which, on one of these *normal* days, will swallow us whole. I don't think it's the poet's job to keep that myth alive. Ninety-nine percent of society is already doing a fine job of that. The biomass at that end of reality is rather thick, to say the least. The everyday hides a multitude of sins and in poetry it's no different. I don't know if there's anything wrong with Canadian culture as such. I don't think I have the ability to make that kind of judgment.

There is a strong leaning towards the accessible poem, the quick read, not just in Canada but across the English-speaking world. There's a real laziness to explore language, to take chances, to leap across meaning and discover new conveyances to deepen our ties with the world. I often worry that it's becoming the age of the McPoem, the McBook. I write away from all that, determined to keep the clown from my door. No, I don't feel my imagination is under attack. No one, so far, has lobbed a grenade through my window. I think I'm writing from a different experience than most poets in Canada and that the work is often misunderstood or not understood at all. Not because it's so terribly erudite or complicated. Just that it's coming from a place that's not held in common with many other poets in this country. This is a normal human reaction, but I can't spend much time worrying about that. My approach is my way of being in the world and, in the end, that's the whole point of art.

SDJ: The images of miners and of poverty in your work are very powerful. How did your childhood and teens on Cape Breton Island influence your poetry?

DD: Yes, it had a strong influence on my work. Growing up surrounded by Celtic culture made a real difference. The use of humour and language was and is very important there, not in a literary way as such, but a language that comes more out of playfulness, out of the sport of words. I've retained much of that sense of play, of simply enjoying language for its own sake, delighting in the linguistic sting that pricks consciousness. It's a potent drug in its own right and habit-forming over time. I should mention here that that sense of attentiveness to words wasn't in my immediate family but in the larger culture. Most of my family were of Celtic descent, but it would be another Maritime cliché to say that all Cape Bretoners have this faculty for language.

     I grew up in a culture that was always on the edge of despair, always fighting to maintain itself, steeped in neglect and poverty. Most of my family were coal miners or steelworkers. Life was hard and often there wasn't any work. There was no real education in my family and my greatest fear growing up wasn't poverty but ignorance, simply having so little knowledge. Yet ignorance has its angel. When I heard a new word or phrase, I was mesmerized by it. It felt like pure light. Those words weren't taken for granted. They were precious, gold that might pay from a larger world. My first impulse early on was to understand nature. So I read as many books on the natural sciences as I could and still have a deep interest in astronomy, paleontology, etc.

     When I was around thirty-two, I became interested in having a better sense of time. It seemed very important to my work just to have a better feel for it, so I collected fossils for fourteen years. After all that, it really is still time out of mind. In the end, how can you understand what 300 million years really means? How can you be present to that? Yet, there's this visceral awareness of time that wasn't there before. So something was gained, albeit through the pores. So there was this hunger for knowledge when I was growing up, this fear of illiteracy, of not understanding. Poverty breeds a silence that engulfs the heart, a fear of everything outside of it, a kind of island mentality, but located in the psyche. Instinctively, I knew that I had to open up, to immerse myself in the larger world. Discovering poetry went a long way to freeing myself of that silence, that fear of the larger sphere of things. I didn't read poetry as much as absorb it, as I absorbed time through paleontology. If there's any such thing as a muse, if I have one, her name is Osmosis.

SDJ: Do you know how the voice in your book *Wolf-Ladder* came into being? Of course the previous books are wonderful as well, but it seems that this is the book where your authentic voice attains its fruition. Did you set out purposely using the wolf as the objective correlative, or did it just unfold, as it seems it must have to me, through serendipity?

DD: This is a difficult question to answer. First of all, I don't think a poet's voice ever attains fruition. That tongue can never be realized. If it did the poetry would stop. There would be no reason for it. Secondly, it seems to me that the voice is always in a state of becoming, the only thing "authentic" is that becoming. There is always something paradoxical about the finished poem or book and that state of becoming. Just because a poem is published doesn't mean it's completed. Poems continue "becoming" through the reader. He or she adds to the work. Through their eyes, their sense of themselves and the world, the poem continues to be added to, altered. It acquires other lives, other points of view and other views of being. The reader is always the second birthplace of the poem. The poem has numerous second births. The poet only gives it one. So after a time, the poet's presence fades. The poem's life, its real life, comes from its readers, from all those other births.

　　　The voice in *Wolf-Ladder* grew out of all the previous books, out of that flow of becoming. I hope with each book I'm getting closer to the centre of something, focusing in a little better. I hope each carries a deeper resonance through deeper structures. At least that's my goal, an all-too-human one, so perhaps I deceive myself. Yes, using the wolf came by way of serendipity. The title came to me one morning as I was waking, so I had to grow into the title. This is very rare for me. Usually the title is the last, or nearly last, piece of the picture, a nail to hang that dimensionality on. In this case, I had a nail but no painting. It took months to come up with something that was worth even considering and that only happened after I stopped thinking about it.

　　　Thinking should always come after you've become open to a multiplicity and oneness in both language and feeling that risk cancelling each other out. The poem strikes below the thinking level and should have its origins there. That's the voice, unreflective and wordless, coming as subversion to thought and intentions, the dark form of becoming that creates each moment, not by our design or our permission, but by us simply stepping aside, retiring from our normal position, which is a kind of sleep away from the world. The voice wakes us to reality, to the process of becoming. To quote Yves Bonnefoy: "Dreaming, in poetry, is to stop dreaming."

SDJ: I apologize for the word "fruition." I meant something which bears fruit, something which has attained a certain degree of success. I didn't mean to imply it was time to chop down the orchard! Clearly your work continues to develop, becoming more and more refined in its music. The Bonnefoy quotation doesn't surprise me. Reading Bonnefoy and other French poets a while ago I noticed you have an affinity with their work, with their inductive reticulation of images. When did you discover French poetry? Would you consider them to be a great influence on your work?

DD: Yes, the French poets have been very important, along with other European poets from other countries. Many names come to mind, including Jean Follain, Robert Desnos, René Char, Max Jacob and Paul Eluard. German poets, such as Rilke, Ingeborg Bachman, Paul Celan, Christian Morgenstern, Georg Trakl and Gottfried Benn. The Greek poet Yannis Ritsos. The Russian poet Osip Mandelstam. The Spanish poets Juan Ramón Jiménez, Lorca and Miguel Hernández. Swedish poets like Tomas Tranströmer and Harry Martinson.

Anyway, the list goes on and on and these are just a few that have been of importance to me. I began reading modern European poets about thirty years ago and felt a very strong affinity for what they were doing, how they were approaching the poem. Yes, "inductive reticulation" makes a lot of sense, a meshwork of images to support the reality of the poem, of experience, the logic of the metaphor, which is the logic of uniting opposites. In that union we can make fire and, for a time, see beyond the narrow confines of a single life, a single moment. It frees us from a bounded scope. Poets writing in Europe first showed me what you refer to as "inductive reticulation." Obviously, they weren't the only ones doing this, but in reading their work it was the first time it really entered my consciousness in any meaningful way.

Much of European poetry strikes me as a kind of qualitative analysis in reverse, finding out what makes reality by putting all the constituent elements back together in a sensory network of perceptions. I see these perceptions as just beyond the reach of language, the poem pushing meaning into an area of primary sensings, which opens up, rather than closes down, our ground of being. Poetry can take us beyond language the way painting and music can. This is what separates it from prose, this metamorphosis of attendance, this transformation of presence. It makes each moment a threshold once again. This idea of "threshold" is what first caught my attention when I began reading European poets. It held infinite possibilities.

SDJ: Why do you think of the "logic of the metaphor" as being "the logic of uniting opposites"? Can you ideate further on the nature of the metaphor?

DD: If there's one thing the poet has to learn, one ability central to poetry, it's the metaphor. There's nothing in the canon of poetry as important as the use of it. Cynthia Ozick has a great line that sums it up: "Metaphor is the mind's opposable thumb." You can't grasp anything without it. You're ham-fisted in its absence. So much of poetry is preverbal. So much depends on leaps across imagery and meanings where language, in the normal sense, can't carry us. Metaphor gives back to us the intuition of our preverbal state, the nostalgia of gnosis. Part of that nostalgia is the marriage of opposites. I believe it was

Delmore Schwartz who said that every time a metaphor was created a marriage was taking place. A good poem is a number of weddings down a page. Metaphors help in freeing us of our singularity. It marries us to a larger sense of who we are and what the world contains. I try in my work to shift my perceptions, my sense of things, by allowing these weddings their place. Out of the confluence of opposites the world is engendered with worlds. Shadows delegate light, light shades the sun, all things exchange essences. The metaphysics of a cricket can sorcerize the night, that night can transform the lovers; they, in turn, can fall into a new metamorphosis well beyond their union.

Metaphors provide the all-important proof that the cosmos exists complete in each pairing of opposites, that there is no existence without it. This is the logic of metaphors, the logic of oneness. My rendering of reality changes with the metaphors which rise up in a poem. My interpretation of things follows their lead. This allows for the unexpected, the irrational, to undermine what is all too frail a human need, the desire for the anticipated, the probable world. There's a story about a Hindu king who disliked the roughness of the ground beneath his feet so he had the idea of covering the entire earth with animal skins. But a wise man pointed out that the same thing could be achieved by cutting out pieces of skin and binding them to his feet. These came to be the first sandals. I would rather not define the world by covering it with one interpretation. It's enough that I can change sandals. Metaphors make for good footwear if you intend to walk along the road where opposites meet, where the unity of all nature is chosen.

SDJ: Adam Zagajewski has a poem in a which a reader complains, "Too much about death,/ too many shadows." Have you ever received such a complaint? Rereading *Stations of the Left Hand* I find the most moving poems to be the poems which are primarily about death, especially "Funereal Poem," addressed to a woman who has died after being in a coma, concluding: "that the flowers/ left on your grave/ are as many comas/ as it will take/ for you to forget the world." Do you know the origin of your need to write about death?

DD: Yes, it's been mentioned a number of times. Not as a complaint as such, or at least I don't think so. My need to write about death is my need to be human. It's not possible to write about life, about the sheer wonder of that, without the backdrop of death. It's the black screen all of life is projected onto. I worked for a while in a morgue and in the emergency room of a hospital. I've seen a lot of people die. I've handled the dead bodies of people, from babies to the elderly, so I have some feeling for the tangible sense of it. The Victorians were death obsessed and hid their sexual natures, so we, of course, have done the opposite. We hide from death behind our sexual desires. We also hide it behind violence itself, in movies and on TV. Sure, there are masses of killings, but no death, no honest sense of that. There's only the ballet of death. We're made to waltz between the *danse macabre* and the *danse du ventre*, between death and sensuality. The world is never that simple. There are so many degrees of temperature between the corpse and the lover, so many perceptual turns of the heart. Poetry should be a place where this can be explored with candour and emotion. There's an obiism to it, a sorcery to call back from the shadows, miraculous spells to act upon, to open us up to its meaning. Death is what opens the rose and invites the kiss.

Beauty itself believes in it, follows its lead. Each moment of reverence owes its intensity to it. Think of Wallace Stevens's line "we should die except for Death." He knew its importance. The poem you mentioned, "Funereal Poem," was about the death of my mother. It wasn't bleak or morbid, but one about loss and love, about grief and tenderness. So often the morphology of death is the morphology of love. My need to write about death is my need to value the world.

SDJ: Although you refer to often attempting to express what is inexpressible with language, and being confronted with a sense of unknowing, your work as a whole to me seems very positive. How have you not fallen into a pit of solipsistic despair?

DD: I see myself as the very centre of the universe and of no importance whatsoever. Both viewpoints hold true for everything. Both coexist in the same space and I see nothing paradoxical in this. Presence moves forth from this position and manages to maintain its hold on reality. The poem moves outward from that same orientation and tries to understand the seeming contradiction in this. For the poem, the solution to this contradiction lies in what's beyond language, in what language fragments through its collective use. Being confronted with a sense of unknowing, coming up against the shadow of the inaccessible, is part of the destination of all art.

The poem longs for the paradox and the oxymoron, for the irrational that takes it to a new level of inarticulateness. It longs for muteness, because out of that silence comes the world itself, anew, spinning on a word. I place great faith in the failure of language. Out of it comes the need for the metaphor. Out of that, the long reach into a deeper life, more felt, more lived and less tormented with duality. I don't really think of my work as positive or negative, but I know what you mean. I think it comes out of an acceptance of opposites, of all the antipodes placed along a meaning, the fusion of opposing forces that goes into the movement of the poem itself, the sway of images that try to answer each other, sometimes across an incredible gulf.

I hope my work, whether dealing with sorrow or delight, manages to point beyond those emotional definitions to something larger and more encompassing. Both despair and hope temper any translation of the world. We can't escape what is essentially human, but we can come to terms with a symmetry created from a unification of our emotions. Art allows for this union, for a vision of what is greater than our own happiness or our fears, and allows for mystery to hold us once again. Poetry asks that we surrender to mystery, that we refuse the constraints of language, that we intuit beyond the mere genre of its expression outward to the larger sphere. When we can accomplish this, we are no longer exiles from being. We are seeing into existence, which has neither joy nor despair, no ambiguity, no discordant longings, just an abounding hereness that takes the present moment and a universe to produce.